THE ROOTS OF UKRAINIAN NATIONALISM: GALICIA AS UKRAINE'S PIEDMONT

Other books by Paul Robert Magocsi

Let's Speak Rusyn—Bisidujme po-rus'ky (1976)
The Shaping of a National Identity (1978)
Let's Speak Rusyn—Hovorim po-rus'kỹ (1979)
The Rusyn-Ukrainians of Czechoslovakia (1983)
Galicia: A Historical and Bibliographical Guide (1983)
Our People (1984, 1994)
Ukraine: A Historical Atlas (1985)
Carpatho-Rusyn Studies, 2 vols. (1988-98)
The Russian Americans (1989, 1996)
The Carpatho-Rusyn Americans (1989, 2000)
The Rusyns of Slovakia (1993)
Historical Atlas of East-Central Europe (1993, 2002)
A History of Ukraine (1996)
Let's Speak Rusyn and English—Besheduime po angliiski i po ruski (1997)
Of the Making of Nationalities There Is No End, 2 vols. (1999)
The Roots of Ukrainian Nationalism (2002)

Books edited by Paul Robert Magocsi

The Ukrainian Experience in the United States (1979)
Wooden Churches in the Carpathians (1982)
Morality and Reality: Andrei Sheptyts'kyi (1989)
Persistence of Regional Cultures (1993)
A New Slavic Language Is Born (1996)
Encyclopedia of Canada's Peoples (1999)
Canada's Aboriginal Peoples (2002)
Encyclopedia of Rusyn History and Culture (2002)

THE ROOTS OF UKRAINIAN NATIONALISM

Galicia as Ukraine's Piedmont

PAUL ROBERT MAGOCSI

UNIVERSITY OF TORONTO PRESS
Toronto London Buffalo

© University of Toronto Press Incorporated 2002
Toronto Buffalo London
Printed in Canada

ISBN 0-8020-4738-6

Printed on acid-free paper

National Library of Canada Cataloguing in Publication Data

Magocsi, Paul R.

The roots of Ukrainian nationalism: Galicia
as Ukraine's Piedmont

Includes bibliographical references
ISBN 0-8020-4738-6

1. Galicia (Poland and Ukraine) – History – Autonomy
and independence movements.   2. Ukrainians – Galicia (Poland and Ukraine) – History.   3. Nationalism – Ukraine –
History.   I. Title

DK608.9.G35M33 2002   947.7'9   C2001-901230-6

University of Toronto Press acknowledges the financial assistance to its publishing
program of the Canada Council for the Arts and the Ontario Arts Council.

University of Toronto Press acknowledges the financial assistance to its publishing
program of the Government of Canada through the Book Publishing Industry
Development Program (BPIDP).

Contents

vi   Contents

Maps, Appendices, and Tables

Maps

Medieval Galicia
Galicia in the Polish-Lithuanian Commonwealth
Galicia in the Austro-Hungarian Empire
Interwar Galicia
Galicia since 1939

Appendices

Preface

As nationalities and nation-states go, Ukraine can be considered a remarkable success story. This might seem at first glance surprising, since for most of its modern history Ukraine's territories have been ruled by states that were in general opposed to Ukrainian national aspirations, whether the Russian Empire and Austria–Hungary before 1914, or the Soviet Union, Poland, and Romania in the twentieth century. One result of such foreign rule is that a sense of Ukrainian national identity and culture, including any normal development for a literary language, was hampered. Less than a hundred years ago, Ukrainians living in most Ukrainian lands had no idea that they even comprised a distinct nationality; rather, they considered themselves a branch of the Russians and their speech merely corrupted dialects of Russian or, in some cases, Polish. Several efforts to change the political status and achieve statehood for Ukraine during the twentieth century, such as at the close of World War I or the outset of World War II, proved unsuccessful.

Despite such an inauspicious recent history, in 1991 Ukraine became an independent state. Moreover, with its over 50 million people, 604,000 square kilometers of territory, rich mineral resources, and industrial infrastructure, Ukraine was suddenly thrust into the position of Europe's second-largest country with one of the fourth-largest nuclear arsenals in the world. That is not bad for a place which, less than one hundred years before, did not exist on any map and whose majority East Slavic inhabitants were not even recognized as being a distinct people.

Does this mean that Ukraine and Ukrainians suddenly appeared *deus ex machina* in 1991? Although it is true that some European states (Belgium, Luxembourg, Austria) may have come into being despite, or even against, the will of their inhabitants, this was not the case with Ukraine. The idea of a distinct Ukrainian people who might have a right to an independent state goes back at least to the early decades of the nineteenth century, during what has been prosaically called in east-central Europe the period of national awakenings.

Political realities at that time did not allow for a Ukrainian national revival to occur for any sustained period of time in the Russian Empire, where most Ukrainians lived. In the neighboring Austro-Hungarian monarchy, however, in particular in the eastern half of Austria's province of Galicia, favorable political and cultural conditions allowed for the gradual growth and preservation of a modern Ukrainian national identity and people. During the seven decades between 1848 and 1914, more and more Ukrainian activists in the Russian as well as the Austrian empires felt that Galicia had become a Piedmont from which a future independent state on all-Ukrainian territory would grow. Therefore, to understand the roots of twentieth-century Ukrainian nationalism, it is necessary to know the historical evolution of the phenomenon in the region popularly called Galicia (in Ukrainian: Halychyna).

The Roots of Ukrainian Nationalism consists of ten essays, eight of which were previously published in scholarly publications in North America. The first two essays are of a general nature and include a historical survey of Galicia from earliest times to the present, followed by the elaboration of a framework for understanding the nineteenth-century Ukrainian national revival, in which Galicia played a crucial role.

The next chapters (3, 4, 5) contain interpretive essays that investigate the manner in which Galician Ukrainians adopted and accommodated to external rule, whether that of the Habsburgs before 1914 or the Soviets after 1945. Three more chapters investigate in detail the mechanisms whereby the national ideology formulated by an elite (intelligentsia) was propagated among the masses, whether through use of a standardized literary language (chapter 6), a proper understanding of national identity (chapter 7), or the activity of reading rooms, theaters, civic events, and publications (chapter 8). The last two chapters review the achievements of Galician Ukrainians in the field of book production (chapter 9) and provide direction for future research using libraries and archives outside the Ukrainian homeland (chapter 10).

With regard to the eight studies published previously, those sections in the original text which were of a general introductory nature have been deleted in order to avoid repetition. Several stylistic changes have been introduced in an attempt to improve the narrative, and some of the bibliographical references have been updated. The basic arguments and factual data have remained the same, however, including interpretive statements (especially in chapter 3) that might now seem moot following the collapse of the Soviet Union.

On a technical note, the Library of Congress transliteration system has been used to render all Cyrillic-language publications. For works written in antiquated Ukrainian and in the nonstandardized language of the Old Ruthenians, the transliteration system for Ukrainian is used with the addition of the following letters: ѣ = î; ы = ŷ; ô = ô. Final hard signs (ъ) have been deleted throughout. The only exception is chapter 10, which discusses holdings in the Austrian National Library in Vienna. Since that institution uses the international transliteration system, it seemed preferable to do so as well in this chapter, so that readers would find it easier to find and consult materials when contacting that library.

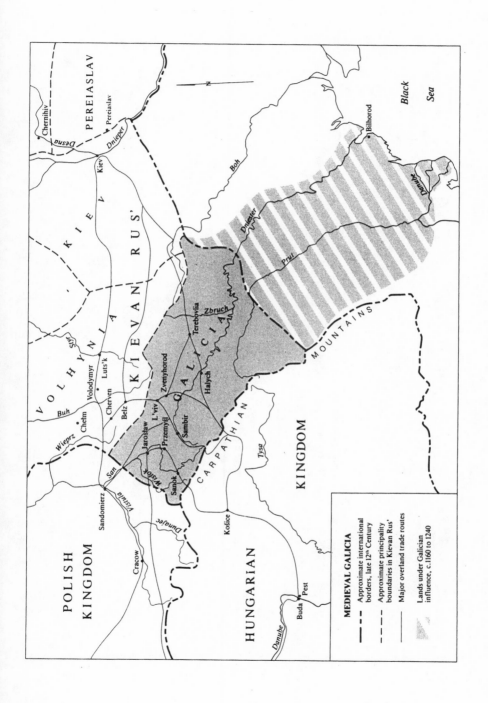

MEDIEVAL GALICIA

- – · – Approximate international borders, late 12ᵗʰ Century
- – – – Approximate principality boundaries in Kievan Rus'
- ——— Major overland trade routes
- Lands under Galician influence, c.1160 to 1240

POLISH KINGDOM

PEREIASLAV

KIEV

VOLHYNIA

KIEVAN RUS'

GALICIA

HUNGARIAN KINGDOM

CARPATHIAN MOUNTAINS

Black Sea

Chernihiv
Pereiaslav
Kiev
Volodymyr
Luts'k
Cherven
Belz
Chełm
Sandomierz
Cracow
Jarosław
Przemyśl
L'viv
Sambir
Zvenyhorod
Sanok
Halych
Terebovlia
Zbruch
Bilhorod
Buda
Pest
Košice

Desna
Dnieper
Boh
Dniester
Prut
Danube
Slyr
Buh
Wieprz
San
Wisłok
Vistula
Dunajec
Tysa

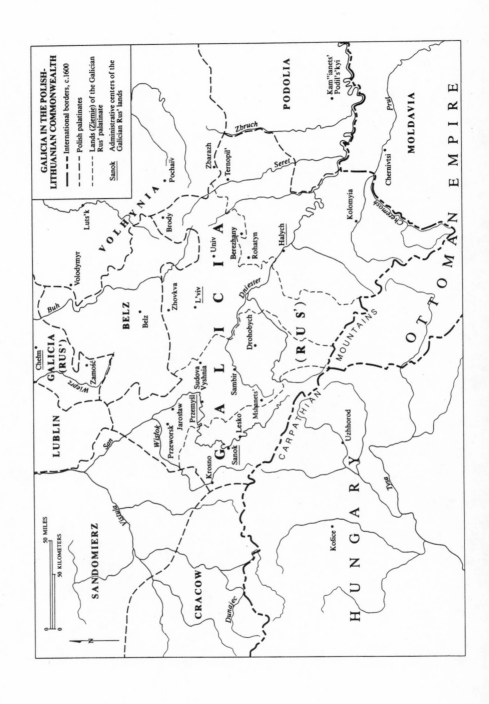

GALICIA IN THE POLISH-
LITHUANIAN COMMONWEALTH

— - — International borders, c.1600
— — — Polish palatinates
- - - - Lands (Ziemie) of the Galician
         Rus' palatinate
Sanok Administrative centers of the
         Galician Rus' lands

PODOLIA

MOLDAVIA

OTTOMAN EMPIRE

• Kam''ianets'
   Podil's'kyi

Zbruch

Seret

Prut

Chernivtsi

Cheremosh

Zbarazh

• Ternopil'

• Pochaïv

• Kolomyia

VOLHYNIA

• Luts'k

• Volodymyr

Buh

Brody

• Univ

Berezhany
• Rohatyn

Halych

Zhovkva

• L'viv

Dniester

G A L I C I A

(R U S')

BELZ

Belz •

• Drohobych

Chełm

GALICIA
(RUS')

Zamość •

Wieprz

LUBLIN

San

Sudova
Vyshnia

• Sambir

Przemyśl •
Jarosław •

Wisłok

Przeworsk •

• Mshanets'

G A L I C I A

Lesko •

Sanok

Krosno •

C A R P A T H I A N   MOUNTAINS

• Uzhhorod

H U N G A R Y

Tysa

• Košice

SANDOMIERZ

Wisła

CRACOW

• Dunajec

50 MILES

50 KILOMETERS

N

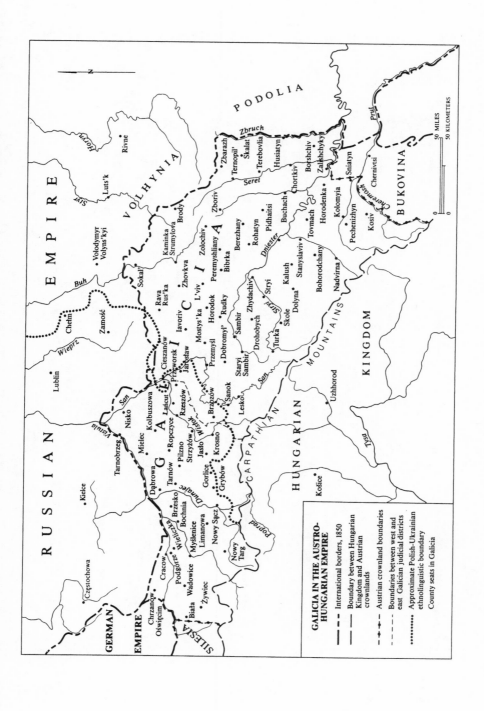

GALICIA IN THE AUSTRO-HUNGARIAN EMPIRE

- – – – · International borders, 1850
- ———— Boundary between Hungarian Kingdom and Austrian crownlands
- –·–·– Austrian crownland boundaries
- – – – Boundaries between west and east Galician judicial districts
- ·········· Approximate Polish-Ukrainian ethnolinguistic boundary
- · County seats in Galicia

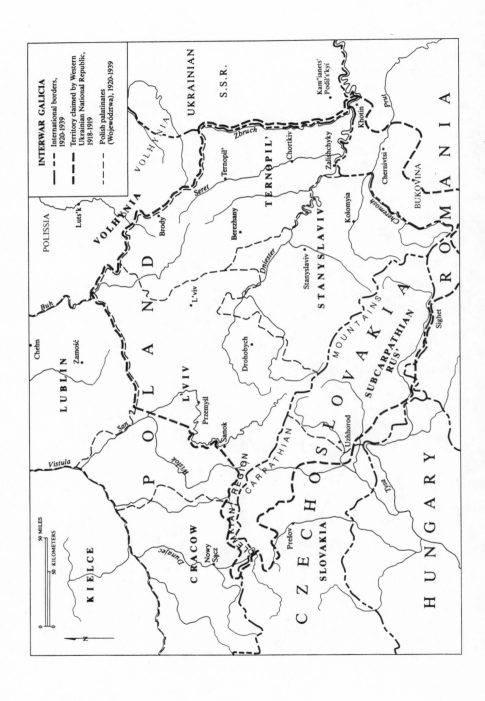

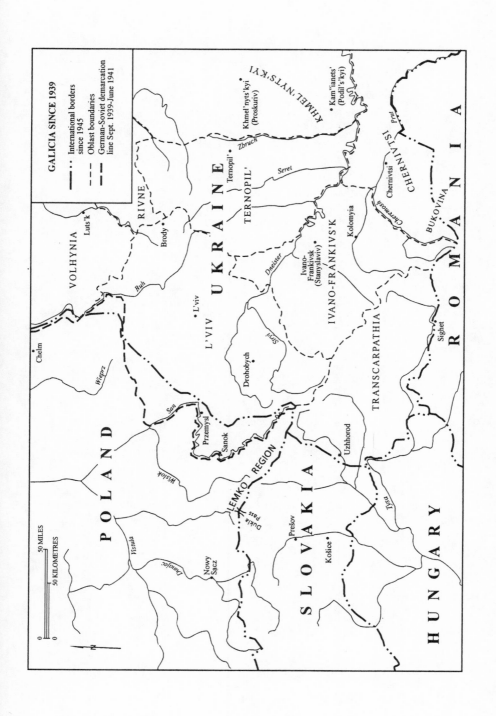

GALICIA SINCE 1939

··· International borders since 1945

‒ ‒ ‒ Oblast boundaries

‒··‒ German–Soviet demarcation line Sept. 1939–June 1941

POLAND

VOLHYNIA

Luts'k

Chełm

Wieprz

Visnula

Bug

Dunajec

Nowy Sącz

Wisłok

San

Przemyśl

Sanok

Dukla Pass

LEMKO REGION

SLOVAKIA

Prešov

Košice

RIVNE

Brody

L'viv

L'VIV

Drohobych

Styr

U K R A I N E

Ternopil'

TERNOPIL'

Zbruch

Seret

Dniester

Ivano-Frankivsk (Stanyslaviv)

IVANO-FRANKIVS'K

Khmel'nyts'kyi (Proskuriv)

Kam"ianets'-(Podil's'kyi)

KHMEL'NYTS'KYI

Kolomyia

TRANSCARPATHIA

Uzhhorod

Tysa

Sighet

Chernivtsi

CHERNIVTSI

Cheremosh

Prut

BUKOVINA

R O M A N I A

H U N G A R Y

N

50 MILES

50 KILOMETRES

THE ROOTS OF UKRAINIAN NATIONALISM: GALICIA AS UKRAINE'S PIEDMONT

chapter one

Galicia: A Brief Historical Survey

Introduction

The term *Galicia* is somewhat imprecise. It is generally associated with the boundaries of the pre-1918 province called in German *Galizien* (in English: Galicia),
located within the Austrian half of the Austro-Hungarian Habsburg monarchy.
The Austrian province of *Galizien* comprised territory north of the Carpathian
Mountains that was divided more or less by the San River and included land to
its west as far as Cracow inhabited mainly by Poles, and to the east as far as the
Zbruch and Cheremosh Rivers inhabited primarily by Ukrainians. In terms of its
territorial extent, Austrian Galicia was much different from historic Galicia.

The concept of historic Galicia derives from the medieval Rus' principality of
Halych. The boundaries of medieval Halych were defined by the crests of the
Carpathian Mountains in the south; the Wisłok and San rivers in the west; and
the Zbruch and Cheremosh rivers in the east. The northern boundary had no
natural frontier, but ran roughly from the mouth of the San River in the west to
the source of the Zbruch River in the east. These boundaries also coincided more
or less with the later Polish palatinate known as Rus' (Polish: Województwo
Ruskie), or Red Rus' (Polish: Ruś Czerwona), which existed from 1434 to 1772.
During the nineteenth century under Austrian rule, what had been medieval Halych
and the later Rus' palatinate was generally called Eastern Galicia. In this survey,
the concept *Galicia* will be understood in its long-term historical sense, meaning, basically, Ukrainian-inhabited lands east of the San and Wisłok rivers.

The Prehistoric Era

Although the history of Galicia traditionally begins with the first documentary
references to the territory that reveal its association with Kievan Rus' in the

late tenth century AD, archeological research has uncovered traces of human habitation going back as far as the Paleolithic Age (300,000 BC). Human settlement and cultural artifacts from this era of "prehistory" are particularly extensive in Galicia beginning with the second century BC.

A transitional period linking archeological "prehistory" with the historical era occurred between the fifth and tenth centuries AD, when Galicia was inhabited by the so-called White Croats. The White Croats have remained to this day a source of controversy among scholars, especially whether their origin was Irano-Alanic, East Slavic, or West Slavic. Whatever their origin, the White Croats had by the seventh century established fortified places known as *horody*, which evolved into centers of commerce and trade. The commercial importance of Galicia was enhanced by its geographical location because it was connected to the two most important water routes in east-central Europe. The upper San and Buh rivers gave access northwestward to the Baltic Sea and the upper Dniester River gave access southeastward to the Black Sea. Several overland trade routes also passed through Galicia, connecting Kiev in the east with Cracow, Buda, Prague, and other cities in the west. It is along Galicia's water and overland routes that the first important towns developed: Przemyśl (Ukrainian: Peremyshl'), Zvenyhorod, Terebovlia, and the territory's first capital, Halych.

By the tenth century, the western parts of Galicia were drawn into the political and cultural sphere of the Greater Moravian Empire, which from its base along the middle Danube River expanded northward and eastward beyond the Carpathians. Przemyśl itself came into being during the 970s (its name, according to some, derives from one of the early Moravian-Czech ruling families, the Přemyslides), and under Moravian influence a hybrid Latin/Byzantine form of Christianity was introduced in western Galicia even before the Christianization of the Rus' in Kiev.

The Kievan Era

The traditional starting point of Galician history is the year 981, when, according to the Rus' Primary Chronicle, the grand prince of Kiev, Volodymyr (reigned 980–1015), went to the Liakhs (Poles) and took Przemyśl, Cherven, and other cities. The same source mentions that in 993 Volodymyr attacked the Croats who inhabited Galicia at the time. These terse statements in the Primary Chronicle have generated numerous and yet unresolved questions about the status of Galicia before Volodymyr's appearance. For example, was the region retaken by the Rus' prince, or did he take it for the first time from Poland or Great Moravia? Whatever answers subsequent writers have provided to such questions, it is certain that after the late tenth century Galicia and its White Croatian inhabitants became part of the political, socioeconomic, and cultural sphere of Kievan Rus'.

Kievan Rus' was itself no more than a loosely knit federation of principalities, each with its own ruler or rulers representing various branches of the founding Riuryk dynasty and nominally subordinate to, though more often than not independent of, the senior or grand prince residing in Kiev. More important as unifying factors were culture and religion. Galicia received Christianity in its eastern Orthodox form from Kiev in the late tenth century and later a cultural language, Church Slavonic, from the same source.

Arrangements reached within the Kievan political order also provided Galicia, in the second half of the eleventh century, with its own branch of the Riuryk dynasty. This was the Rostyslav dynasty founded by Prince Rostyslav (d. 1065), the grandson of the powerful prince of Kiev, Iaroslav the Wise (reigned 1019–1054). Rostyslav's three sons, the real founders of the Galician dynasty, divided the realm and ruled from the fortresses of Zvenyhorod, Przemyśl, and Terebovlia. Their successors during the twelfth century— Volodymyrko (reigned 1124–1153) and Iaroslav Osmomysl' (reigned 1153– 1187)—united these cities, founded a new capital at Halych (1141), and extended the principality's territorial extent from its original base along the upper Buh and Dniester rivers toward the southeast as far as the Black Sea. It was also during this period that Galicia's economic wealth increased, mainly because of its exports of salt (mined near Halych) to Kiev and the revenue derived from international trade with Byzantium, Kiev, and cities in east-central Europe.

Like other lands within Kievan Rus', Galicia experienced several periods of chronic wars caused by interprincely rivalry for the throne of Kiev and for other principalities within the realm. During the eleventh and twelfth centuries, the princes of Kiev and especially of neighboring Volhynia frequently attempted to take the Galician throne. Galicia also had problems that distinguished it from other Kievan Rus' principalities. Both the neighboring Hungarian kingdom south of the Carpathians and the Polish principalities to the west claimed Galicia as their patrimony, and on numerous occasions armies from those lands invaded the region (sometimes at the invitation of Galician princes or discontented boyars). Finally, the boyars (a social estate represented by wealthy landowners) grew to be a politically and economically influential group, and after the twelfth century they served as an effective restraint on centralized princely authority. The boyars also contributed to the internal chaos that was often exploited by the neighboring Poles and Hungarians.

In 1199, the Rostyslav dynasty died out, and the local boyars invited Prince

Roman of Volhynia (reigned 1199–1205) to be their ruler. This heralded the establishment of a new branch of the Riuryk dynasty—the Romanovyches—as well as the unification of Galicia and Volhynia through the person of their ruling prince. After a period of civil war, foreign invasion, and declining economic fortunes, Galicia–Volhynia reached its apogee under Danylo (reigned 1238–1262) and his son Lev (reigned 1264–1301). Since Kiev had by the early thirteenth century lost its preeminent political and economic role, Galicia–Volhynia replaced it as the dominant force within the southern Rus' lands. This position was maintained even after the Mongol invasion, which devastated Kiev and other southern Rus' principalities, including Galicia, in 1240–1241. Danylo reached an accommodation with the Mongols, while at the same time negotiating with western states, including the Pope, from whom he received a crown in 1253. As king of Rus' (*Rex Rusiae*), Danylo was recognized as a full-fledged monarch in the context of the western-European feudal order. The Kingdom of Galicia–Volhynia (*regnum Galiciae et Lodomeriae*) continued to flourish, especially in the economic sphere, under Danylo's successor, Lev. It was also at this time (1260s) that L'viv was made the capital of Galicia. In order to enhance further the prestige of the Galician-Volhynian Kingdom, its ruler succeeded in obtaining its own Orthodox metropolitanate independent of Kiev, established in 1303 with a seat in Halych.

At the moment of its seeming height, however, the kingdom entered a period of decline, which ultimately was to prove fatal. The first decades of the fourteenth century witnessed the death of the last male in the Romanovych dynasty (1323); an increase in antiprincely activity on the part of the boyars; new friction with the Mongols; and frequent incursions on the part of the Poles, Hungarians, and a new power from the north, the Lithuanians. In 1340, the last Romanovych ruler (on the female side) was poisoned by the boyars. This act immediately plunged the kingdom into a period of internal civil war and anarchy as well as foreign invasion and diplomatic maneuvering that was to last for almost half a century, at the end of which Galicia was annexed by the Polish Kingdom.

The Polish Era

The years 1340 to 1772 comprise the Polish era of Galicia history. This era actually began with a transition period marked by the assassination in 1340 of Iurii II, the last Romanovych ruler of the Galician-Volhynian Kingdom, and the entry of Polish armed forces dispatched by Poland's King Casimir ("the Great," reigned 1333–1370). As part of his expansive drive toward the east, Casimir put forth dynastic claims to Galicia. For the next half-century, from

1340 to 1387, Galicia was to experience almost continuous instability because of foreign invasion by Tatars, conflicts provoked by various foreign claimants to rule Galicia and Volhynia, and revolts against princely rule led by local boyars. Among the claimants to the Galicia and Volhynian patrimony were its neighbors, Poland, Lithuania, and Hungary, each of which ruled the territory for varying periods of time. Finally, by 1387, Poland reached agreements with Lithuania and Hungary, as a result of which Galicia would remain under the jurisdiction of the kings of Poland. As for the neighboring principality of Belz (which since 1234 had been part of Galicia), it too came under Polish sovereignty, first as part of Mazovia, then after 1462 as a distinct palatinate. Neighboring Volhynia was incorporated into the Grand Duchy of Lithuania.

Within Poland, Galicia was initially known as the Rus' land (Polish: Ziemia Ruska, or Ruś Czerwona). Its boundaries more or less coincided with those of the medieval principality of Galicia (before the 1234 acquisition of Belz), and it was ruled by deputies (*starosta*) appointed by the king to handle administrative, legal, and military affairs. During the first decades of the fifteenth century, Galicia was administratively integrated with other lands in the Polish Kingdom, and in 1434 it became the Rus' palatinate (Polish: Województwo Ruskie) with its administrative center in L'viv. The Rus' palatinate was further divided into four administrative-territorial units known as lands (*ziemie*): L'viv, Halych, Przemyśl, and Sanok. During the sixteenth century, a fifth land, Chełm, was added. From its establishment, the Polish court system was introduced into the Rus' palatinate and the Galician nobility was given more clearly defined privileges by the king.

Poland's rulers set out to make Galicia politically, socially, and culturally a part of their kingdom. Attention was first directed at Galicia's influential boyar estate, and those who had fought against Polish expansion were forced to give up their landholdings. Consequently, many emigrated to Orthodox Rus' lands held by Lithuania in the east or to Orthodox Moldavia and Walachia in the south. On the other hand, many boyars received charters from Polish kings confirming their property rights and even awarding them new lands. A portion of the Galician ruling elite was thereby co-opted into the new political system, and although they retained their Rus' faith, as members of Poland's heraldic nobility (*szlachta*), they gradually came to consider themselves Poles in terms of political loyalty. Noble status was particularly important in Poland, because by the sixteenth century that kingdom had, in essence, become a "republic of nobles." This meant that at the national and in particular at the local level, political, legal, socioeconomic, and to a large extent cultural life was controlled or directed by the nobility. To be sure, there were great discrepancies in the wealth and therefore political power among the different strata of the nobility—magnates, gentry, petty gentry—although in theory all were legally equal and all held hereditary rank. The desire among Galicians to enjoy all the privileges and social prestige of noble status in Poland led many to abandon their Rus'-Ukrainian faith and language for Roman Catholicism and Polish culture. This assimilatory trend among the upper strata of Galician-Ukrainian society was particularly marked beginning with the second half of the sixteenth century.

Polish rule brought into the Galician countryside an influx of nobles of Polish and central-European origin, as well as Roman Catholic peasants. Meanwhile, in towns and cities the numbers of Germans, Poles, and Armenians increased, and they were later joined by Jews. Since a noble's wealth depended on landed property and the exploitation of agriculture, and since Poland's economy was restructured to respond to the demand for grain exports during the sixteenth century, the need for a fixed labor supply became paramount, resulting in the legal enserfment of the peasantry. Although there were variations throughout Galicia, by the end of the sixteenth century serfdom had become the norm, and some peasants were obliged to provide an ever-increasing number of work days for the domains of their lords.

The early centuries of the Polish era, at least until the mid-seventeenth century, brought economic prosperity to Galicia. International trade routes continued to flourish, connecting Galicia with the Ukrainian steppe in the east, with Cracow and central Europe in the west, with the lower Vistula River and the Baltic Sea to the north, and with the Hungarian Kingdom to the south. Protected by Polish military might and enriched by the growing wealth of the country's grain exports, Galicia's cities maintained prosperous commercial and artisan activity until the mid-seventeenth century.

By far the most important urban center in Galicia was L'viv, which was in fact the largest city throughout all Ukrainian territory during the era of Polish rule. As early as 1356, L'viv received from the Polish king the right of self-rule as outlined in the privileges of Magdeburg Law, and it became the administrative center of the Rus' palatinate when it was created in 1454. To enhance its importance, the city was heavily fortified. Polish rule also brought demographic change, with an influx of German and to a lesser degree Armenian settlers, who came to dominate the city's merchant and artisan classes until the late fifteenth century. Urban life was organized according to guilds, whose number increased to thirty by the mid-seventeenth century. Among the city's chief manufactures were iron works and weapons. By the seventeenth century, most of the Germans and Armenians in L'viv became polonized as the city took on a distinctly Polish character. Only Roman Catholics (Poles and polonized Germans) enjoyed the urban privileges of Magdeburg Law, while the growing

Jewish population was restricted to living in ghettos and to engaging only in those economic activities (especially money lending and certain trades) permitted them by royal decrees. The Orthodox Ukrainians had no particular privileges, and they were limited to one section of the city (*Rus'ka ulytsia*) and especially to its suburbs. It was this generally unfavorable situation among the Ukrainians in L'viv that provided the stimulus to the brotherhood movement and the Orthodox cultural revival of the sixteenth century.

The Polish presence in Galicia also affected culture. As in the rest of Poland, Latin became the official language of administration. The Roman Catholic church expanded its activity, establishing in 1365 a Latin-rite archdiocese in Halych, which was later transferred to L'viv in 1414. The L'viv archdiocese became the metropolitan see for Roman Catholic dioceses not only in the Rus' palatinate (L'viv–Halych, Przemyśl, Chełm), but in other Ukrainian lands as well. Concomitantly, there was a decline in the status of the Orthodox church (comprising the eparchies of Halych–L'viv, Chełm, and Przemyśl in Galicia). A distinct Galician Orthodox metropolitanate was formed at the outset of the fourteenth century to unite these various eparchies, but it eventually fell victim to the complexities of eastern church politics. In particular, the idea of a distinct Galician Rus' metropolitan jurisdiction was opposed by the metropolitan of Kiev and all Rus' residing in Moscow. As a result of this opposition, the Galician metropolitanate was abolished in 1401, and its eparchies were made subordinate once again to the metropolitan see of Kiev. Even more serious was the fact that the office of Orthodox bishop of Halych was not filled after 1406, and for the next 130 years the eparchy was administered by lay persons, many of whom were appointed by the Roman Catholic archbishop of L'viv–Halych. Although an Orthodox bishop of Halych was finally appointed in 1539, the fate of the Orthodox church in Galicia—which was the symbol of Rus'-Ukrainian culture in the region—continued to decline.

The Ukrainian reaction to these developments took different forms. Whereas the increase in serfdom prompted sporadic peasant uprisings (the most famous being one in southeastern Galicia in 1490–1492, led by a Moldavian named Mukha), a more typical pattern was flight eastward. In fact, much of the empty Ukrainian steppe in the lower Dnieper valley was settled during the sixteenth and seventeenth century by peasants fleeing Galicia.

On the cultural front, the sixteenth century was characterized by a revival aimed at restoring the legal and moral status of the Orthodox church and improving its intellectual standards. First led in the 1570s by Orthodox nobles from Galicia and most especially Volhynian magnates headed by Prince Kostiantyn of Ostrih (1527–1608), the cultural and religious revival soon came to be centered in the cities, especially L'viv. There, in the 1580s, a group of townspeople and petty nobles founded a brotherhood in association with the Orthodox Church of the Assumption. Although established at lay initiative, the L'viv Assumption Brotherhood strove to enhance the status of the Orthodox church and community through the founding of schools, print shops, hospitals, and orphanages. Most important, the L'viv brotherhood received, in 1589, the status of stauropegia. This meant it was responsible only to the ecumenical patriarch, or nominal head of the Orthodox church in Constantinople, and not to the local Orthodox bishop. The L'viv Assumption, or Stauropegial Brotherhood, also provided a model for other brotherhoods that were established not only in Galicia (Zamość, Przemyśl, Rohatyn, Horodok) but also in Kiev and other cities of Volhynia and Belarus'.

In a sense, by the late sixteenth century, Galicia, and especially L'viv, had become the most important center of religious and intellectual life for all Orthodox Rus' lands within Poland. It is, therefore, not surprising that the controversial question of church unity was related in large measure to developments in Galicia. Since the split between Rome and Constantinople in 1054, there had been several attempts to unite the Catholic and Orthodox worlds. Even the magnates who led the Orthodox Rus' cultural revival in Poland during the 1570s discussed the feasibility of church union.

It was actually the Orthodox bishop of L'viv, Gedeon Balaban (1530–1607, consecrated 1569), who initiated a new attempt at union. Jealous of the prerogatives and what he perceived as interference in church affairs by the Stauropegial Brotherhood, Balaban turned to the Roman Catholic archbishop of L'viv and began to discuss the possibility of union. Balaban was joined by several other Orthodox bishops and by the metropolitan of Kiev. Encouraged by the Polish king, two Orthodox hierarchs journeyed to Rome and declared for union. Upon their return they convened a synod at Brest in 1596 and proclaimed the union. In the meantime, however, Bishop Balaban had changed his mind. Backed by several Orthodox magnates and the brotherhood, he opposed the Union of Brest that had brought into being the so-called Uniate church, that is, one whose liturgy and practices (including a married clergy) remained Eastern Orthodox but which considered the Pope as its supreme authority. For his part, the Polish king not only recognized the new Uniate church as legal, he at the same time outlawed the Orthodox church and its supporters.

The precarious position of Orthodoxy in Galicia and other Rus' lands within Poland was somewhat improved by the issuance of several decrees legalizing once again the church's existence and culminating in a royal charter of 1632. Political events connected with the Zaporozhian Cossacks farther east were, however, to change the situation once again. After the failure of the Cossack revolution of 1648 to attain political independence for Ukrainian lands, the position of the Orthodox church worsened considerably. More and more Orthodox hierarchs in Galicia secretly and then openly passed over to the Uniate church. Finally, in 1708, the Stauropegial Brotherhood, which from its establishment in the sixteenth century had been the primary defender of Orthodoxy, became Uniate.

While the more than century-long struggle since the Union of Brest resulted in the demise of Orthodoxy in Galicia, it also prompted a spirited Uniate–Orthodox polemical debate enhanced by numerous publications produced on local printing presses and written by talented authors such as Ivan Vyshens'kyi (ca. 1550–1620) and Lavrentii Zyzanii (ca. 1570–1621), who were either natives of, or who worked in, Galicia. The region also produced a number of Orthodox leaders who emigrated eastward, where they played an important role in larger Ukrainian developments; these included the Zaporozhian Cossack hetman, Petro Konashevych Sahaidachnyi (d. 1622); the archimandrite of the Monastery of the Caves in Kiev, Ielysei Pletenets'kyi (1550–1624); and the metropolitan of Kiev, Iov Borets'kyi (d. 1631). Finally, while the Uniate church was jurisdictionally subordinate to Rome, it did maintain the liturgy and traditions of the Orthodox world, so that by the eighteenth century this hybrid ecclesiastical structure was well on its way to becoming the symbol of Galician-Ukrainian culture and identity.

Galician society during the Polish era was divided into several social strata, or estates, that essentially coincided with different ethnic groups. The Ukrainians comprised the vast majority of the enserfed peasant masses as well as a small number of Orthodox and later Uniate clergy. The traditional Ukrainian elite, that is, the few magnates and larger number of gentry who had at least retained their ancestral Orthodox faith before the Union of Brest, rapidly converted to Latin-rite Catholicism and assimilated totally to Polish culture during the seventeenth century. This process was less prevalent among the petty gentry (especially in the villages), many of whom remained adherents of the eastern church and continued to use Ukrainian in their everyday lives. As for townspeople, they were primarily Jews and smaller numbers of Armenians and Germans who dominated urban and small-town commercial and artisan activity. The Poles, including some rural peasants and urban dwellers, dominated the administrative/noble estate, which was made up either of individuals who had immigrated from western Polish lands or of local polonized Ukrainians.

Polish domination over Galicia—both political and cultural—seemed complete during the late seventeenth and most of the eighteenth centuries. The only brief threat came during the Zaporozhian Cossack revolution of 1648 led by Hetman Bohdan Khmel'nyts'kyi (ca. 1595–1657). Khmel'nyts'kyi invaded Galicia twice and laid siege to L'viv in 1648 and 1655. It was also during the

Khmel'nyts'kyi era that the town of Zboriv in far eastern Galicia experienced one of its most important historical moments. In August 1649, just outside the town, Khmel'nyts'kyi's Cossacks surrounded the army of the Polish king. That same month, the so-called Peace of Zboriv was signed, resulting in a military truce between Poles and Cossacks and the recognition of a Cossack state encompassing the Polish palatinates of Kiev, Bratslav, and Chernihiv. Galicia itself, however, remained outside the boundaries of the new Cossack state, and despite Khmel'nyts'kyi's presence in the region on two occasions, the existing sociopolitical system did not change. Polish rule over Galicia remained intact, although discontented peasants did revolt during the Khmel'nyts'kyi era and then flee eastward when the Cossacks retreated.

Other forms of protest against Polish rule consisted of peasant uprisings and the brigand movement (*opryshky*), which occurred during the late-seventeenth and early-eighteenth centuries. The peasant movement was sporadic, while the brigands restricted their activity to the Carpathian Mountains and the Pokuttia region. Thus, Polish rule remained firmly entrenched in Galicia. On the other hand, beginning in the second half of the seventeenth century, Poland's general economic situation took a turn for the worse, which was symbolized in Galicia by the precipitous decline in prosperity of the territory's leading center, L'viv. In the wake of the Khmel'nyts'kyi revolution, Poland–Lithuania was subjected to ongoing military conflict known as the "period of ruin," which in turn led to a change in trade patterns, the unfavorable influence of the landowning nobility on the country's economic policies, and eventually interference by outside powers, especially Russia, during the eighteenth century. Faced with such difficulties, the country was unable to withstand international pressure, which during the 1770s resulted in the First Partition of Poland by its neighbors. This First Partition was to have a decisive impact on Galicia.

The Austrian Era

In 1772, Prussia, Austria, and Russia carried out the first of what were to become three partitions of Polish territory that, less than a quarter of a century later, in 1795, were to result in the removal of Poland from the map of Europe. During the First Partition, the Austrian Habsburg empress Maria Theresa (reigned 1740–1780) laid claim as sovereign of Hungary to the lands of the medieval Galician-Volhynian Kingdom, which since the thirteenth century the Hungarian royal house had considered to be part of its own patrimony. On the basis of this claim, the Habsburgs received territory known as the Kingdom of Galicia and Lodomeria (the Latin name for Volhynia), which became one of the crownlands or provinces of the Austrian Empire.

Despite its official name, Austria's new territorial acquisition included hardly any of Volhynia (except for a small region around the town of Zbarazh). On the other hand, the province of Galicia did include virtually the entire former Polish palatinate of Rus' (minus the northern half of the Chełm land), the Bełz palatinate, and a small part of the Podolia palatinate west of the Zbruch River. Added to these core lands, which were inhabited primarily by Ukrainians and which had formed the medieval principality of Halych, were Polish-inhabited lands farther west (the Sandomierz and Cracow palatinates south of the Vistula River), which Austria also received in 1772.

Austria's new province of Galicia comprised 82,000 square kilometers and an estimated 2.7 million inhabitants. During the first decades of Habsburg rule, Galicia's boundaries changed many times. In 1787, Austria added the territory of Bukovina (75,000 inhabitants), which it had recently (1774) acquired from Moldavia, a vassal of the Ottoman Empire. Then, as a result of the Third Partition of Poland in 1795, Austria expanded farther northward, thereby almost doubling Galicia's size. This last acquisition, known as West Galicia, was lost in 1809 to the Duchy of Warsaw, which eventually became the Congress Kingdom of Poland within the Russian Empire. The only other territorial change came in 1847, when the Austrian-administered autonomous city-state of Cracow (including the city and some territory north of the Vistula River) was made an integral part of Galicia. With the exception of this last minor acquisition, the boundaries of Austrian Galicia were more or less fixed in 1809. Thus, from the outset of the nineteenth century, the Austrian province of Galicia–Lodomeria included historic Galicia (medieval Halych) inhabited primarily by Ukrainians (71 percent in 1849), as well as some Polish-inhabited territory west of the San and Wisłok rivers. In keeping with the principles outlined in the introduction, this discussion of the Austrian era will deal with developments in historic, or "eastern," Galicia.

Galicia entered the Austrian Empire at a time when that state was ruled by the "enlightened" co-rulers Maria Theresa and her son Joseph II (reigned 1780–1790). Both were anxious to strengthen their realm through a program of national planning and governmental centralization. By 1786, Austrian laws replaced Polish ones; the old dietines (*sejmiki*) were abolished; and, after a while, the elected urban councils (whose privileges had been guaranteed under Magdeburg Law) were replaced by an administration of bureaucrats appointed by the Habsburg imperial administration in Vienna. As in other Austrian provinces, an Assembly of Estates was set up. Located in L'viv, which under the German name of Lemberg remained the administrative capital, the assembly comprised magnates, gentry, and clergy. It could only send petitions to the emperor, however. Real power rested in the hands of the emperor's appointee, the governor (*gubernator/naczelnik*), who ruled with his administration from

L'viv. To administer the province more effectively, the Austrian authorities divided Galicia into nineteen regions (*Kreise*).

The era of the enlightened, or reforming, Austrian rulers which Galicia first experienced had a profound effect on the province's life. The formerly all-powerful position of the Polish nobility (*szlachta*) was broken. The theoretical equality of all nobles was ended by the creation of two separate estates—magnates and gentry; the tax-exempt status for nobles was abolished; their domination of the legal system ended; and their control over the serfs was strictly defined. Emperor Joseph II even went so far as to abolish serfdom in 1781, although this social experiment ended after his death, when serfdom was restored. Nonetheless, despite these and other reforms from above, life for the masses of the population remained the same. Galicia still remained an overwhelmingly agrarian society in which the vast majority of the populace was composed of enserfed peasants whose existence, especially in the economic sphere, was dependent on a small stratum of magnates and gentry.

Separated from the trade routes and markets of the Polish economic sphere of which it had been a part, the economic life of Galicia stagnated. Although the Austrian government did initially make some investments in the province, it soon decided Galicia should remain an agricultural region and source of food products and other raw materials for the rest of the empire. At the same time, it would itself become a market for products from the more industrialized western provinces. Hence, investments were not encouraged; industry was limited to a few ineffectual textile mills, iron works, glass works, and breweries; and the urban areas were neglected. In short, Galicia became a kind of internal colony and one of the most economically depressed and backward areas within the Austrian half of the empire.

Agriculture declined as well. The Josephine reforms, which were aimed at improving the status of the enserfed peasantry, were either short-lived or their intention was distorted. Most of the land remained in the hands of Polish magnates and gentry, and peasant obligations remained in force. The socio-economic situation was made worse by a rapid growth in population that could not be absorbed by a nonexistent industrial sector, and by an agricultural sector with no access to credit and smaller and smaller plots of arable land.

In one area, however, Austrian rule did bring a distinctly positive change. In their efforts to strengthen the internal structure of the Habsburg realm, Maria Theresa and Joseph II established a network of schools and addressed the problem of religion. While the activity of the monasteries was curtailed, the Uniate church (renamed the Greek Catholic church in 1774) was made the legal and social equal of the Roman Catholic church. Although supported by the state, educational advances for Ukrainians in Galicia remained closely linked to the

Greek Catholic church. To ensure that the church would be able to fulfill its new role, cadres of priests had to be educated, and for that purpose theological seminaries were established in Vienna (the Barbareum, 1775–1784) and L'viv (1783). Also, at the University of L'viv (est. 1784), a special collegium, the Studium Ruthenum (1787–1809), was set up to instruct Ukrainians who were still unable to understand Latin. Finally, the prestige of the Greek Catholic church was raised substantially when, in 1808, the Galician metropolitanate was restored with its seat in L'viv and eparchies in L'viv and Przemyśl. The result of these developments was the creation of a Galician-Ukrainian intelligentsia, albeit mostly clergy, trained in a Catholic and Western-oriented educational tradition.

Nevertheless, at the very time when the cultural status of Galicia's Ukrainians seemed to be steadily improving, there occurred a change in Austrian policy. The reform era of Maria Theresa and Joseph was over, and in the wake of the Napoleonic wars, the Viennese government under the influence of its chancellor, Prince Clemens von Metternich, was more interested in maintaining the status quo both within its own empire and within Europe as a whole. All of these factors affected the Ukrainians of Galicia. By the early nineteenth century, the Barbareum and the Studium Ruthenum had ceased functioning, the University of L'viv after 1817 offered instruction only in German, and the network of elementary schools taught for the most part in Polish. As a result, the younger generations who received a clerical or secular education were becoming rapidly polonized.

Nonetheless, the late-eighteenth-century Austrian enlightenment did have a lasting and positive impact on Ukrainians. One result was the formation of a Galician-Ukrainian intelligentsia. Though small in number and composed almost exclusively of Greek Catholic clergy, this group did become exposed to the ideas of romantic nationalism that dominated contemporary thought in Germany and east-central Europe and that placed an almost mystical faith in the supposed virtues of the *Volk*, that is, unique ethnolinguistic groups. Imbued with this new interest in the *Volk* (people), a few local leaders, mostly Greek Catholic clergy, inaugurated a national awakening in Galicia during the first half of the nineteenth century. Folk songs were collected, local histories were written, and several grammars were published. The first publication in the vernacular also appeared, the literary anthology *Rusalka dnistrovaia* (1837). This work was the result of collaboration among three Greek Catholic seminarians in L'viv who came to be known as the Ruthenian Triad—Markiian Shashkevych (1811–1843), Iakiv Holovats'kyi (1814–1888), and Ivan Vahylevych (1811–1866).

To be sure, all of these activities marked only the very embryonic stage of national development. Illiterate and impoverished serfs still comprised the vast majority of the population, while the small intelligentsia that was not polonized confined itself to struggling over issues of education and the question of formulating an acceptable literary language. There were no newspapers or journals in the native tongue, and the few attempts at establishing cultural societies had failed. In such circumstances the survival of the Galician-Ukrainian national movement would require the mobilization of a larger number of people than just a handful of clerical intellectuals. The participation of the masses, however, had to await political and social change, which finally came in 1848.

That year witnessed the outbreak of revolutionary activity throughout large parts of the European continent. Galicia was to remain under Austrian rule, but during the next six decades its Ukrainian population was to experience a profound political, social, and cultural transformation. The revolutionary activity that began in March 1848 and that eventually threatened to overthrow Habsburg rule spread quickly to Galicia. One month later, an imperial decree repealed serfdom. As a result of this act, a whole stratum of people (making up more than 90 percent of the Ukrainian populace) had for the first time to be reckoned with as a factor in political and cultural life. In May, the liberated serfs participated in elections to Austria's first parliament (the Reichstag). At the same time, a small group of Ukrainian leaders, mostly Greek Catholic clergy, set up political and cultural organizations. Even though Habsburg authority was by 1850 reinstated throughout the empire and a period of neoabsolutist rule had begun, this did not erase the fact that Ukrainians, because of the events of 1848, came into existence as a group. From now on, their political and cultural needs were taken into account by the imperial government in Vienna as well as by the provincial authorities in Galicia.

The abolition of serfdom, an increase in the number of Ukrainian elementary and secondary schools, and the resultant advances in literacy contributed, after the 1870s, to the growth of civic consciousness and to the organizational strength of the peasant masses as well as to the evolution of a new, more secular Ukrainian intelligentsia. Along with this came the establishment of numerous Ukrainian newspapers and journals, publishing houses, cultural societies, theaters, credit associations, economic cooperatives, and, in the 1890s, political parties. Thus, by the end of the nineteenth century, Ukrainians in Galicia had created a comprehensive infrastructure for national life that in turn prompted demands for more and more political autonomy.

During this rapid advancement of Galician-Ukrainian society, it is not surprising that the group's political and cultural leaders often suffered because of the inability of Austrian society to fulfill their ever-rising expectations. Whereas the Habsburg imperial government permitted and even at times promoted Ukrainian national life, political realities dictated that Vienna reach an accommodation with the most powerful force in Galicia—the Poles. The failure of the post-1850 neoabsolutist approach to Austria's internal problems and its military defeats at the hands of France and Sardinia (1859) and of Prussia (1866) forced Vienna to embark on a period of experiment in reorganizing its empire. The result was the establishment of a new parliament (1861), which ushered in Austria's constitutional period, and the creation of the Dual Monarchy (1867), which permitted self-rule for Hungary. The Galician Poles, who had just witnessed the failure of another Polish revolt (1863) against Russia, were ready to cast their lot fully with the Habsburgs. They expected, however, to receive the same degree of autonomy that the Hungarians had received. Vienna was not prepared to go so far, although in return for their political support the Poles were allowed to control the internal affairs of Galicia as they saw fit. As a result, the provincial administration remained basically in Polish hands at least until the outbreak of World War I in 1914.

For their part, the Ukrainians were left to struggle as best they could to obtain a greater control over the life of the province. It was an uphill battle, fought primarily for more schools, for more seats in both the Austrian imperial parliament (Vienna) and the Galician provincial diet (L'viv), and for more funds for cultural and economic activity. Like all peoples living within a multinational state and struggling for political autonomy and even independence, the Ukrainians in Austrian Galicia were never satisfied that they had gained enough concessions. Nevertheless, despite continued Polish dominance in the affairs of the province and the generally underdeveloped agrarian-based economy that left the region one of the poorest in the whole Habsburg Empire, the Ukrainians of Galicia did make remarkable progress in the political and especially cultural spheres. Their region, small by comparison with Ukrainian-inhabited lands in the neighboring Russian Empire, became the leading center for the Ukrainian national revival during the second half of the nineteenth century.

Because of the significance of Galicia for the Ukrainian national revival in general, it might be useful to look in somewhat more detail at political, socioeconomic, and cultural developments from 1848 until the outbreak of World War I. During this period, Ukrainians in Galicia entered the modern political sphere for the first time, and their activity was played out in three places: in Galicia itself, at the Slav Congress in Prague, and at the newly elected Reichstag, which carried on its short-lived parliamentary career in Vienna and then in the Moravian town of Kroměříž/Kremsier.

In Galicia itself, the enterprising governor, Count Franz Stadion (1806–1853), tried to stay on top of the revolutionary situation. He pushed through a decree on April 22, 1848, that liberated the serfs (actually months ahead of lands in the rest of the empire), and in early May he encouraged a group of Ukrainian Greek Catholic clergy centered at the St. George Cathedral (from which the term *sviatoiurtsi* derives) to form a political organization, the Supreme Ruthenian Council (Holovna Rus'ka Rada). The latter development gave rise immediately to Polish accusations that Stadion had created a Ruthenian problem, even the Ruthenian nationality. Consequently, polonized nobles of East Slavic Rus' origin set up a rival Ruthenian Council (Rus'kyi Sobor) composed of "Ruthenians of the Polish nation" (*gente Rutheni natione Poloni*). During 1848, the Ukrainians also established their first newspapers—*Zoria Halytska* and *Dnewnyk ruski*; their first cultural societies—the Congress of Rusyn Scholars (Sobor Rus'kykh Uchenykh) and the Galician-Rus' Matytsia (Halytsko-russka Matytsia); and their first military units—a peasant frontier defense organization, a national guard, and a sharpshooter division.

Outside Galicia, two rival delegations of Ukrainians, one representing the Supreme Ruthenian Council, the other the pro-Polish Ruthenian Council, journeyed to Prague in June, where they and other national leaders put forth cultural and political demands at the first international Slavic Congress. Even more important was Ukrainian participation in Austrian political life. During debates in the Austrian imperial parliament (Reichstag) between July 1848 and March 1849, thirty-nine Ukrainian deputies (elected in May 1848) called for greater social reform and the division of the province into Ukrainian and Polish halves.

The importance of these developments for Galicia's Ukrainians cannot be overstated. For the first time, Ukrainian interests were considered in Austria, as Ukrainians participated directly in political life not only within their own province but also at the national level in the imperial capital. Furthermore, by their presence at the Slavic Congress in Prague, Ukrainians were recognized as a distinct nationality by fellow Slavs within and beyond the Austrian Empire.

Indeed, these political advances depended entirely on the course of the 1848 revolution. After the Austrian imperial army (with tsarist Russian military assistance) defeated the Hungarian revolutionaries in August 1849 and quickly consolidated its control throughout the empire, the government in Vienna under the new emperor, Franz Joseph I (reigned 1848–1916), embarked on a policy of neoabsolutism. This meant that the empire as a whole was to be governed directly from Vienna. In Galicia, martial law was imposed, lasting until 1854. Then, for the next quarter of a century, the province was to be administered by a Polish governor, later renamed viceroy, Count Agenor Gołuchowski (1812–1875). His policies had the full support of the Vienna

government, even if his pro-Austrian sympathies were not yet fully appreciated by Polish political circles, whether conservative or liberal.

As for the Ukrainians, the Supreme Ruthenian Council dissolved itself at
the urging of the authorities in 1852. Subsequently, most of the group's concerns revolved around cultural issues, such as the maintenance of Ukrainian
cultural institutions, the use of the Ukrainian language in public life, and a
preference for German instead of Polish as the official language in the school
system. The main cultural concern at the time was the language question, a
problem that took on elements of a Ukrainian *cause célèbre* when
Gołuchowski's administration proposed in 1859 that the Latin alphabet, instead of the traditional Cyrillic, be introduced for all Ukrainian publications.
These efforts were aborted following concerted protests by Ukrainian leaders
that blocked the implementation of any alphabet reform.

With the failure of the imperial government's policy of neoabsolutism, the
decade of the 1860s witnessed the inauguration of the constitutional period in
Austrian history. In February 1861, a two-chamber imperial parliament
(Reichsrat) consisting of a House of Lords (Herrenhaus) and House of Deputies (Abgeordnetenhaus) was established by imperial patent in Vienna, while
during the same year the Galician Diet (Landtag/Sejm) in L'viv was transformed into a representative assembly. The diet consisted of representatives
elected by four *curiae*, or estates: great landowners, chambers of commerce,
towns, and rural communes. A few Ukrainians were chosen from the last three
estates. Initially, representatives to the House of Deputies of the imperial parliament in Vienna were designated by the Galician Diet; then, after 1873, the
four-*curiae* system was initiated for elections to the imperial parliament as
well. In 1895, a fifth *curia* was created and opened to all male voters, and
finally in 1907 the *curia* system was abolished and replaced by universal male
suffrage. In the upper house of the imperial parliament, Ukrainian Greek Catholic bishops were members ex officio from the very beginning.

Despite their rough demographic equivalency to the Poles, the Ukrainians
were always underrepresented in both the Austrian imperial parliament and
the Galician Diet. Between 1861 and 1914, the number of Ukrainians in any
one session ranged from 38 (1861) to 3 (1867) in parliament and from 46
(1861) to 13 (1883 and 1901) in the diet, which meant at best never more than
30 percent of the total allotment in either of the representative bodies.

In terms of goals, most Ukrainian politicians had throughout this period
basically accepted the existence of the Habsburg Empire, although they hoped
to institute certain administrative changes. These included: (1) the division of
Galicia into two parts, each with its own diet, administration, and board of
education—"eastern Galicia" thereby becoming a "Ukrainian" province; (2)

the principle of equality for Ukrainian-language usage in schools and public life; (3) the establishment of a Ukrainian university; and (4) the implementation of universal suffrage.

At the provincial level, the Ukrainians were opposed by the Poles, whose own political interests were in most cases diametrically opposed to Ukrainian interests. Polish-Ukrainian relations did vary, however, and ranged from efforts at compromise (as during the so-called New Era of the 1890s) to total alienation (as during the first decade of the twentieth century) that culminated in 1908 with the assassination by a Ukrainian student of Galicia's Polish viceroy.

Initially, Ukrainian political desires were expressed by umbrella-like organizations similar to the 1848 Supreme Ruthenian Council. More influential were political parties, which came into being during the 1890s. The first of these was the Ukrainian Radical party (est. 1890). It called for the complete transformation of Galician society according to socialist principles, and after 1895 its program included the proposal of one of its members, Iuliian Bachyns'kyi (1870–193?), for the eventual creation of an independent Ukrainian state that would include Ukrainian territory in Austria–Hungary as well as in the Russian Empire. The more influential National Democratic party was founded in 1899, and it hoped to work through existing channels in Austria to create a separate Ukrainian province of eastern Galicia, which someday might become the Piedmont of an independent Ukrainian state on both sides of the Austro-Russian border. The other two orientations in Ukrainian political life, the Old Ruthenians and the Russophiles, also had their own political parties, but these never attained more than 15 percent of the representatives in either the Galician Diet or the Austrian parliament.

Of the four basic political goals of Galicia's Ukrainians, only universal suffrage was attained in 1907, as part of a general Austrian law that affected elections to the imperial parliament. At the provincial level, the Poles continued to be the dominant force. Only in 1914 did the Ukrainians and the Poles finally reach a compromise that promised political and cultural equality for the two nationalities. The agreement never went into effect, however, because within a few months war broke out, changing entirely the situation in Galicia and in Europe as a whole. Nonetheless, during the last seventy-five years of Austrian rule, Galician Ukrainians did participate in the political process, so that by the outbreak of World War I a whole new generation of leaders and a politically aware populace had come into being.

Despite certain achievements in Austrian political life, the mass of the Ukrainian population remained rural peasants and agricultural laborers. And although the serfs were legally freed from bondage in 1848, they in essence remained economically bound to their landlords. This situation was largely due to the fact that the right of the peasants to use the gentry-owned woods and pastures (the traditional "servitudes") was revoked. Because they were frequently unable to pay for the use of woods and pastures, the peasants were forced to rely on their own land, which was constantly being subdivided among offspring. Such a situation resulted in chronic indebtedness among Ukrainian peasants, who effectively were transformed into "economic serfs." Despite repeated demands by Ukrainian political activists for a favorable resolution of the "servitude" issue and for more equitable distribution of the land, the Polish gentry, in particular the so-called Podolians in eastern Galicia, successfully opposed (at least until the end of the century) any real reform. Thus, by 1900 as much as 40 percent of the farmland remained in the hands of large landlords (each owning at least 100 hectares). The vicious cycle of indebtedness, the subdivision of land into smaller holdings, and rapid demographic growth (the population rose by 45 percent between 1869 and 1910) led at the turn of the century to a series of agricultural strikes, the largest of which took place in 1902, involving an estimated 200,000 peasants.

In an attempt to alleviate the economic distress of the peasantry, the new secular-oriented populist intelligentsia created a strong cooperative movement, which, beginning in the 1880s, led to the formation of numerous agricultural and dairy cooperatives, trade and credit associations, and insurance companies. The cooperatives were not only run by Ukrainians, they also published widely in the Ukrainian language and thereby helped to promote the national movement. Thus, organic social growth in the crucial economic sphere was combined with and carried out in a Ukrainian national spirit.

The cooperative movement was unable to alleviate the oppressive economic conditions suffered by most peasants, however. When all else failed, emigration to North America seemed the only solution. Encouraged by steamship agents who visited the Galician countryside, the first emigrants began to depart in the 1880s. Hearing about the success of their brethren through avidly read letters, they established a pattern of chain migration that reached large-scale proportions during the first decade of the twentieth century. By 1914, an estimated 420,000 Galician Ukrainians had emigrated to the New World, mainly to the United States and Canada. Smaller numbers went to South America and other European countries.

The reluctance of the large landowners in eastern Galicia to change the economic status quo (which assured them an unlimited supply of cheap labor) and the general Habsburg policy that considered Galicia to be an agricultural zone and marketplace (a kind of "internal colony") for products from the empire's industrially advanced western provinces (Bohemia, Silesia, Lower

Austria) are two factors that caused the province to remain economically under-developed. Hence, while Galicia accounted for 25 percent of the land area in the Austrian half of the monarchy, it had only 9.3 percent of the industrial enter-prises—and most of these were in western Galicia. A few sawmills, tanneries, and brick factories existed in eastern Galicia; then in the 1890s oil fields near Drohobych were developed. The small enterprises, however, were mostly owned by Jews, who made up as much as 75 percent of the population in the towns, while the oil industry (which by 1905 accounted for 5 percent of world produc-tion) was largely in the hands of foreign investors (English and Austrian).

In contrast to their poor economic situation and only limited achievements in political life, Ukrainians in Galicia made marked advances in their national culture, most especially between the 1860s and 1914. That half-century wit-nessed a phenomenal growth in popular and scholarly cultural organizations, in the press and other publications, in schools, and in literary activity. More-over, all this was taking place at a time when, in the Russian-controlled Dnieper Ukraine, Ukrainian cultural activity was severely curtailed (1863–1905). To be sure, Galician-Ukrainian cultural life was not without difficulties, such as the internal controversies over national identity and an acceptable literary lan-guage, or the continued reluctance on the part of the provincial administration to allow more Ukrainian schools. On the other hand, these factors may have stimulated as much as hampered the vibrant cultural activity that was the mark of the last half-century of Austrian rule in Ukrainian eastern Galicia.

National identity became a serious factor in Galician life only after 1848. Before then there were basically two orientations: the Polonophiles, or Ruthenians of the Polish nation; and the Rus' patriots. Soon after 1848, the Polonophiles disappeared while the Rus' intelligentsia became divided into three groups: the Old Ruthenians (*starorusyny*), the Ukrainophiles (*narodovtsi*), and the Russophiles (often described by their antagonists with the pejorative term *moskvofily*). The Old Ruthenians had a vague sense of belonging to East Slavdom, although their national horizons did not really transcend the bound-aries of Galicia. The populist Ukrainophiles (*narodovtsi*) considered them-selves part of a distinct Ukrainian nationality stretching from the Carpathians to the Caucasus Mountains. The Russophiles rejected both the vagueness of the Old Ruthenians and the "separatism" of the Ukrainophiles and considered the population of eastern Galicia (as well as the Dnieper Ukraine) to be part of a common Russian nationality, the so-called *obshcherusskii narod*.

Each of the national orientations had its own cultural organizations. The Old Ruthenians controlled the Galician-Rus' Matytsia (est. 1848), the Stauropegial Institute, the National Home (est. 1864), and the Kachkovs'kyi Society (est. 1874). The Ukrainophiles founded the Rus'ka Besida (est. 1861), the Prosvita Society (est. 1868), and the prestigious Shevchenko Scientific Society (est. 1873). The Russophiles never founded new cultural organizations, but by the end of the century they took over most of those that had been run by the Old Ruthenians.

The Galician-Ukrainian cultural movement was also accompanied by a burst of publication activity during the second half of the nineteenth century. Hundreds of titles in thousands of copies made their appearance. Literature flourished, and the region produced one of the greatest Ukrainian writers anywhere, the prolific Ivan Franko (1856–1916). The press prospered, and each of the national orientations had its own newspapers, cultural magazines, and scholarly journals. Among the most important were, for the Old Ruthenians, *Slovo* (1861–87), *Nauka* (1871–1939), *Naukovyi/Lyteraturnyi sbornyk* (1865–97); for the Ukrainophiles, *Pravda* (1867–96), *Dilo* (1880–1939), *Zoria* (1880–97), *Literaturno-naukovyi vistnyk* (1898–1932), *Zapysky Naukovoho tovarystva im. Shevchenka* (1892–1937); and for the Russophiles, *Besieda* (1887–98), *Prikarpatskaia Rus'* (1909–15), *Golos naroda* (1909–14), and *Nauchno-literaturnyi sbornik* (1901–34).

Closely related to the growth of the Ukrainian press in Galicia was the language question. The need for publications, prompted by the increase in the size of the secular intelligentsia and educated general public, forced editors to face a practical question that at the same time was laden with cultural and national implications. Namely, what literary language should be used in publications? By the beginning of the twentieth century, the Galician recension of Church Slavonic (described as the *iazychiie* by its detractors), the language used by the Old Ruthenians, and literary Russian, the language used by the Russophiles, were both rejected by the majority of the populace (as well as by the Austrian government) in favor of the Ukrainophile solution of a vernacular-based language. After protracted debate between Galician Ukrainians and their brethren in the Russian Empire, the language finally adopted was standard Ukrainian based on the Poltava dialects in Dnieper Ukraine.

Galician-Ukrainian political and cultural leaders also placed great emphasis on expanding the group's educational facilities during the last decades of the nineteenth century. A closely related problem was the legal status of language. After 1867, Polish replaced German as the language of instruction in secondary schools, while at the elementary level the decision was left up to local community councils. As a result of these provisions, Ukrainian leaders were forced to begin a long campaign to pressure the provincial and imperial governments to increase the number of Ukrainian schools at all levels.

By the outbreak of World War I, the Ukrainians had achieved a certain success. They did have 2,510 elementary schools (71 percent of the total number in the region) and six *gymnasia* with Ukrainian as the language of instruction, as well as two *gymnasia* with parallel classes in Ukrainian and ten teacher's colleges (seminaries) where Ukrainian was taught alongside Polish. Ukrainians remained dissatisfied, however. For instance, while there was one Polish *gymnasium* for every 60,400 Poles, there was only one Ukrainian *gymnasium* for every 546,000 Ukrainians. Consequently, the Ukrainians founded private schools run by educational societies or by the Greek Catholic church, so that by 1914 there were sixteen privately run elementary schools, ten *gymnasia*, and three teachers' colleges.

Whereas the Ukrainians never had their own university in Galicia, they did have departments (*katedry*) at the University of L'viv, which provided Ukrainian-language instruction in Ukrainian-related and some non-Ukrainian disciplines. The first such department (*katedra*) was established by the Vienna government during the revolutionary era of 1848. By the end of Austrian rule there were a total of ten Ukrainian departments, the most famous being the department of history, held from its establishment in 1894 down to 1914 by the distinguished scholar and national leader Mykhailo S. Hrushevs'kyi (1866–1934).

The direction of the national movement in Galicia was affected as well by other internal and external developments, namely, the church, and relations abroad. Ever since the first national awakening at the outset of the nineteenth century, the Greek Catholic church had supplied the vast majority of national leaders, who by the 1870s had formed the stronghold of the Old Ruthenian orientation in cultural life. Relations with the Ukrainophile orientation were initially cool until the outset of the twentieth century, when Andrei Sheptyts'kyi (1865–1944, consecrated 1899) became metropolitan of the Greek Catholic church. He eventually supported the Ukrainophile orientation in national life, thereby restoring the close historic bonds between religion and nationality. Meanwhile, some Old Ruthenians in the 1880s and the Russophiles after the 1890s favored Orthodoxy as the "true" faith of the local populace. As a result, peasants in certain areas (especially the Zboriv and later Lemko regions) were encouraged "to return to the Orthodox faith." Orthodoxy was also frequently equated with acceptance of a Russian national identity and hope in "liberation" someday by the Russian tsar. Reacting to what was perceived as a threat to its own security, in 1882 and again on the eve of World War I, the Austrian government held treason trials in Galicia in which local Old Ruthenians and Russophiles were accused of promoting Orthodoxy and thereby tsarist Russian political aims against the Habsburg Empire.

In such circumstances, Galicia became the focus of much attention among Ukrainian and Russian political and cultural leaders in the Russian Empire who, in turn, had a great influence on the national life of Galician Ukrainians.

Figures from Russia's Dnieper Ukraine, such as Mykhailo Drahomanov (1841–1895), Panteleimon Kulish (1819–1897), and Oleksander Konys'kyi (1836–1900). interacted closely with the Galician Ukrainophiles. Analogously, Russian cultural leaders—especially the Pan-Slavists—and tsarist officials gave varying kinds of support to Galicia's Russophiles. Such cultural interest was transformed by the first decades of the twentieth century into foreign-policy goals, so that one important cause of friction between Austria–Hungary and Russia was the latter's interest in "liberating" the "Russians" of Galicia from the "yoke of Austrian rule." Such goals became reality following the outbreak of World War I in August 1914.

World War I and the Struggle for National Independence

The last phase of Austrian rule in Galicia began in August 1914, with the outbreak of World War I. It ended four years later with the dissolution of the Habsburg Empire in October 1918. From the outset of hostilities, Galicia, especially its eastern, Ukrainian-inhabited half, was a theater for military operations. After a brief advance onto Russian territory, the Austro-Hungarian army was turned back by a series of swift Russian victories that began on August 5; one month later, the tsarist armies reached the San River and the well-defended walls of Przemyśl. During their rapid retreat, Habsburg troops, especially the Hungarian *Honvéds*, took revenge upon many inhabitants whom they considered to be Russian spies. Several hundred people—both local Russophiles and Ukrainophiles, Orthodox and Greek Catholics—were summarily shot, hanged, or herded off to concentration camps, the most infamous being in Styria near the former hamlet of Talerhof (now under the Graz airport).

Militarily in control of eastern Galicia, the Russian government installed a civilian administration headed by Count Georgii Bobrinskoi, who immediately cooperated with local Russophiles and pro-Russian Poles. Ukrainian cultural and educational institutions were closed, plans were made to dismantle the Greek Catholic church, and several leaders, including Metropolitan Andrei Sheptyts'kyi, were arrested and deported to Russia. Those Ukrainians who managed to flee westward before the Russian advance settled in refugee camps, the largest of which was at Gmünd in Upper Austria. The tsarist army captured Przemyśl in March 1915 and advanced even farther westward into Galicia as far as Gorlice and Tarnów on the Dunajec River. Finally, an Austrian counter-offensive (with German help) began in May 1915. Within a month the Russian government was driven out of L'viv, and the tsarist army was pushed back so that it managed to retain only the far eastern section of Galicia, south of Ternopil' between the Seret and Zbruch rivers. The rest of Galicia remained under the control of an Austrian military and civilian administration until November 1, 1918. The Russians held most of eastern Galicia again briefly during the summer of 1916, but by the fall of that year they were driven back to the region around Ternopil', which they were finally forced to abandon as well in July 1917.

During the war years, Galician-Ukrainian leaders set up new interparty political organizations in Vienna. The first of these, the Supreme Ukrainian Council (Holovna Ukraïns'ka Rada), within a week of its establishment on August 1, 1914, united the Ukrainian units in the Austrian army into a military formation known as the Ukrainian Sich Riflemen (Ukraïns'ki Sichovi Stril'tsi). This unit fought within the Austrian ranks against the tsarist army on the eastern front. The Supreme Ukrainian Council cooperated with the Union for the Liberation of Ukraine (Soiuz Vyzvolennia Ukraïny), also founded in Vienna in August, but by Ukrainians from the Russian Empire.

Eventually, two factions arose among the Galician Ukrainians. They were in basic agreement about their ultimate goals but not about tactics. The General Ukrainian Council (Zahal'na Ukraïns'ka Rada, est. May 5, 1915), led by the Austrian parliamentary deputy Kost' Levyts'kyi (1859–1941), supported the idea of an independent state for Dnieper Ukrainians in the Russian Empire but called only for national autonomy for Galicia within Austria. The other faction, the Ukrainian Parliamentary Representation, led by another member of the parliament in Vienna, Ievhen Petrushevych (1863–1940), and supported by the Ukrainian Sich Riflemen, was after 1916 less conciliatory toward the Austrians, demanding the separation of Galicia and a guarantee of Ukrainian autonomy even before hostilities ceased. The imperial Habsburg government made some token concessions but never fulfilled the basic demands of either Ukrainian faction.

Despite such procrastination, which was a hallmark of Vienna's governmental policy, Galicia's Ukrainians basically remained loyal to the Habsburgs, thereby confirming their prewar reputation within the Austro-Hungarian Empire as the "Tyroleans of the East." As ultra-loyal "Tyroleans" until the very last months of 1918, the Ukrainian Sich Riflemen fought with distinction on the side of the Austrian imperial army, while politicians continued to plan for the division of the province and the "restoration" of the medieval Galician-Volhynian Kingdom, to be ruled, they hoped, by the Habsburg Archduke Wilhelm Franz (Vasyl' Vyshyvanyi, 1895–ca. 1950). Finally, in October 1918, when the end of the war was in sight and it became clear that Austria was to be on the losing side, Ukrainian politicians were forced to consider other solutions to their homeland's future. On October 19, several leaders gathered in L'viv, where they stated their intention to declare an independent western-

Ukrainian state comprising Ukrainian-inhabited northern Bukovina and north-eastern Hungary as well as eastern Galicia.

Ukrainian activity was similar to that of other nationalities (and branches of nationalities) in the rapidly disintegrating Austro-Hungarian Empire, who also created national councils, declared their independence and then set out to achieve in fact what they had declared in word. Ukrainian military and political preparations for the imminent collapse of the Habsburg state had already begun with the establishment in L'viv of a Central Military Committee at the end of September and a Ukrainian National Council (Rada) headed by parliamentarian Ievhen Petrushevych on October 18. Prepared militarily and politically, the Galician Ukrainians took the initiative on November 1 by seizing the Austrian government buildings in L'viv and by establishing a Western Ukrainian National Republic (Zakhidno-Ukraïns'ka Narodna Respublyka) headed by Ievhen Petrushevych.

Seizing control from a disintegrating empire was one thing; maintaining control in the face of a well-armed and antagonistic rival claimant for the same territory was quite another. Local Poles, who had always claimed all of Galicia as part of their own political and cultural patrimony, were hardly willing to give up their claims to the very same Ukrainians over whom they had had political ascendancy even during the Austrian era. Thus, in the absence of Habsburg authority, war broke out immediately between local Polish militia and the Ukrainian Galician Army, which had evolved from the Sich Riflemen.

After several battles, by the last week of November 1918, the Poles had driven the Ukrainians out of L'viv. The Ukrainian government moved first to Ternopil' and then at the end of December to Stanyslaviv. Despite a rapidly changing military situation, the Ukrainians managed to establish a government administration and to set up diplomatic representation abroad. The Galicians also decided to unite with their brethren in Dnieper Ukraine, who had previously declared their independence from Russia with the establishment of the Ukrainian National Republic on January 22, 1918. Now, exactly one year later—on January 22, 1919—Galician representatives went to Kiev where in a solemn act they proclaimed the unity (*sobornist'*) of all Ukrainian lands.

Despite this act of union, the Western Ukrainian National Republic maintained its own administration and its well-equipped Ukrainian Galician Army. That army was still fighting against the Poles for control of Galicia in a fierce struggle that had reached a stalemate by early 1919. The situation changed radically, however, in April. Under General Józef Haller (1873–1960), a battle-hardened Polish army which had fought alongside the French during World War I was dispatched eastward by the Allies ostensibly to fight the Bolsheviks in Soviet Russia. Instead, it entered Galicia. In such circumstances, the Ukrainian Galician Army and the Western Ukrainian government were, by July 1919, militarily overwhelmed and pushed east of the Zbruch River and entirely out of Galicia.

Forced from its homeland, the Ukrainian Galician Army first fought along-side the forces of the Ukrainian National Republic and thereby became em-broiled in the Ukrainian struggle for independence and the civil war that was raging in lands of the former Russian Empire. In November 1919, acting with-out the consent of the Western Ukrainian government, the Ukrainian Galician Army joined the anti-Bolshevik White Russian Army of General Anton Denikin (1872–1947), only later to switch sides and become the Red Ukrainian Galician Army (January 1920), a unit that operated with Bolshevik forces until its final dissolution in April 1920.

For its part, the Western Ukrainian government set up an administration in exile, first in Kamianets'-Podil's'kyi (July–November 1919) and then in Vienna (to March 1923), where, under the leadership of Ievhen Petrushevych, it tried to convince the Entente powers of the need to guarantee the existence of an independent and neutral Galician-Ukrainian state in the face of Polish aggres-sion.

The Interwar Era

Following the exile of the Ukrainian army and government in July 1919, Galicia came under the control of the new Polish state that had just come into exist-ence after World War I. The idea of Polish statehood had been a war aim of the victorious Entente, so that when the Entente leaders gathered in Paris in early 1919 to redraw the map of Europe they were in general positively predisposed to the Poles. In fact, even before the Ukrainian army and government were driven entirely out of Galicia, the Entente recognized Polish control of lands up to the Zbruch River until the final "decisions to be taken by the Supreme Council [of the Allied and Associated Powers] for the settlement and political status of Galicia."

The Galician-Ukrainian government-in-exile under Petrushevych placed high hopes in the declaration of the Supreme Council, assuming that the Entente would indeed eventually resolve the Galician matter in its favor. Even the Treaty of Versailles signed on June 28, 1919, expressly postponed a decision on the eastern frontiers of Poland (including Galicia), which would be "subsequently determined by the principal Allied and Associated Powers." For its part, the new government in Warsaw began to administer all of Galicia as if it were already an integral part of Poland. By 1920, the former Austrian crownland of

Galicia (with its local diet and educational administration) was abolished and divided into four Polish provinces (*województwa*): Cracow, L'viv, Stanyslaviv, and Ternopil'. The last three of these provinces, comprising the core area of pre-1772 historic Galicia and inhabited predominantly by Ukrainians, were renamed Eastern Little Poland (*Małopolska Wschodnia*). Not only were Ukrainians denied autonomous status in Eastern Little Poland, they were also deprived of the political, cultural, and educational achievements made previously under the Austrians, even to the degree of replacing the name *Ukrainian* with the Polish noun and adjective for Ruthenian (*Rusini, rusiński*) in official matters.

Finally, in March 1923, the uncertain international status of Galicia was clarified. The Entente's Council of Ambassadors, overwhelmed with more pressing international problems in western Europe, tired of the Galicia question, relinquished its theoretical authority over the region, and awarded the whole province as far as the Zbruch River to Poland. Thus, the naive faith placed in the Entente by the leaders of the Western Ukrainian National Republic proved unwarranted, because after 1923 all of Galicia was internationally recognized as Polish territory.

With no recourse to outside aid, Galicia's Ukrainians were faced with the long-term prospect of being ruled directly by the Poles; moreover, they had no recourse to higher authority, as had been possible with the central government in Vienna during the prewar Habsburg days. Basically, the Ukrainian leadership and the vast majority of the population considered the Poles as representatives of a regime of occupation, and this attitude was to remain throughout the entire interwar period. In practical terms, the Ukrainian reaction ranged from participation in the political process and in socioeconomic and cultural developments to boycotts of elections or an outright rejection of Polish rule resulting in acts of sabotage against installations. After the Entente decision of 1923, which made it clear that Poland was to rule all of Galicia, the two Ukrainian political approaches—participation in, or outright rejection of, Polish rule— were to prevail at varying times and in varying strengths throughout the whole interwar period.

Beginning in 1925, the largest Galician political parties united to form the Ukrainian National Democratic Union (Ukraïns'ke Natsional'ne Demokratychne Ob"iednannia—UNDO), which, carrying on the tradition of the prewar Ukrainian National Democratic party, followed the model of organic work adopted under Austrian rule and attempted to improve the status of the Ukrainian population through constructive political, social, and economic action. This group included both older politicians (Kost' Levyts'kyi, Dmytro Levyts'kyi, Stepan Baran) and younger leaders (Vasyl' Mudryi, Liubomyr Makarushka, Ostap

Luts'kyi). There were also several other Galician parties that participated in interwar Polish political life. Among them were the old prewar Ukrainian Radical, later Ukrainian Socialist-Radical, party and the Ukrainian Social-Democratic party, as well as the Ukrainian Catholic National party, a few Russophile parties, and finally the Communist party of the Western Ukraine.

The policy of organic work aimed at strengthening the social fabric of the nation from within—a policy that had met with success under Austrian rule—was also adopted by the cooperative movement and in the educational sphere. Despite opposition from the Polish government, several self-help cooperative societies from the Austrian days, such as the Audit Union of Ukrainian Cooperatives (Reviziinyi Soiuz Ukraïns'kykh Kooperatyv), the Central Union (Tsentrosoiuz), the Dairy Union (Maslosoiuz), and the Agricultural Association (Sil's'kyi Hospodar), continued to prosper. These cooperatives not only increased the economic potential of Galician-Ukrainian agriculturalists, they also continued important work in raising national consciousness.

Much attention continued to be devoted as well to education, although the growth of a Ukrainian educational system at all levels that had made such steady progress under Austrian rule was to be curtailed in interwar Poland. In 1921, the provincial school administration based in L'viv was abolished and the local county school boards had to give up whatever effective power they had once had to the centralized Ministry of Education and Religion in Warsaw. Although the total number of schools increased in eastern Galicia between 1919 and 1939, their character changed. Initially, the Ukrainian system, especially at the elementary level, was left largely intact, while new Polish schools were founded. Then, as a result of a 1924 law sponsored by the government of Prime Minister Władysław Grabski (1874–1938), Ukrainian and Polish schools were unified and made bilingual. By the 1930s, many of these officially bilingual schools became Polish. At the university level, all but one of the departments in Ukrainian studies and other appointments were abolished at the University of L'viv in 1919.

The Ukrainian reaction to these developments was to expand, at the community's own expense, the number of private schools. The result was that by the 1937–38 school year, 59 percent of all Ukrainian *gymnasia*, teachers' colleges, and professional schools, which together represented approximately 40 percent of Ukrainian students at those levels, were privately operated. The growth of private schools was due largely to the Ukrainian Pedagogical Society, founded in 1881 and renamed Ridna Shkola in 1926. At the university level, courses sponsored by several Ukrainian cultural institutes began in 1919, and an underground Ukrainian University was founded in L'viv in 1921. The university operated with as many as 1,500 students until 1925 when, after constant pressure by Polish authorities, it was closed, forcing Galician Ukrainians to attend universities abroad, especially in Prague in neighboring Czechoslovakia. Thus, the constructive efforts at participation in political, socioeconomic, and cultural life led to only limited achievements for Ukrainians in interwar, Polish-ruled Galicia.

The second approach, that of revolutionary activity and military action, was represented by the Ukrainian Military Organization (UVO), which by 1929 provided the initiative for the formation of the Organization of Ukrainian Nationalists (OUN). Led by Ievhen Konovalets' (1891-1938) and sharing many of the ideological tenets of integral nationalism developed by Dmytro Dontsov (1883-1973), the OUN demanded strict discipline from its members and advocated a Ukrainian national ideal that would embrace all aspects of Galician society. The assassinations, bombings, and isolated acts of terror and sabotage directed by the UVO during the 1920s against Polish authority prompted acts of government retaliation that reached their most intense pitch during the so-called pacification campaign carried out by the Polish army and gendarmerie between September 16 and November 30, 1930. Pacification took the form of beatings and arrests leveled against Ukrainians, especially in villages, and the sacking and closing of Ukrainian reading rooms, cultural centers, newspaper offices, and cooperatives.

As a result of the pacification campaign, Polish and Ukrainian societies became largely polarized, so that the more moderate tactics of the UNDO were rapidly superseded by an increase in the number of violent acts carried out by the OUN. There still were attempts at Polish-Ukrainian political compromise during the mid-1930s (the so-called period of normalization), but this resulted in no real change in the situation. By 1938, both Ukrainian and Polish societies were wracked by anxiety over the imminent outbreak of armed conflict in Europe. On September 1, 1939, that conflict did come, and within a few weeks Polish control of Ukrainian eastern Galicia came to an end.

World War II and Its Aftermath

September 1, 1939, marked the beginning of World War II. It also marked the beginning of a five-year holocaust during which society in Galicia was completely torn apart. The initial invasion of the Red Army resulted in the decimation of segments of the Ukrainian and Polish populations and the establishment of a radically new form of government; warring factions of the Organization of Ukrainian Nationalists (OUN) fought with each other, with the Germans, with the Poles, with Soviet partisans, and with the Red Army; Ukrainians sympathetic to Soviet rule were ousted by those who accepted Nazi-

German rule, who were in turn forced to flee in the face of the returning Red Army in 1944. The local German populace was "voluntarily" relocated to the German fatherland, while the large and vibrant Galician Jewish community was physically exterminated. It seemed that during these five years, no matter what side an inhabitant chose, it would sooner or later be the wrong one. And if individuals tried to remain apolitical, they still would be hard-pressed to avoid the raids, artillery, or bombing of one of the many competing factions.

Galicia's fate was decided on August 23, 1939, when the Ribbentrop–Molotov nonaggression pact was signed between Nazi Germany and the Soviet Union. Both countries agreed not to attack each other while they were engaging in the total destruction of Poland. Germany's attack from the west on September 1 was followed by a Soviet attack from the east on September 17. By mutual agreement, the Red Army occupied L'viv and the rest of Galicia east of the San River. As a result, only Ukrainian-inhabited areas around Przemyśl and the Lemko region in the Carpathians remained under Nazi-German control as part of a large area stretching as far as Warsaw and known as the Generalgouvernement Polen.

In lands under the control of the Red Army, Soviet-style elections were organized on October 22 for a People's Assembly of Western Ukraine. Four days later, this body, which in large part was composed of local Communists and their sympathizers as well as delegates sent from Soviet Ukraine, requested to be incorporated into the Ukrainian Soviet Socialist Republic. The request was granted on November 1, and immediately a Soviet administration was set up throughout eastern Galicia.

Under Soviet rule, changes were instituted in Galicia that were designed to make it similar to other Soviet territory. Collectivization of the land was begun, industries were nationalized, and the educational system was reorganized on the Soviet model, with Ukrainian replacing Polish as the language of instruction. Older Ukrainian cultural institutions, such as Prosvita and the Shevchenko Scientific Society, were closed, while the polonized University of L'viv and Polish cultural institutions like the Ossolineum were "Ukrainianized." The Greek Catholic church, still under the leadership of Metropolitan Sheptyts'kyi, was allowed to exist, although more and more restrictions were being placed on its activity.

The efforts at a complete transformation of Galician society according to the Soviet model were cut short, however, when on June 22, 1941, the Germans broke their nonaggression pact and invaded the Soviet Union. Within a few days, Galicia east of the San River was overrun by German troops, and on August 1 it was made the fifth province of the Generalgouvernement.

For almost three years, eastern Galicia was ruled by the Nazis. Ukrainians were employed only at the lowest levels of the administration, and a few organizations were permitted: a branch of the Cracow-based Ukrainian Central Committee, some schools, a publishing house, and a theater. None of the older political parties abolished by the Soviets were permitted to be revived, and both factions of the OUN, which before 1941 had reached an accommodation with the Germans, were banned. A military force was allowed, however. In April 1943, the Galician Division was formed from Ukrainian volunteers and it fought within the ranks of the German Waffen SS.

As the war progressed, Nazi-German rule became increasingly burdensome and unpopular among the Galician Ukrainians. And in this era of war, rapid political change, and extreme violence, it is not surprising that the OUN, although banned by the Germans, came to play a dominant role in Ukrainian political life. After the generally respected head of the OUN, Ievhen Konovalets', was assassinated in 1938 by a Soviet agent, the directorate (*Provid*) of the organization chose Andrii Mel'nyk (1890–1964) as its new leader. Mel'nyk had fought with the Ukrainian Sich Riflemen during World War I and was arrested in 1924 by the Poles for being the leader of the underground Ukrainian Military Organization (UVO). But his generally moderate attitude toward political change and his reluctance to use violent methods as well as his close relationship with Metropolitan Sheptyts'kyi—all of which made Mel'nyk a leader who could appeal to a broad spectrum of Galician-Ukrainian public opinion—were at the same time characteristics deplored by the younger, more radical, and military-minded members of the OUN. These included Stepan Bandera (1910–1959), Mykola Lebed' (b. 1910), Roman Shukhevych (Taras Chuprynka, 1907–1950), and Iaroslav Stets'ko (1912–1986), who were suspicious of anything that suggested compromise, a policy that had been adopted by older Ukrainian leaders and that they believed had failed totally.

These differences in attitude came to the fore when, as a result of Germany's defeat of Poland, many imprisoned younger members of the OUN were released. They proceeded to denounce Mel'nyk and the OUN directorate, and in February 1940 established a rival Revolutionary Directorate of the OUN headed by Stepan Bandera. This was the origin of the struggle between the Melnykites (*Mel'nykivtsi*) and the Banderites (*Banderivtsi*), which severely weakened Ukrainian political and military efforts during World War II. The activist Banderites formed military units (Nachtigall and Roland) that fought with the German Army against the Soviets, but when Germany took over Galicia, Banderite leaders proclaimed a Ukrainian National Government in L'viv on June 30, 1941. The German government was displeased by such an act and put Bandera and some of his associates under house arrest in Berlin. Nonetheless, the interned Banderite leaders were still able to maintain contact with

Galicia, where in the spring of 1943 the Ukrainian Insurgent Army (Ukraïns'ka Povstans'ka Armiia—UPA) was established. The UPA, led by Roman Shukevych (General Taras Chuprynka), fought against the Germans and, following the rapid disintegration of the eastern front in 1944, against the Red Army as well. As for Mel'nyk, who like Bandera was confined to Berlin until 1944, some of his supporters also conducted partisan warfare, although most were arrested by the Germans or eliminated by their Banderite rivals.

Galicia's future was not to be determined by Ukrainian political infighting, however, but by the evolution of the war, especially along the eastern front. As the Germans began their retreat from Soviet territory, Galicia once again became a theater of military operations. By mid-1943, Ukrainian nationalist and some Soviet partisans were already operating in the region against the Germans. But no decisive change was to occur until the arrival of the Red Army. The Red Army's advance into Galicia began with its victories after the siege of Ternopil' (March–April 1944) and the Battle of Brody (July 7–22, 1944) and ended in the fierce struggle to acquire the Dukla Pass in the Carpathian Mountains (September–November 1944), which opened the way to the Danube Basin. In the wake of these military victories, it was once again possible to install a Soviet regime.

The Red Army's success in driving the Nazis out of Galicia by the autumn of 1944 and the area's reincorporation into the Ukrainian Soviet Socialist Republic did not mean the end of military hostilities. The Ukrainian Insurgent Army (UPA), together with the political wing of the movement, the Ukrainian Supreme Liberation Council (Ukraïns'ka Holovna Vyzvol'na Rada—UHVR, est. July 1944), continued to fight against what they considered the Soviet aggressor and its allies, the Communist-controlled governments of Poland and later Czechoslovakia. Against overwhelming odds, the UPA held out in the Carpathian Mountains and continued to make raids into the Galician lowlands until the early 1950s. By then, most of the UPA members had been killed, had accepted Soviet amnesties, or had escaped to Austria and West Germany via Czechoslovakia.

Despite such continued military resistance to Soviet rule, the new government proceeded with the transformation of Galician society. Ukrainian-inhabited Galicia was divided by the new Polish-Soviet border that ran northward from the Carpathians along the San River, then followed a northeast line, leaving Przemyśl within Poland. This meant that the Lemko region and other Ukrainian areas around Przemyśl were returned to Polish rule. Under a Communist government, Polish authorities began to encourage the Lemko population to emigrate eastward to the Soviet Ukraine. Then, in the spring and summer of 1947, those Lemkos who remained were forcibly deported westward and northward to lands (Silesia and Pomerania) acquired by Poland from Germany after the war.

The larger part of Galicia came under Soviet rule. The old administrative divisions were abolished and four new Soviet Ukrainian oblasts were created—L'viv, Drohobych (made part of L'viv after 1959), Stanislav (renamed Ivano-Frankivs'k in 1962), and Ternopil'. The very term *Galicia* dropped out of general usage, and its three oblasts (L'viv, Ivano-Frankivs'k, Ternopil'), together with neighboring Transcarpathia and Chernivtsi (formerly northern Bukovina), were referred to as western Ukraine. The new Soviet regime proceeded to nationalize industries, banks, and the entire private business sector, as well as to collectivize the land and to reorganize educational and cultural facilities according to the Soviet model.

In contrast to previous regimes, the Soviets were determined to transform Galicia by implementing its centralized command economy and introducing several new industries, in particular, machine building and metalworking, chemical products, and light industry such as clothing manufacturing. In the collectivized agricultural sector, the biggest change came with the introduction of industrial crops (sugar beets and corn). Industrialization also changed the demographic balance in Galicia's three oblasts, so that in contrast to pre-Soviet times the percentage of the urban population more than doubled, from 23 percent (1931) to 47.3 percent (1989).

With regard to cultural developments, Ukrainianization according to the Soviet model was promoted. This meant that education and cultural life were to be Ukrainian in form but socialist in content. Consequently, pre-Soviet cultural and organizational life was all but forgotten in official discourse. The long-time symbol of Galician-Ukrainian identity, the Greek Catholic church, was abolished in March 1946, when a group of priests "voluntarily" annulled the 1596 union with Rome and joined the Russian Orthodox church. Those Greek Catholic priests and hierarchs who opposed this move were jailed, while the legal Russian Orthodox church was restricted in its activity. Besides this, several hundred thousand persons, including most of the prewar Galician-Ukrainian intelligentsia, were uprooted. A large number had fled westward before the advancing Red Army in 1944, settling first in camps in Germany before eventually emigrating as deported persons (DPs) to the United States and Canada. Of those remaining behind, many were suspected of being opposed to the government or of having familial ties to known resisters and, therefore, were deported to other parts of the Soviet Union.

As a result of the administrative, socioeconomic, cultural, religious, and demographic changes implemented by the Soviet regime after 1945, Galicia ceased to exist as a distinct entity. Such a situation began to change only during the second half of the 1980s, when the Soviet Union came under the leadership of Mikhail S. Gorbachev (b. 1931). Gorbachev's attempts to reform the Soviet system through what he called transformation (*perestroika*) and openness (*glasnost'*) put an end to the centralized command economy and to the domination of the Communist party in political life.

In Galicia, as in other parts of Soviet Ukraine, old institutions were revived and new ones opposed to Communism appeared. Among those that were restored were the Shevchenko Scientific Society and the Prosvita Society in 1990 and the Greek Catholic church in 1991. The end to Soviet censorship stimulated a renewed interest in the historical past, resulting in an attempt to fill in the "blank spots" of history that were created by Soviet-Marxist authors and to write about the activity of forgotten Galician institutions and movements, such as the World War I Ukrainian Sich Riflemen, the Organization of Ukrainian Nationalists (both the Melnykite and the Banderite factions), and the World War II Galicia Division.

The tradition that Galicia might continue to form a distinct administrative or even autonomous territorial entity was revived in 1990 in the form of an umbrella organization, the Galician Assembly, whose goal was to lobby on behalf of the region before the central government in Kiev. It was not long, however, before the assembly's members began to fear that a distinct Galician body such as theirs would lend support to those political forces who favored seeing a future independent Ukraine become a federal state. Consequently, the Galician Assembly dissolved itself. The region then became home to other political movements, the most notable being the Ukrainian National Assembly (UNA), which came into being during the summer of 1991 and which created its own paramilitary wing, the Ukrainian Self-Defense Force (UNSO). Supporters of the UNA–UNSO rejected the idea that Galicia might, as in the late nineteenth century, again serve as the basis (piedmont) to lead the way toward the creation of a Ukrainian nation-state. Instead, UNA–UNSO leaders argued that an independent state must be established first, and that the state should take the lead in forming a nationally conscious Ukrainian populace based on all inhabitants—of whatever ethnolinguistic background—living in Ukraine.

By the summer of 1991, most Galician Ukrainians considered themselves part of a nationally conscious vanguard that stood in the forefront of the struggle for an independent Ukraine. It is not surprising, therefore, that when independence was confirmed during a national referendum in December 1991, fully 94 percent of the inhabitants in Galicia's three oblasts (L'viv, Ivano-Frankivs'k, Ternopil') voted in favor of Ukrainian sovereignty. Since that time, Galicians, whether national democrats or right-wing integral nationalists (UNA–UNSO), have favored the adoption of a new constitution that would define Ukraine as a centralized and unitary state with only limited local government for existing oblasts and no administrative recognition for historic regions such as Galicia. In the end, the results of the referendum of 1991 and the centralized constitution which was adopted in 1996 reflected the continuation of a tradition by which Galician Ukrainians have viewed themselves—and are still viewed by other Ukrainians—as the most avid supporters of an independent and unitary Ukrainian nation-state.

chapter two

The Ukrainian National Revival:
A New Analytical Framework*

The Ukrainians are but one example of the many Slavic and other peoples in east-central Europe that experienced a national revival in the course of the nineteenth century. In comparative terms, the Ukrainian case is usually seen as one that entered the process of national revival relatively late, and as one that in the end was not successful in fulfilling the ultimate goal of national movements—political independence. Such a perception—that national movements should be analyzed and implicitly judged by the degree to which they were or were not successful in obtaining political independence—has inevitably determined the philosophical and intellectual thrust of the literature on the subject.

Before turning to the existing literature and the proposals for a new analytical framework, we need to glance at the specific background of the Ukrainian case. When the process of the national awakening or revival was in its earliest stages during the last decades of the eighteenth century, Ukrainian ethnolinguistic territory—that is, lands inhabited by Ukrainians—was located within the boundaries of two multinational empires: the Russian Empire and the Austrian Empire. This political division was to remain without substantial change until World War I. From the standpoint of numbers, the Ukrainian lands within the Russian Empire were by far the more important, since it was there that 90 percent of all Ukrainian ethnolinguistic territory was located and that 85 percent of all Ukrainian inhabitants resided. On the other hand, despite the smaller percentages of territory and people within the Austrian Empire, Ukrainians there, especially in the province of Galicia, were to play a significant

* This is a revised version of an article that first appeared in the *Canadian Review of Studies in Nationalism*, XVI, 1–2 (Charlottetown, P.E.I., 1989) pp. 45–62. A Ukrainian translation by Marco Carynnyk appeared in *Ukraïns'kyi istorychnyi zhurnal*, XXXV, 3 (Kiev, 1991), pp. 97–107.

and even decisive role in determining the direction of the Ukrainian national revival.

Within both empires, Ukrainians did not have any administrative unit that corresponded either in whole or in part to the lands they inhabited. Rather, they remained divided among the administrative units of those two multinational states, neither of which recognized any specific Ukrainian territorial entity. Within the Russian Empire, Ukrainians lived primarily within nine *guberniia*, or provinces (Chernihiv, Poltava, Kharkiv, Kherson, Katerynoslav, Taurida, Volhynia, Kiev, and Podolia), which in whole or in part were sometimes loosely referred to as South Russia or Little Russia. Within the Austrian Empire, Ukrainians were to be found in certain parts of three regions: in the provinces (crownlands) of Galicia and Bukovina in the "Austrian half" of the empire, and in several counties of northeastern Hungary which were sometimes referred to as Subcarpathian Rus' (Ruthenia), later Transcarpathia.

Although by the nineteenth century Ukrainian lands enjoyed neither administrative unity nor autonomy, the inhabitants of certain regions, especially those descended from the Cossacks, still had strong memories of self-rule. This was particularly the case in Ukrainian lands within the Russian Empire, three regions of which had enjoyed varying degrees of political autonomy until as late as the second half of the eighteenth century—the Sloboda Ukraine (to 1765), Zaporozhia (to 1775), and the Hetmanate (to 1785).[1]

As for the socioeconomic basis of Ukrainian lands, the situation was essentially the same in both empires. Ukrainian lands were overwhelmingly agrarian. Moreover, the basic structure of Ukrainian society did not really change during the late nineteenth century, a time when industrialization began, especially in the eastern-Ukrainian lands of the Russian Empire. This is because urban areas throughout Ukraine and the new burgeoning industrial centers in the east were for the most part not inhabited by Ukrainians, so that despite the increasing industrialization in their midst, ethnic Ukrainians *per se* were hardly touched at all. The Russian census of 1897 revealed that only 5.7 percent of Ukrainians lived in urban areas, while up to 81.1 percent worked in agriculture or as day laborers and servants. In the Austrian Empire there was an even smaller percentage of Ukrainians living and working in cities and a larger percentage engaged in agriculture. In a sense, urban areas throughout Ukrainian territories remained islands inhabited by varying national minorities (Russians,

---

1 For a survey of the ethnogeographic and administrative structure of Ukrainian lands, see Paul Robert Magocsi, *Ukraine: A Historical Atlas* (Toronto, Buffalo, and London, 1985), esp. the commentary and maps 2, 15–21.

Poles, Jews, etc.) who had little or nothing to do with the Ukrainian masses in the surrounding countryside. Finally, Ukrainian agrarian life was characterized by small-sized holdings worked by chronically impoverished peasants who had only recently obtained liberation from serfdom: in 1848 in Austria and in 1861 in Russia.[2]

Thus, throughout the nineteenth century, which coincided with the period of the national revival, Ukrainian society could be characterized as an underdeveloped agrarian society divided between two multinational empires—Russia and Austria. Nowhere did Ukrainian lands enjoy administrative or political autonomy, and at best certain groups retained the memory of past self-rule that seemed beyond any possibility of being resurrected within the given imperial circumstances. Therefore, the idea of something specifically Ukrainian could not hope to survive through the continuance of some past political tradition. Something new had to be found. That new catalyst was found, and it did come from beyond Ukraine. It was nationalism.

We will not be concerned here with the ideology of nationalism *per se* or its specific Ukrainian manifestation, nor will we be concerned with discovering the ideological origins of the Ukrainian national revival and the manner in which it evolved during the nineteenth century. These are problems which have, at least in their barest outline, been discussed more than once before. What we are concerned with is to see what, if any, framework or frameworks have been used in previous studies to analyze the Ukrainian national revival and in the end to propose a new one that will not only place the Ukrainian example in the larger European context, but also respond to the specific characteristics of the Ukrainian experience.

In general, the literature has been dominated by two basic approaches—the Soviet-Marxist and the non-Marxist view. The Soviet-Marxist model is straightforward and related to the framework of general historical and socioeconomic evolution in which each society must go through five stages: a slave-owning stage; feudalism; bourgeois capitalism; imperialism; and finally socialism and Communism.[3] The time frame for these stages varies, depending on the specific nature of individual societies, although in the classic Soviet-Marxist un-

---

2 Bohdan Krawchenko, "The Social Structure of Ukraine at the Turn of the 20th Century," *East European Quarterly*, XVI, 2 (Boulder, Colo., 1982), pp. 171–181; and John-Paul Himka, "The Background to Emigration: Ukrainians of Galicia and Bukovyna, 1848–1914," in Manoly R. Lupul, ed., *A Heritage in Transition: Essays in the History of Ukrainians in Canada* (Toronto, 1982), pp. 11–31.

3 The following discussion on the relationship of Marxism to nationalism is based largely on Walker Conner, *The National Question in Marxist-Leninist Theory and Strategy* (Princeton, N.J., 1984), esp. pp. 5–42.

derstanding every society must inevitably pass through each of these increasingly "progressive" phases of human evolution.

As for the concept of nationality and the ideology of nationalism, Soviet Marxists believe that these are historical phenomena which come into existence only with the demise of the feudal stage and the rise of capitalism—that is, during a period marked by the development of new economic relations and changes in modes of production, in particular during the capitalist stage. Therefore, since the transition from feudalism to capitalism on Ukrainian lands is "officially" decreed to have occurred only in 1848, the phenomenon of Ukrainian nationalism is present only during the latter half of the nineteenth century. It lasts, moreover, only as long as the era of capitalism and its sequel, imperialism—that is, until the transition to socialism begins after 1917.[4] Moreover, nationalism is considered in Soviet-Marxist terms to be reflective only of the bourgeois class, which uses it in an attempt to identify its own interests with the interests of society as a whole.

Given such ideological premises, it is understandable that the national revival is not treated as a phenomenon unto itself in Marxist histories of Ukraine. Rather, it is seen as a potentially "progressive" force which might contribute to breaking down the remnants of the feudal order during the early capitalist phase of the country's evolution. Yet nationalism "inevitably" becomes obsolete, even "counterrevolutionary," as the capitalist-imperialist phase ends and is replaced by the socialist phase. Since it is not individual nationalities but rather a classless society that, allegedly, is the ultimate and desirable goal of humanity, national revivals are given only passing notice in Marxist histories of individual nationalities. This applies as well to Ukraine, where the national revival and its leaders (Shevchenko, Kostomarov, Kulish, etc.) are judged by Marxists in terms of their individual contributions to the progressive evolution of history.[5] And this ultimate goal is not independent statehood but rather a classless socialist society in union with other classless societies, regardless of their national or linguistic background.

---

4 Among the more recent versions of this interpretation is that found in the multivolume *Istoriia Ukraïns'koï RSR*, 8 vols. in 10 (Kiev, 1977–79); volume 3 is subtitled: "Ukraine during the Era of the Breakdown and Crisis of the Feudal-Serf System: The Abolition of Serfdom and the Development of Capitalism (19th Century)"; and volume 4: "Ukraine during the Imperialist Era (1900–1917)." The "remnants" of nationalism remained alive longer in western-Ukrainian lands (eastern Galicia, northern Bukovina, and Transcarpathia), which did not undergo their socialist transformation until after their incorporation into the Soviet Ukraine during the 1940s.

5 For instance, in the recent multivolume history mentioned in note 4, the Ukrainian "national movement" is given a scant nine pages in volume 3 (pp. 441–450) and eight pages in volume 4 (pp. 66–74).

In sharp contrast, non-Marxist historiography is in large measure determined by the acceptance, or at least recognition, of national and/or state boundaries as the primary organizational factor in historical development. In that regard, those who are interested in the formation of nationalities see them as ends in themselves, governed by an ideology called nationalism, which accepts the premise that humanity is divided into nationalities and that the ultimate goals of national revivals or movements are (1) independence—the acquisition of a nation-state in which a given nationality is dominant; and (2) national unity—the incorporation within the independent nation-state of all groups that are considered, whether by themselves or by those who claim to speak of them, to belong to the nationality.[6]

As for the Ukrainian national revival, it has generally been viewed either as (1) a unilateral process of ever-increasing national consciousness occurring first among the intelligentsia who then propagate it among the masses;[7] or (2) as a somewhat more complex development marked by various stages whose number and chronological extent vary from author to author.[8] The underlying assumption of both these approaches is that independent statehood is the ultimate, if long-term, goal. Although in its specific quest the Ukrainian movement may have gotten close to independence during the revolutionary period,

6 From the enormous literature on nationalism, this definition has been based on the cogent introductory formulation of Hugh Seton-Watson, *Nations and States* (Boulder, Colo., 1977), p. 3.

7 The general linear approach in descriptions of the Ukrainian national revival is evident in the standard one-volume non-Marxist histories by Mykhailo Hrushevs'kyi, *Illiustrovana istoriia Ukraïny* (Winnipeg, 1924), pp. 477-519 and Dmytro Doroshenko, *Narys istoriï Ukraïny*, Vol. 2, 2nd ed. (Munich, 1966), pp. 274-328, as well as in the more recent survey by the Polish Ukrainianist Wladyslaw A. Serczyk, *Historia Ukrainv* (Wrocław, Warsaw, Cracow, and Gdańsk, 1979), esp. pp. 225-326 passim.

8 Ivan L. Rudnytsky, "The Intellectual Origins of Modem Ukraine," *The Annals of the Ukrainian Academy of Arts and Sciences in the U.S.*, VI, 3–4 (New York, 1958), pp. 1381–1405, limits his discussion to the Russian Empire and speaks of three stages: the aristocratic period (1780s–1840s), populism (1840s–1880s), and modernism (1890s–1914). The three stages were later reiterated in his "The Role of the Ukraine in Modern Society," *Slavic Review*, XXII, 2 (Seattle, Wash., 1963), pp. 199–216, to which John S. Reshetar responded that it would be better to speak of five stages based on the geographic region in which they were played out: Novhorod-Sivers'kyi and Kharkiv (circa 1798–1830s); Kiev/Right Bank (1840–1860s); Geneva (1870s–1880s), Galicia (1890s–1914). See his remarks in Omeljan Pritsak and John S. Reshetar, Jr., "Ukraine and the Dialects of Nation-Building," *Slavic Review*, XXII, 2 (Seattle, Wash., 1963), esp. pp. 241–255.

More recently, Omeljan Pritsak has spoken of six Ukrainian cultural zones (Sloboda Ukraine, Hetmanate, New Russia, Right Bank, Galicia/Bukovina, Transcarpathia), but despite his promise to present a "new solution," his inconclusive essay provides no new schema for the national revival. Compare his "Prolegomena to the National Awakening of

1917–1921, it is generally assumed that the movement ultimately failed.

Based on such teleological premises, the Ukrainian national revival and its propagators are judged to the degree that they contributed to the idea of a distinct Ukrainian identity and political cause. On the other hand, those orientations or individuals who were less than committed to Ukrainian distinctiveness are considered at best assimilators or more likely some kind of aberrants who are detrimental to the Ukrainian movement as a whole.

What I believe would be useful, nay necessary, is to avoid this kind of historical predeterminism, and to look at the phenomenon of nationalism or the national revival in Ukrainian lands on its own terms and not from any preconceived notion whereby the only criterion for judging the movement is whether it evolved "progressively" toward a future classless society or toward an independent and territorially unified Ukrainian nation-state. As a corollary, it would also be useful to reject the idea of uniqueness—though a popular approach, especially to non-Marxist Ukrainian historians—and to place the Ukrainian movement in the context of other European national revivals.

In the past two decades, several scholars in east-central Europe (Poland, Czechoslovakia, Hungary) have undertaken comparative analyses of national movements among peoples in their own region as well as among stateless peoples in western and northern Europe with the intent to discover, if possible, some common elements or to formulate a model or framework that could be used to analyze the various national revivals. As the comparative studies of Miroslav Hroch, Józef Chłebowczyk, and Emil Niederhauser have shown,[9] there are obvious parallels in the national revivals among peoples who did not yet have political independence, whether among the Flemings, Norwegians, and Finns in western and northern Europe or among the Czechs, Lithuanians, and Slovenes in east-central Europe. The Ukrainians are rightly considered to be among the stateless peoples of Europe, and their national revival to have had much in common with those of the others.

Despite their different approaches to the subject, all three—Hroch, Chłebowczyk, and Niederhauser—attempt to combine aspects of the Marxist and non-Marxist approaches. Thus, while maintaining the basic historical stages

---

the Ukrainians during the Nineteenth Century," in Roland Sussex and J.C. Eade, eds., *Culture and Nationalism in Nineteenth-Century Eastern Europe* (Columbus, Ohio, 1983), pp. 96–110.

9 All three studies were originally published between 1968 and 1976 in Czechoslovakia, Poland, and Hungary, but they are now available in English: Miroslav Hroch, *Social Preconditions of the National Revival in Europe* (Cambridge, 1985); Jozef Chłebowczyk, *On Small and Young Nations in Europe* (Wrocław, Warsaw, Cracow, and Gdańsk, 1980); Emil Niederhauser, *The Rise of Nationality in Eastern Europe* (Budapest, 1982).

and rhetoric or class interests associated with Marxist writings, they also em-phasize—as do non-Marxists—"the exceptional role" (to quote Chłebowczyk) of the local leadership or nationalist intelligentsia that is responsible for for-mulating the substance of national ideology, for propagating the ideology among the group in whom a national identity is created, and for implementing nation-alist demands that result in varying forms of political autonomy or even inde-pendence.

Thus, one may speak of intelligentsia-inspired national movements or na-tionalism in contrast to state-imposed nationalism. The first category emanates from below, or from the bottom up, and it occurs among groups who live in multinational states where a language, culture, and identity other than their own is dominant. The stateless group's often self-proclaimed leaders—the na-tionalist intelligentsia—work to convince the group's members that they form a distinct nationality and as such deserve at the very least cultural autonomy if not political autonomy or even independence. The second category, state-im-posed nationalism, emanates from above, or from the top down, and it occurs within already existing independent states whose governments hope to gain the allegiance of their subjects by convincing them that they are united be-cause they belong to a given nationality whose primary function is loyalty to the existing nation-state and its social structure. As a stateless people living within the Russian and Austrian empires, the Ukrainians and their national revival obviously fall into the intelligentsia-inspired variety of nationalism.

In order to analyze those many European peoples whose movements are of the intelligentsia-inspired category of nationalism, some of the writers referred to above speak of progressive stages. Hroch, for instance, speaks of three stages: (1) the period of scholarly interest, when individual intellectuals "rediscover" the nationality and formulate the outlines of an identity; (2) the period of patri-otic revival, when the masses of a given population become involved in the revival; and (3) the rise of a mass national movement with political implica-tions. These three categories were applied by an American specialist on mod-ern Ukraine (Roman Szporluk), who when surveying the nineteenth-century Ukrainian national revival spoke of the academic, cultural, and political phases.[10]

At about the same time, I, too, had spoken of three stages, referring to them somewhat more specifically as (1) the heritage-gathering stage, when indi-vidual scholars and, even more often, untrained enthusiasts collect the linguis-tic, folkloric, literary, and historical artifacts of a given people; (2) the organi-zational stage, when cultural organizations (reading rooms, theaters, libraries, museums, national homes, etc.), schools, and publications are formed to dis-

10 Roman Szporluk, *Ukraine: A Brief History* (Detroit, Mich., 1979), pp. 41–54.

seminate knowledge about the national heritage already or still being gathered; and (3) the political stage, which witnesses the creation of parties and other civic organizations established to allow group participation in the political process.[11]

As with any schematic historical framework, none of these stages begins or ends abruptly, and frequently there is some overlap in terms of chronology or activity. Nor is it even necessary that these stages occur in a linear progression, beginning always with stage one and ending with stage three. Different historical and political circumstances can affect the order, as we shall see in the Ukrainian case. Despite such caveats, however, it is possible to observe three stages— the heritage-gathering, organizational, and political—in the Ukrainian national revival, so that, by approaching the nineteenth century with these categories in mind, we can give some order to otherwise seemingly disparate events while at the same time placing the specific Ukrainian case in a comparative context.

Nonetheless, each historical phenomenon has its own uniqueness, and the Ukrainian national revival is no exception. As with all national minorities living in multinational states, it is likely that before, during, and even after the national revival a certain proportion of the local intelligentsia would not necessarily opt to identify with the "new movement," but instead would associate in one degree or another with the ruling or dominant nationality. This phenomenon has heretofore been described by most commentators on the Ukrainian national revival as assimilation. Moreover, the assimilators are often considered to be lost sons or even traitors to the national cause and to their own people.

Such a simplistic appraisal often leads to outright distortion of the historical record or to frustration when faced with the careers of real persons who in the course of one lifetime may have changed from assimilator to national patriot and back again. Such intellectual phases could be and often were repeated more than once in a single career; moreover, the phases might even have occurred simultaneously, as in the case of some belletrists whose use of varying genres and written languages may have reflected their own differing national allegiances.

In recent years, social scientists have begun to argue that situational or optional ethnicity, in which an individual's identification can be "consciously emphasized or deemphasized as the situation dictates," is as widespread as the so-called primordialist or primordialist approach, in which an individual's identity is viewed as a fixed and unchangeable phenomenon ostensibly predetermined by blood ties, shared descent, and a particular language and

11 Paul R. Magocsi, "Nationalism and National Bibliography: Ivan E. Levyts'kyi and Nineteenth-Century Galicia," *Harvard Library Bulletin,* XXVIII, I (Cambridge, Mass., 1980), pp. 81–82.

culture.[12] Historians of nationalism would be well advised to keep in mind the situational as well as the primordialist approach when analyzing individual national movements.

In an attempt to understand better and put some order into this aspect of the Ukrainian national revival, I suggest we keep in mind what might be called the principle of the hierarchy of multiple loyalties or identities as opposed to the principle of mutually exclusive identities.[13] Such formulations derive from the following premises.

In most social settings, there are few persons loyal to one object. Most operate within a network of loyalties—family or tribe, occupational group, church, clubs, et cetera. In political systems, those loyalties may be to a village or city, region, state, and country, all of which are compatible with each other. In multinational states, it is quite natural to find individuals who feel perfectly comfortable with one or more what we might call "national" loyalties or identities. Thus, in the case of Ukrainian lands in the nineteenth century, it seemed perfectly normal for some residents to be simultaneously both a Little Russian (Ukrainian) and a Russian. The most well-known example of such types comprised the Cossack officer stratum, whose members, because they strove to become recognized as members of the Russian noble estate, seemed to become assimilated and therefore russified. Besides these Cossacks-turned-nobles, there were several intellectuals who followed the same path, the most well known being the great writer Nikolai Gogol', a Ukrainian who published only in Russian. These and other "Little Russians" who consciously felt that there was a harmonious union between their attachment to Little Russia and Russia as a whole are perhaps too simplistically described in the literature as russified and therefore of little or no interest to the evolution of the Ukrainian national revival.[14] Instead, they should be seen as representing part of the "natural" hierarchy of multiple loyalties present in many national revivals, including the Ukrainian.

On the other hand, as the Ukrainian national revival evolved, some of its leaders became convinced that, in order for the movement to survive, the otherwise natural hierarchy of multiple loyalties or national identities had to be

---

12 For a useful introduction to the problem of situational and primordial ethnicity, see the review of the literature in Chew Sock Foon, "On the Incompatibility of Ethnic and National Loyalties: Reframing the Issue," *Canadian Review of Studies in Nationalism,* XIII, 1 (Charlottetown, P.E.I., 1986), pp. 1–11

13 The author still recalls a seminal study that eventually led him to formulate such categories: David M. Potter, "The Historian's Use of Nationalism and Vice Versa," *American Historical Review,* LXVII, 4 (New York, 1962), esp. pp. 924–938.

14 Although concerned with somewhat different issues, David Saunders has recently elaborated upon the relations of "Little Russians" to the larger Russian world in his *The Ukrainian Impact on Russian Culture, 1750–1850* (Edmonton, 1985).

replaced by a framework of mutually exclusive identities. Thus, one could not be a Russian from Little Russia, or a Pole from Ukraine, one had to be either a Russian or a Ukrainian (the term that was favored over *Little Russian* precisely to accentuate the degree of perceptual difference), or a Pole or a Ukrainian. One simply could not be both.

In a real sense, the whole course of the Ukrainian national revival down to World War I (and in a different context the status of Ukrainians in Soviet and even post-Soviet Ukraine) can be seen as the story of the conflict between the framework of multiple cultural and national loyalties on the one hand and mutually exclusive identities on the other and of how this conflict sometimes had and still has a traumatic and/or creatively inspirational effect upon the individuals involved.

Therefore, when examining the intelligentsia-inspired Ukrainian national revival, it might be useful to keep in mind a nexus of several patterns and principles. This nexus includes (1) the three stages of intelligentsia-inspired national movements (heritage-gathering, organizational, political); (2) the principles of multiple and mutually exclusive identities; and, finally, (3) geopolitical distinctions that depend on whether the discussion concerns Ukrainian lands within the Russian or the Austrian Empire. With these various patterns as a basis for a new analytical framework, let us look, at least briefly, at how this nexus can be applied specifically to the Ukrainian case.

Turning first to Ukrainian lands in the Russian Empire, we find that the chronological limits of the three stages are (1) the heritage-gathering stage (1780s to 1840s); (2) the organizational stage (1840s to 1900); and (3) the political stage (1900 to 1917).[15] The first stage began with a search to "rediscover" the Ukrainian historical past. The original motivation was not a desire for knowledge, however, but rather a practical socioeconomic need. The Cossack elite, who had just lost their privileged status following the abolition in the early 1780s of the last vestiges of autonomy in the Hetmanate, began to scour busily through familial and local historical records in an effort to "prove" their equality and therefore worthiness to be classified as nobles (*dvoriane*)

---

15 Further details for the following outline of the Ukrainian national revival in the Russian Empire can be found in Zenon Kohut, *Russian Centralism and Ukrainian Autonomy: Imperial Absorption of the Hetmanate, 1760s–1830s* (Cambridge, Mass., 1988); George S.N. Luckyj, *Between Gogol and Ševčenko* (Munich, 1971); Georges Luciani, *Le livre de la genèse du peuple ukrainien* (Paris, 1956); Orest Pelech "Toward a Historical Sociology of the Ukrainian Ideologies in the Russian Empire of the 1830s–1840s" (Ph.D. diss., Ann Arbor, Mich., 1976); Pavlo Zaitsev, *Taras Shevchenko: A Life* (Toronto, 1988); Thomas M. Prymak, *Mykola Kostomarov: A Biography* (Toronto, 1996); George Luckyj, *Panteleimon Kulish: A Sketch of His Life and Times* (Boulder, Colo., 1983); and Paul Robert Magocsi, *A History of Ukraine* (Toronto, 1996), pp. 351–382.

within the imperial Russian social structure. One byproduct of this practical search to legitimize Cossack noble status was an enormous interest in the past that soon resulted in several manuscripts and publications, whether tracts in defense of historic Cossack rights (Roman Markovych, ca. 1800; Tymofii Kalyns'kyi, ca. 1800 and 1808; Vasyl' Poletyka, 1809; Adrian Chepa, 1809) or more general histories of Ukraine, sometimes in several volumes (Dmytro Bantysh-Kamens'kyi, 1822; Mykola Markevych, 1842–43). The most famous historical tract from this period was the *Istoriia Rusov* (History of the Rus' People), circulated widely in manuscript during the 1820s and 1830s before being published in 1846.

Besides historical works, the heritage-gathering stage was also marked by the compilation of works in Ukrainian ethnography (Nikolai Tsertelev, 1819; Mykhailo Maksymovych, 1827, 1834, 1849; Izmail Sreznevskii, 1833–80) and language (Oleksander Pavlovs'kyi, 1818; Ivan Votsekevych, 1823), as well as the birth of modern Ukrainian literature, from its hesitant beginnings in the early decades of the nineteenth century as a language appropriate only for burlesque and other minor literary genres (Ivan Kotliarevs'kyi, Petro Hulak-Artemovs'kyi, Hryhorii Kvitka-Osnovianenko, Ievhen Hrebinka) to its full-fledged development in the early 1840s in the works of Taras Shevchenko.

The 1840s also marked the beginnings of the second, or organizational, stage. Here the role of the Russian imperial government was particularly helpful. Already in 1834, as part of its *Drang nach Westen* to "reacquire" in cultural terms the Right Bank Ukraine and other lands recently obtained from Poland, the government established a new university in Kiev, one of the goals of which was to promote research into local history and culture. In essence, research became the primary activity of the Archeographical Commission established in Kiev in 1843, the results of which were reflected on the pages of new scholarly publications that began to appear both within and beyond Ukraine (*Kievlianin*, 1843-50; *Chteniia Obshchestva istorii i drevnostei rossiiskikh*, 1846–48, 1858–1915).

The existence of such institutions and publications in turn stimulated and made possible the work of a new generation of cultural activists, the most important for the Ukrainian national revival being the triad Mykola Kostomarov, Panteleimon Kulish, and Taras Shevchenko. Besides their own historical, ethnographic, and literary work—so typical of the first, heritage-gathering stage of intelligentsia-inspired national movements—this trio, together with a few other patriots, were directly or indirectly involved in the establishment during the mid-1840s of the secret Brotherhood of Saints Cyril and Methodius, whose program included the propagation of Ukrainian nationalism. Before the brotherhood had a chance to develop, however, the tsarist Russian government arrested its members in 1847. The arrests and the dissolution of the brother-hood heralded a new tone in tsarist Russia's attitude toward the embryonic Ukrainian movement.

For the rest of the century, tsarist policy swung back and forth between periods of tolerance (1850s to 1863, 1880s to 1890s) and periods of restriction and repression (1863 to the 1870s). Because of governmental concern, the Ukrainian revival was unable to move beyond the organizational stage, although during the periods of liberalization various publications (*Osnova*, 1861–62; *Kievskaia starina*, 1882–1907), theaters, and grassroots cultural organizations (the Hromada movement) were able to function, even if it must be admitted that the dissemination of a national identity among the broad masses of the population—so characteristic of the second organizational stage—did not really occur on Ukrainian lands in the Russian Empire.

Despite the incompleteness of the organizational stage, the third political stage could be said to have begun at the outset of the twentieth century. This was related to the increasing number of illegal political movements throughout the Russian Empire and the general discontent among ever broader segments of the population that was to culminate in the Revolution of 1905 and the subsequent experiment in governmental reform, including the establishment of an elected parliament or Duma. As part of these changes, several political parties came into existence (Revolutionary Ukrainian party, 1900; Ukrainian People's party, 1902; Ukrainian Democratic party, 1905; Ukrainian Social-Democratic Labor party, 1905) whose express goals were cultural and political autonomy or even independence for Ukraine. In the first and second Dumas (1906 and 1907), Ukrainian representatives (respectively forty and forty-seven) formed a Ukrainian bloc to press for their specific demands. Although tsarist repression had severely limited the electoral base and mandate of the third and fourth Dumas (1907–1912 and 1912–1917), the Ukrainian movement, with its political parties and participation, had clearly entered the political stage. That stage was to culminate in the events of 1917–1918 and the concrete efforts toward autonomy and then independent statehood.

Turning to western Ukraine, that is, to those Ukrainian lands within the Austrian Empire, all three stages of intelligentsia-inspired national movements are easily discernible.[16] Not only were the individual stages more fully devel-

16 Further details for the following outline of the Ukrainian national revival in the Austrian Empire can be found in Magocsi, *History of Ukraine*, pp. 397–457; A.S. Markovits and F.E. Sysyn, eds., *Nationbuilding and the Politics of Nationalism: Essays on Austrian Galicia* (Cambridge, Mass., 1982); Jan Kozik, *The Ukrainian National Movement in Galicia, 1815–1849* (Edmonton, 1986); and Paul R. Magocsi, *The Shaping of a National Identity: Subcarpathian Rus', 1848–1948* (Cambridge, Mass., 1978).

oped than in the Russian Empire, but their order was somewhat different. In effect, the new historical era began in the 1770s, when Habsburg Austria acquired the partially Ukrainian-inhabited provinces of Galicia (1772) and Bukovina (1775). At the time, Austria was under the rule of the enlightened emperors Maria Theresa (reigned 1740–1780) and her co-regent son, Joseph II (reigned 1780–1790), whose government was interested in improving the cultural and socioeconomic status of the inhabitants of these new territorial acquisitions and thereby making them loyal Habsburg subjects. As a result of such governmental intervention from above, it could be said that the Ukrainian national revival in the Austrian Empire began its second or organizational phase before having gone through the heritage-gathering phase.

The structures given to Ukrainians from above included legal decrees to equalize the Greek Catholic church with the dominant Roman Catholic church (1774); elementary schools in the vernacular speech of the inhabitants (1777); the first institutions of higher learning, mostly seminaries, designed specifically for the Ukrainian intelligentsia (the Barbareum in Vienna, 1775, and the Studium Ruthenum in L'viv, 1787); and the revival of a metropolitanate at L'viv for the Greek Catholic church (1807), whose membership virtually coincided with the Ukrainian nationality.

The organizational stage, imposed as it was from above during the last decades of the eighteenth century, was really dependent on the policies of the Austrian imperial government. Before long those policies changed, so that by the outset of the nineteenth century the Ukrainian educational institutions had either ceased to exist or had begun to offer instruction in Polish. This meant that the Ukrainian national revival had to start again from scratch.

The new sequence of stages in the western or Austrian Ukrainian lands could be chronologically defined as follows: (1) the heritage-gathering stage, 1816–1847; (2) the organizational stage, 1848–1860; (3) the political stage, 1861–1918. As elsewhere, the heritage gatherers compiled, codified, and published works about language, folklore, and history, and they began to create a new literature. As was the case in the Russian Empire, the Austrian Empire had its own trio of Ukrainian nationalist intelligentsia who were working at about the same time, in the 1830s and 1840s. The three figures were Markiian Shashkevych, Iakiv Holovats'kyi, and Ivan Vahylevych, who in subsequent literature have come to be known as the Rusyn Triad (*Rus'ka Triitsa*). Again, as with many other contemporaneous national revivals in east-central Europe, Ukrainian leaders in Austria were most concerned with the so-called language question, that is, with deciding which linguistic form was most appropriate for use in publications and schools and, therefore, most representative of the nationality as a whole.

The second, organizational stage among Austria's Ukrainians began rather abruptly in 1848, triggered by external events—namely, the revolution of that year, which began in March in the imperial capital of Vienna and soon affected the entire Habsburg realm. Events moved rapidly, and within a year and a half, the Ukrainians established their first newspaper (*Zoria Halytska*), their first cultural organizations (Galician-Rus' Matytsia, National Home), their first political organization (Supreme Ruthenian Council), and their first permanent center of higher learning (the Department/*Katedra* of Rus'/Ruthenian Language and Literature at the University of L'viv). Because of profound changes in the political system of Austria, Ukrainian peasants (who made up more than 90 percent of the group) were liberated from serfdom. Almost immediately, they and other Ukrainians were elected to a national parliament (Reichstag). Although such promising political achievements were to be curtailed as early as 1850 with the reimposition of autocratic Austrian rule, the cultural achievements survived and the number of Ukrainian organizations, publications, and schools were to increase in subsequent decades.

The third, or political stage can be said to have begun effectively in 1861, when Austria created provincial diets to which Ukrainian deputies were elected. Six years later, in 1867, an imperial parliament (Reichsrat) began to function once again in Vienna, and Ukrainians became members of that body as well. With such political structures set up in the relatively democratic parliamentary environment that Austria allowed, political interest groups promoting Ukrainian issues arose, first as umbrella organizations during the 1870s (Rus' Council) and 1880s (National Council), then as political parties in the 1890s (Ukrainian Radical party, 1890; National Democratic party, 1899; Ukrainian Social-Democratic party, 1899; Russian National party, 1900). The political stage, which lasted until the end of World War I, saw not only the growth of Ukrainian political organizations and activity, especially in Galicia, but also the flowering of the organizational stage, with its burgeoning expansion of schools, cultural organizations, theaters, publications, and scholarly centers, all of which disseminated a sense of national identity not only among the intellectual elite and a new generation of students but also among the populace as a whole.

The other important element to keep in mind as part of the proposed analytical framework for the Ukrainian national revival concerns the concept of the hierarchy of multiple loyalties versus that of mutually exclusive identities. These seemingly conflicting principles were present in each stage of Ukrainian national revival in both the Russian and the Austrian empires. For instance, in the heritage-gathering stage within the Russian Empire, most of the early histories of Ukraine expressed a deep sense of local patriotism and love for the Ukrainian past. Yet all were written in Russian and were imbued with the notion that

Ukraine, or Little Russia (as it was commonly known at the time), was a natural and integral part of the Russian imperial world, a view that implicitly accepted the idea of a hierarchy of multiple loyalties or identities. On the other hand, the *Istoriia Rusov,* which was circulating in these very same years, treated Little Russia not as a province of a larger Russian world but rather as an independent country and culture that only recently had come under Russian imperial hegemony. The theme of Ukrainian distinctiveness in the *Istoriia Rusov* clearly reflected the concept of mutually exclusive identities.

Analogously, while linguists like Pavlovs'kyi were arguing that Ukrainian was but a dialect of Russian and while the patriotic folklorist Mykhailo Maksymovych (1840) was proclaiming that "Little Russian" was "artificial" and that therefore Ukrainians could never have their own literature, their contemporary, Taras Shevchenko, was publishing works that encompassed "a wide range of feelings and ideas in Ukrainian of the highest artistic form."[17] Shevchenko's writings heralded a perceptual process whereby some of his contemporaries and subsequent followers came to believe that the "Little Russian dialect" could indeed function as a full-fledged literary language. But language alone was insufficient. Shevchenko not only created the medium, he provided the message as well—national pride in the form of heartrending and memorable literary passages, so that in marked contrast to most of his contemporaries, who accepted a hierarchy of multiple loyalties, Shevchenko thought solely in terms of mutually exclusive Russian or Ukrainian identities.

Nonetheless, one should not expect that the Ukrainian national awakening was ideologically unidirectional and that after Shevchenko a gradual but increasing number of leaders would move from the idea of multiple loyalties to that of mutually exclusive identities. In fact, while many figures like Volodymyr Antonovych or Ivan Franko evolved into the mutually exclusivist position, some, such as Kostomarov, Kulish, or Holovats'kyi, moved later in their careers from the mutually exclusivist position to the concept of multiple loyalties. This should be considered not an opportunistic political move, as some might imply, but rather a reflection of the Ukrainian cultural setting not only during the period of the national revival but also before and for that matter after it as well. In that regard, it is interesting to note that the political theorist Mykhailo Drahomanov, who was the first to equate social and cultural issues

---

17 The appraisal of Shevchenko is by Luckyj, *Between Gogol and Ševčenko,* p. 137. The views of Maksymovych were expressed in an 1840 letter to the Galician-Ukrainian activist Denys Zubrys'kyi: "Everything written here in Little Russian is in some sense artificial and has only a regional character like Germans writing in the Alemannic dialect. We cannot have a literature in the South Russian language." Cited in Luckyj, *Between Gogol and Ševčenko,* p. 30.

within Ukrainian developments, even argued that in some cases Ukrainians needed to pass first through the stage of multiple loyalties (that is, believing they were Rus'/Little Russians/Russians) before they could appreciate the intellectual propriety of a mutually exclusive Ukrainian national identity.[18]

The fluidity with which national activists changed their attitudes about multiple and mutually exclusive identities was particularly evident in western-Ukrainian lands within the Austrian Empire. Initially, all three members of the Rusyn Triad—Markiian Shashkevych, Iakiv Holovats'kyi, and Ivan Vahylevych—were firm believers in the idea of mutually exclusive identities. But after 1848 there was a change. Shashkevych died young—remaining, in the view of patriotic Ukrainian writers, ideologically pure—while Vahylevych accepted the idea of a Ukrainian/Polish multiple identity and Holovats'kyi a Little Russian/Russian one. In fact, the whole second half of the nineteenth century, which coincided with the organizational stage of the national revival among Austria's Ukrainians, was marked by a struggle between mutually exclusivist Ukrainophiles and two variant hierarchies of multiple loyalties (Old Ruthenian and Russophile), each of which had its own press, cultural organizations, and political parties.[19]

Assuming that the concepts of a hierarchy of multiple loyalties and mutually exclusive identities are both equally impartial aspects of Ukrainian historical development, it might be useful when analyzing the national revival not to prejudge Ukraine's intellectual leaders and the organizations they created solely in terms of whether they implicitly or explicitly contributed to the idea of national exclusivity. To put it another way, one might argue, when considering the whole course of the national revival from its beginnings in the late eighteenth century through its culmination in World War I, as well as its evolution since then under Soviet rule, that the principle of a hierarchy of multiple loyalties, which assumes the existence of what social scientists call situational ethnicity, and which was evident during the nineteenth century within the Russian and Austrian empires as well as more recently in the Soviet Union, is as "natural" a phenomenon in Ukrainian culture as the concept of mutually exclusive identities that allegedly can function successfully only with the attain-

---

18 Drahomanov had in mind the Subcarpathian Rusyns, "the wounded brother I can never forget," about whom he commented: "whoever wants to spread populism among the Uhro-Rusyn [Subcarpathian Rusyn] intelligentsia must approach the problem from what already exists, Muscophilism, and therefore begin to propagate Russian books, although only of a living, democratic progressive orientation. ..." M. Drahomanov, *Spravi Uhorskoi Rusy* (L'viv 1895), p. 9.

19 For a revised understanding of these orientations, see below chapter 7.

ment of independent statehood. Such a premise raises issues that go beyond the scope of this essay and that require further study of the Ukrainian national revival. Let us hope that studies by others will be enhanced by the analytical framework proposed here.

chapter three

A Subordinate or Submerged People: The Ukrainians of Galicia under Habsburg and Soviet Rule[*]

In the context of the Center for Austrian Studies conference, "Great Power Ethnic Politics: The Habsburg Empire and the Soviet Union," the Ukrainians are unique. They are the only indigenous people in the former Habsburg Empire subsequently to have experienced direct rule by the Soviet Union. The Soviet-ruled territories that before 1918 had been part of the Habsburg Empire comprised three areas in western Ukraine known as eastern Galicia, northern Bukovina, and Transcarpathia. The largest of these lands was eastern Galicia, which will be the focus of attention here.[1]

In comparing Habsburg and Soviet methods of rule in eastern Galicia, it is possible to address factors such as the administrative, economic, military, and nationality policies of the two regimes. The concern here will be primarily with the nationality question. The chapter will not only compare and contrast the Habsburg and Soviet approaches to the Ukrainian nationality question in the past, it will also try to see what practical value, if any, the Habsburg approach may still have for present and future Soviet policy makers.

Eastern Galicia occupied only a quantitatively small part of the Ukrainian problem as a whole. Even the three Habsburg lands combined—eastern

---

[*] This is a revised version of a paper presented at a symposium, "Great Power Ethnic Politics: The Habsburg Empire and the Soviet Union," April 26–28, 1990, sponsored by the Center for Austrian Studies at the University of Minnesota, and published in Richard L. Rudolph and David F. Good, eds., *Nationalism and Empire: The Habsburg Empire and the Soviet Union* (New York: St. Martin's Press, 1992), pp. 95–108. A Polish translation by Benedykt Heydenkorn appeared in *Zeszyty Historyczne*, XCVII (Paris, 1991), pp. 91–100.

1 For an introduction to the extensive literature on eastern Galicia during both Habsburg and Soviet rule, see Paul Robert Magocsi, *Galicia: A Historical Survey and Bibliographic Guide* (Toronto, Buffalo, and London, 1983), esp. chapters 5, 6, 8, and 9.

Galicia, northern Bukovina, and Transcarpathia—accounted at most for 12 to 15 percent of the total Ukrainian land mass and population. Yet, despite their relatively small size within the total Ukrainian context, Habsburg-ruled Ukrainian lands, in particular eastern Galicia, were to play an enormously positive role in preserving the Ukrainian national idea during the nineteenth century. In fact, at the very same time that tsarist oppression had stopped the Ukrainian movement dead in its tracks in the Russian Empire, the Ukrainians living under the relatively benign rule of the Habsburgs were able to develop Ukrainian nationalism into a viable movement for themselves and their descendants.

When examining the Ukrainian nationality question, whether in eastern Galicia or in Ukraine as a whole, it is useful to keep in mind certain conceptual issues. Nationalist movements can be divided into two basic categories, which might be called intelligentsia-inspired national movements and state-imposed nationalism.[2] Intelligentsia-inspired national movements emanate from below. They occur among groups who live in multinational states where a language, culture, and identity other than their own is dominant. Self-proclaimed leaders—the nationalist intelligentsia—seek to convince the group's members that they form a distinct nationality and that consequently they deserve at the very least cultural autonomy, if not political autonomy or even independence. The second category, state-imposed nationalism, emanates from above, and occurs within already existing independent states. The governments of these states hope to gain the allegiance of their subjects by convincing them that they are united because they belong to a given nationality whose primary function is loyalty to the existing nation-state's government and social structure.

Because Ukrainians were a stateless people, their national revival fell within the intelligentsia-inspired variety of nationalism. Living in the Habsburg and neighboring Russian empires, however, Ukrainians were exposed as well to the state-imposed nationalisms of those states. Thus, at the very same time that the Ukrainian national revival was unfolding, the Habsburg and tsarist Russian authorities were also trying to implement their own respective state-imposed nationalisms. The manner in which those two imperial authorities tried to transform Ukrainians into loyal Habsburg or tsarist subjects was to have an indelible imprint on the Ukrainian self-image and on the manner in which Ukrainians identified themselves. In short, the Ukrainian national revival of the late nineteenth century—as well as the Ukrainian national psyche ever since

---

2 The following discussion is pursued at greater length in chapter 2, above.

then—has been marked by two seemingly contradictory phenomena: an acceptance of a hierarchy of multiple loyalties versus an emphasis on mutually exclusive identities.

Put another way, some East Slavs living on Ukrainian territory might have several "national" loyalties or identities, so that it did not seem problematic to be both a Little Russian (Ukrainian) and a Russian, or an ethnic Ruthenian (Ukrainian) of the Polish nation—*gente Ruthenus, natione Polonus*. Others, however, were dismayed by what they considered uncertainty, or even a lower status on a hierarchical ladder of identities. Hence, they argued that national identities such as Russian or Ukrainian, or Polish and Ukrainian, were mutually exclusive, and that an individual must choose between one or the other.

But how did these conflicting concepts of multiple loyalties versus mutually exclusive identities affect the manner in which Ukrainians could function in the specific territory of eastern Galicia, which was ruled by both the Habsburg Empire and later the Soviet Union? In effect, both the Habsburg Empire and the Soviet Union tried to impose their respective versions of a state-imposed nationalism upon Galicia's Ukrainians. In the case of the Habsburgs, this took the form of promoting loyalty to an imperial dynasty; in the case of the Soviets, the goal was to create loyalty to a classless and eventually nationality-less Communist state. What were the results of the Habsburg and Soviet approaches to the phenomenon of Ukrainian nationalism in Galicia?

In the case of Habsburg rule, which lasted from 1772 until 1918, the final balance sheet was, from the standpoint of Ukrainian nationalism, quite positive. Already in the 1770s, when Galicia first became a Habsburg land, Empress Maria Theresa together with her co-regent and successor, Joseph II, initiated a series of reforms that were to have a positive impact on what was still the very embryonic stage of Ukrainian nationalism. From the outset, the Habsburg authorities clearly distinguished Galicia's Ukrainians, whom they called Ruthenians (*Ruthenen*), from Russians, the nationality with which they frequently had been and were still to be confused.[3] Other Habsburg contributions included (1) an improvement in the status of the Greek Catholic church, which was virtually the exclusive religion of Galicia's Ukrainians and which was made equal to the Roman Catholic church (1774); (2) the introduction of universal elementary education in the vernacular language (1777); and (3) the establishment of the first modern schools of higher learning

---

3 The confusion, which existed not only among the Habsburg authorities but also among the Galician-Ukrainian populace itself, derived in part from the fact that the people called themselves *rus'kyi* (i.e., Rusyn/Ruthenian), which when pronounced aloud sounded virtually the same as *russkii* (i.e., Russian).

specifically for Ukrainians—the Studium Ruthenum at the University of L'viv (1787) and the Greek Catholic seminary called the Barbareum in Vienna (1775).

These positive precedents were to be developed further at certain critical periods in Habsburg history. Thus, in 1848 it was at the instigation of the Habsburg authorities that the Ukrainians as a group began to participate in the political world and, thereby, to enhance the status of their national movement. In that year alone, Ukrainians established their first political organization (Supreme Ruthenian Council), their first newspaper (*Zoria halytska*), their first cultural societies (Galician-Rus' Matytsia and National Home), and their first modern military formations (Ruthenian National Guard and Sharpshooters Battalion). Furthermore, they participated actively as members of the newly established Austrian parliament (Reichstag), and they received their first permanent center of higher learning, the Department (*Katedra*) of Ruthenian Language and Literature at the University of L'viv. All of these achievements led some contemporary Polish nationalists to quip that it was the Habsburgs (especially Galicia's governor, Franz Stadion) who "invented" the Ukrainians.[4]

This mid-century boost to the Galician-Ukrainian national movement was subsequently tempered by the ups and downs of Austrian political life during the next seven decades of Habsburg imperial history, from 1849 to 1918. Yet despite the increasing dependence by the Habsburg authorities on Galicia's Poles as the group of choice to rule the province (in particular after 1868), the Ukrainian national movement continued to make remarkable advances through the creation of numerous cultural organizations, publishing houses, newspapers, and political parties. In the critical area of education, the number of Ukrainian-language elementary schools rose from 1,293 to 2,510, and secondary schools from one to five during the last four decades of Habsburg rule.[5] Moreover, nine new Ukrainian university departments were created at the University of L'viv. Finally, the Habsburg authorities even stepped in on the side of Ukrainians during the internal nationality conflicts that were raging between rival members of the intelligentsia, some of whom argued that the local East Slavic population was Russian, while others said that it was part of a distinct Ukrainian nationality.[6] In the end, the Habsburg authorities clearly favored the pro-Ukrainian orientation. The most significant contribution in this

---

4   For details on the early stages of the Ukrainian national revival in Galicia before 1849, see Jan Kozik, *The Ukrainian National Movement in Galicia, 1815–1849* (Edmonton, 1986).

5   Ann Sirka, *The Nationality Question in Austrian Education: The Case of Ukrainians in Galicia, 1867–1914* (Frankfurt-am-Main, 1980), pp. 75–95 *passim*.

6   The Galician-Ukrainian national movement actually experienced an internal struggle between an intelligentsia who accepted the principle of a hierarchy of multiple loyalties

regard was the 1893 decision of Galicia's provincial school board in favor of vernacular Ukrainian as the only acceptable language to be taught in schools and to serve as the linguistic medium to represent the Ukrainian nationality.

This is not to say that Galicia's Ukrainians attained all their national goals. The province was never territorially divided into separate Polish and Ukrainian administrative entities, nor was a Ukrainian university ever established. Nor did Polish domination of the upper and middle levels of the Galician provincial administration ever change. Yet, while Galicia's Ukrainians did not fare terribly well in comparison with Galicia's Poles, the contrast between their status and that of their national brethren across the border in the Russian Empire could not have been greater.

In tsarist Russia, there were until 1905 no legal Ukrainian political parties, no cultural organizations, and no newspapers. There were no Ukrainian-language schools at any level, and the Ukrainian language itself was officially banned from 1863/1876 to 1905. It was in the context of these realities that, despite criticism leveled by political and civic activists against certain aspects of Habsburg rule, Galicia's Ukrainians were until the very end of the empire's existence in late 1918 to remain its loyal "Tyroleans of the East."[7]

Even before the Soviet Union came to rule eastern Galicia in 1939–1941 and then after 1945, the achievements in Ukrainian national life stemming from the Habsburg era had already been largely undermined. This is because when the Habsburg Empire collapsed in 1918, all of Galicia came under Polish rule. Under Poland during the interwar years, the number of Ukrainian cultural institutions decreased dramatically, most Ukrainian-language elementary schools became bilingual Polish-Ukrainian schools, and all but one of the university departments in Ukrainian subjects were abolished.[8] Then, when the Soviet Union first annexed the region in the aftermath of the Nazi-German– Soviet destruction of Poland in September 1939, many of the remaining institutions from the "feudalistic" Habsburg and "bourgeois" Polish days were closed. Soviet rule was interrupted by the German invasion of June 1941, but it was renewed with the return of the Soviet Army in the fall of 1944.

With the close of World War II, the Soviet Union became the dominant force throughout all of east-central Europe, and a new version of state-imposed nationalism was instituted for the inhabitants of eastern Galicia. Although the

---

(the Old Ruthenians and Russophiles) and an intelligentsia who favored the idea of mutually exclusive identities (the Ukrainophiles). See below, chapter 7.

7   On the question of Ukrainian loyalty to the Habsburgs, see below, chapter 4.

8   The decline in Ukrainian national life among Galicia's Ukrainians during the interwar years is outlined in Bohdan Budurowycz, "Poland and the Ukrainian Problem, 1921– 1939," *Canadian Slavonic Papers*, XXV, 4 (Toronto, 1983), pp. 473–500.

new rulers were to foster the Ukrainian aspects for eastern Galicia, they did this only to the degree that such Ukrainianism fit into the Soviet predilection for an acceptable hierarchy of multiple loyalties.

On the one hand, the Ukrainianization of eastern Galicia as carried out by the Soviets took the form of the expulsion through population exchange of most of the remaining Poles living in the towns and rural countryside.[9] The Polish language was also replaced in the educational system, as elementary and secondary schools were made either purely Ukrainian or bilingual Ukrainian and Russian. Analogously, the former dominant Polish presence in cities such as L'viv as well as in numerous towns throughout eastern Galicia came to an end, as Polish cultural organizations and Roman Catholic churches were abolished and replaced by Soviet-Ukrainian institutions.

All Ukrainian political, cultural, and religious institutions that had existed before 1945 were also abolished. And if their association with the Habsburg "feudal" and Polish "bourgeois" past was not enough to make them unacceptable, the fact that some may have existed (or have been restored) during the three years of Nazi-German occupation (1941–1944) provided the Soviets with the ultimate justification for their abolition—their very existence during the war years made them "collaborationist" and "fascist." The most important of such organizations was the Greek Catholic church, which, under the nearly half-century leadership of its patriarch-like leader, Metropolitan Andrei Sheptyts'kyi (1865-1944), had in itself become an integral part, if not the very essence, of Galician-Ukrainian national identity. Following the precedent of nineteenth-century tsarist Russia, the Soviet authorities arranged for a church council (*sobor*) at L'viv, which in 1946 abrogated the union with Rome. This meant that Greek Catholicism was made illegal, and all its former adherents, should they wish to remain Eastern-rite Christians, had to become adherents of the Russian Orthodox church.[10]

Thus, under Soviet rule, all the former institutions, national symbols, and historical events that until then had been associated with a Ukrainian self-identity in Galicia were outlawed and removed from public life. For instance,

9 During the interwar years, when Poland ruled "Ukrainian" eastern Galicia, the number of Polish settlers increased by 300,000, so that by the 1930s ethnic Poles comprised 39.5 percent of the urban population and 21.1 percent of the rural population. With the onset of Soviet rule in 1945, nearly three-quarters of a million of the Poles still remaining moved westward to the restored state of Poland. For details on the fate of Poles, see Joseph B. Schectman, *Postwar Population Transfers in Europe, 1945–1955* (Philadelphia, 1962), pp. 151–179.

10 On the importance of Sheptyts'kyi in Galician-Ukrainian life and the subsequent demise of the Greek Catholic church, see Paul Robert Magocsi, ed., *Morality and Reality: The Life and Times of Metropolitan Andrei Sheptyts'kyi* (Edmonton, 1989).

the pre-Soviet Ukrainian national flag and national anthem, or the heros of Galician-Ukrainian history, most especially during the recent twentieth-century struggle against Polish and German rule, were branded as examples of Ukrainian "bourgeois nationalism," a phenomenon that could be and frequently was considered a crime against the Soviet state. Galician Ukrainians could remain Ukrainian, but only if they were specifically Soviet Ukrainian.

And what did *Soviet Ukrainian* mean? In essence, it meant forgetting everything that previously had been considered positive in the Galician past, in particular since the onset of Habsburg rule in 1772, as well as events, regardless of when they happened, that were associated with the Polish presence in the area. There were a few exceptions to this general condemnation of the historical heritage of the last two centuries. The most outstanding of such exceptions was the late-nineteenth-century belletrist and publicist Ivan Franko (1856–1916), who because of his socialist inclinations could be claimed as a precursor to Communist activities in the twentieth century. Franko was posthumously raised by the Soviets to the level of national hero, with the University of L'viv and several streets and squares being named after him, not to mention the frequent republication of his writings, and the organizing of numerous conferences about his career. Soviet-Ukrainian ideology also included the glorification of a group of otherwise little-known and relatively unimportant leftist and Communist leaders and events in interwar eastern Galicia, and, in particular, of the World War II struggle against local "collaborationist" Ukrainian bourgeois-nationalist leaders.

Even more problematic for Ukrainians living under Soviet rule was the unresolved issue of multiple loyalties versus mutually exclusive identities. Under Habsburg rule, these seemingly contradictory principles coexisted because, in Austrian Galicia, Ukrainians could function within the socially and politically acceptable imperial Habsburg framework of a hierarchy of multiple loyalties without having to give up their own national identity. In other words, an East Slav from Galicia could be simultaneously a Ukrainian national patriot and a loyal Habsburg subject. Both identities were compatible.

This was in decided contrast to the situation within the Russian Empire and, for that matter, the Soviet state that succeeded it. In tsarist Russia, accepting the idea of a hierarchy of loyalties effectively meant that a resident of the Ukraine or, as it was known then, Little Russia, was at best a Little Russian. In the absence of any Little Russian or Ukrainian language schools, all means of written and oral communication outside one's native village were in Russian. In such a situation, being a Little Russian became, *nomens omens*, merely a lower or less advanced form of Russian identity. Moreover, according to the *Weltanschauung* of tsarist society, the Ukrainian or Little Russian past was merely an appendage of Russian civilization. Hence, the residents of medieval Ukrainian territory and the language they spoke were considered "Old Russian," the states they inhabited were referred to as "Kievan Russia" or the "Galician-Russian" principality, and a leader such as the seventeenth-century hetman Bohdan Khmelnyts'kyi became just another Russian Cossack.

Whereas the Soviets recognized Ukrainian as a distinct literary language and Ukrainians as a distinct people, their interpretation of the historical past as presented to several generations through a centralized school system proved to be not much different from what was taught in tsarist days. Even the view that Ukrainian is a distinct language was at times undermined by Soviet policy, which already in the late 1930s argued that all Ukrainian students must be fluent in the Russian language and that Ukrainian must be brought steadily closer to the Russian language in alphabet, vocabulary, and grammar.

Finally, the Soviet understanding of the hierarchy of multiple identities was best represented by a three-stage evolution that Marxist-Leninist ideologists expected to take place among all nationalities living in the Soviet Union, but most especially among the three closely related East Slavic peoples—Russians, Belorusans, and Ukrainians. Those three stages—*rastsvet* (flowering), *sblizhenie* (drawing together), and *slianie* (fusion)—were expected to culminate in a situation which would replace distinct nationalities with a new Soviet nation (*sovetskaia natsiia*) or "historical community of people—the Soviet people (*sovetskii narod*)." Thus, while the hierarchy of multiple loyalties in the Austro-Germanic Habsburg world allowed for the survival and even flourishing of a Ukrainian nationality, in the Soviet Union multiple loyalties allowed for a gradual process of Russian assimilation or at the very least the persistence of a "lower" form of Russian identity, whether it was called by its old name, *Little Russian*, or its new one, *Ukrainian*.

The organizers of the conference at the University of Minnesota's Center for Austrian Studies hoped that comparative exercises such as this one might illuminate present-day policy debates and even have some "practical value for Soviet and East European policy makers." In a real sense, the traditional conflict within the Ukrainian national psyche between the concepts of multiple national identities and mutually exclusive identities persists to this day. While it is true that the Habsburg heritage had contributed to making Galicians the most nationally conscious segment of the Ukrainian population, they are the exception in today's Soviet Ukraine. In fact, it is the persistence of a hierarchy of multiple loyalties among perhaps three-quarters of the Ukrainian population that has led to only a passive commitment on the part of Ukrainian society as a whole to the kind of demands for national autonomy or even independence that, since the beginning of the Gorbachev era, have been heard with increasing frequency in other parts of the Soviet Union, in particular the Baltic and Caucasian republics. The Ukrainian situation reminds one of what Václav Havel has recently repeated so eloquently about his own Czechoslovak society—that the more dangerous problem for the well-being of a people comes not from the external forces of a repressive state but from the moral failings within individuals whose very personas are crossed by walls that divide our souls.[11]

This internal division is precisely what is of most concern to organizations such as the Popular Movement of Ukraine for Reconstruction, better known by its acronym RUKH, which at present is in the forefront of the effort to renew Ukrainian cultural and spiritual life. While RUKH is not calling for independent statehood, it does wish to see the Soviet Union become a true federation of equal republics and, most especially, to transform the Ukrainian S.S.R. into a country that is Ukrainian in fact and not simply in name. RUKH's greatest difficulty is to become accepted among the people whom it ostensibly represents and to convince Ukrainians, as it were, to give up their multiple loyalties for a single national identity. In short, the battle against Little Russianism is far from won in Soviet Ukraine and, until it is, there is little that nationalist organizations such as RUKH can do to mobilize society as a whole to carry out the kind of changes it would like to see.[12]

But what about Soviet policy makers at the center in Moscow? Most are committed to the idea that the Soviet Union should survive, even if the relationship of the center to the constituent republics will probably have to change in the direction of a real federation of national states. If that is the goal, then the Habsburg experience in Galicia might be worthy of emulation. Like the Habsburgs, the Soviets could, in theory, satisfy the instinctive need for national self-pride if they encouraged an end to the tsarist and now Soviet version of multiple loyalties, one in which the Russians play the role of the supposedly older and wiser brother vis-à-vis the Little Russians or Ukrainians. The encouragement of multiple loyalties has always contributed to a blurring of

---

11 Havel expressed these views in his 1990 New Year's speech to the Czechoslovak people and again in an address to the Polish parliament, the latter reprinted in English translation as Václav Havel, "The Future of Central Europe," *New York Review of Books*, XXXVII, 5 (New York, 1990), pp. 18–19.

12 On the persistence of Little Russianism in the Ukrainian mentality at present, see Mikola Riabchuk, "Ukrainskaia literatura i malorossiiskii 'imidzh'," *Druzhba narodov*, L, 5 (Moscow, 1988), pp. 250–254, and, in particular, the interview conducted by Roman Solchanyk: "Mykola Ryabchuk Speaks on 'Little Russianism'," *Ukrainian Weekly*, September 3 and 10, 1989, pp. 2 and 12.

distinctions between Russian and Ukrainian cultures and to suspicions on the part of Ukrainians that they are constantly under the threat of national assimilation. Like the Habsburgs before them, the Soviets need to view Ukrainian national self-pride not as a threat but as a complement to their rule. The Habsburgs were, after all, able to maintain the loyalty of their Galician-Ukrainian "Tyroleans of the East," whose support they lost only *after* Austria–Hungary ceased to exist because of external circumstances. In the absence of some catastrophic external threat or profound internal transformation within the Soviet Union, it may be possible, following the Habsburg experience, for the Soviet Union to accommodate Ukrainian national needs and therefore guarantee its own survival.

chapter four

The Tyroleans of the East: Galicia's Ukrainians and the Revolution of 1848

Throughout the nineteenth century, Ukrainians lived within the borders of two multinational states, the Russian Empire and the Austrian or Habsburg Empire. Although no more than 15 percent of the Ukrainian populace lived within the Habsburg realm, the political, social, and cultural conditions that prevailed there made that relatively small group of far greater importance to general Ukrainian developments than their numbers (3.1 million in 1848) might suggest. The focus here is on one aspect of Ukrainian activity in the Habsburg Empire, namely, the reaction of Ukrainians, most particularly from eastern Galicia, to the revolutionary events of 1848 in the imperial capital of Vienna.

At the outset, it may be useful to clarify a conceptual and terminological problem: what is meant by the term *Ukrainian*? Traditionally, most of the populace in question as well as its leaders referred to themselves as *rusyny* (Rusyns) or *rus'ki liudy* (the Rusyn people), terms that derived from Rus', the medieval designation for all East Slavs. In nineteenth-century Habsburg Austria, the substantive *rusyn* and the adjective *rus'kyi* were rendered officially in German as *Ruthenen* and *ruthenisch*, forms which in English are respectively Ruthenians and Ruthenian. These, of course, are the proper historical names. But because in the twentieth century the vast majority of the group in question has defined itself as Ukrainian and is defined by others as such, it seems appropriate to employ present-day terminology. Thus, the term *Ukrainian* will be used here to describe the group, *Ruthenian* to describe some of its historic organizations.[1]

Although there is no study devoted specifically to the question of Ukrainian

---

1 For a discussion of terminology used to describe Ukrainian-inhabited Galicia and its inhabitants, see Paul Robert Magocsi, *Galicia: A Historical Survey and Bibliographic Guide* (Toronto, Buffalo, and London, 1983), pp. xv–xvi.

attitudes toward the events in Vienna in 1848, there is a substantial body of archival material, printed sources, and secondary literature that can shed light on the subject.[2] One of the best sources for gauging Ukrainian views is the first newspaper published by Galicia's Ukrainians, called *Zoria halytska* (L'viv, 1848–57), of which the inaugural issue appeared on May 15, 1848. It was the official organ of the Holovna Rus'ka Rada (Supreme Ruthenian Council), which, with its many branches throughout eastern Galicia, was the most representative body for Ukrainians at the time. Another important source from the period is the newspaper *Dnewnyk ruskij* (L'viv, 1848), whose nine issues reflected the pro-Polish attitudes of a few Ukrainian leaders. Published documents from 1848 include a Soviet collection that is useful for its inclusion of petitions by peasants and local organizations, the protocols of the Polish-Ukrainian section of the Slav Congress in Prague (June 1848), and the stenographic record of Ukrainian speeches at Austria's parliament (Reichstag).[3] Finally, there are numerous Ukrainian political pamphlets from 1848 as well as some memoirs that provide an insight into contemporary public opinion.[4]

The secondary literature on Ukrainian Galicia during the 1848–1849 revolutionary period is rather well developed. Among the better works are an excellent monograph by the Polish specialist Jan Kozik; a history of eastern Galicia on the eve of and during 1848 by the Soviet Marxist writer Evdokiia Kosachevskaia; and a comparative study of developments in all Ukrainian lands in Austria–Hungary by the Slovak scholar Michal Danilák.[5] There is as well a

2 For a survey of these, see ibid., pp. 123–128.

3 Hryhorii Ia. Serhiienko, ed., *Klasova borot'ba selianstva skhidnoï Halychyny (1772–1849)* (Kiev, 1974), esp. pp. 380–529; W.T. Wisłocki, "Kongres słowianski w roku 1848 i sprawa polska," *Rocznik Zakładu Narodowego imienia Ossolińskich*, I–II (Cracow, 1927–28), pp. 517–731; *Verhandlungen des österreichischen Reichstages nach der stenographischen Aufnahme*, 5 vols. (Vienna, 1848–49).

4 Several of the political pamphlets are listed in Magocsi, *Galicia*, pp. 124–125, notes 28–29. For a more complete list, see Ivan E. Levyts'kii, *Halytsko-ruskaia bybliohrafiia*, Vol. I: *1801–1866* (L'viv: Iz tip. Stavropigiiskogo instituta, 1885–95), pp. 30–50, *passim*. Among the important memoir literature describing 1848–1849 are works by the Ukrainians Iustyn Zhelekhovs'kyi and Anatol Vakhnianyn, and the Polish official Leon Sapieha; for full references, see Magocsi, *Galicia*, p. 120, notes 10–11.

5 Jan Kozik, *Między reakcją a rewolucją: studia z dziejów ukraińskiego ruchu narodowego w Galicji w latach 1848–1849*, Zeszyty Naukowe Uniwersytetu Jagiellońskiego, CCCLXXXI: Prace Historyczne, Vol. LII (Warsaw and Cracow, 1975)—published together with his monograph on the 1830s and 1840s in an abridged English translation: *The Ukrainian National Movement in Galicia: 1815–1849* (Edmonton, 1986); Evdokiia M. Kosachevskaia, *Vostochnaia Galitsiia nakanune i v period revoliutsii 1848 g.* (L'viv, 1965); Mikhal Danylak, *Halyts'ki, bukovyns'ki, zakarpats'ki ukraïntsi v revoliutsiï 1848–1849 rokiv* (Bratislava, 1972).

concise introduction to Ukrainian developments in 1848 in a pamphlet by Marta Bohachevsky-Chomiak.[6] Finally, there are several studies on Ukrainian political, cultural, and military activity during 1848–1849 and biographies of the key Austrian and Polish officials in Galicia during those years, Franz Stadion and Wacław Zaleski.[7] The data presented in this essay are drawn from the 1848 issues of the newspaper *Zoria halytska*, from some of the available documentary collections and memoirs, and from the most important secondary literature.

The Ukrainian reaction to events in Vienna in 1848 was based on the actions of Ferdinand I, the Habsburg emperor, who reigned until December. For Ukrainians, Vienna *was* the emperor, or more properly the emperor *was* Vienna. He was the embodiment of everything that mattered in the capital and in the administrative heart of their Habsburg homeland. Thus, it is not surprising that contemporary Ukrainian views, as they pertain to Vienna, focus almost exclusively on the Habsburg throne and its occupant. Before examining what those views actually were, it is perhaps necessary to survey, however briefly, Ukrainian developments within Austria during the crucial year 1848.

In most writings about Austria, it has become a cliché to talk about 1848 as the "Spring of Nations." Clichés sometimes reflect truths, and in the case of Galicia's Ukrainians, the cliché could not be any truer. The year 1848 did indeed witness the rebirth of Ukrainian life on lands under the Habsburg scepter. Within that year alone, Ukrainians established their first political organization, their first newspaper, their first cultural organization, and their first military units in modern times. They also took part in their first elections. Of enormous importance was the fact that the vast majority of the group—over 95 percent of whom were peasants—were liberated from serfdom. In a sense, a social class that virtually coincided with the nationality as a whole had come into civic existence, so that, for the first time, the peasants were treated as human beings and as such had to be reckoned with in political, cultural, social, and economic life.

Ukrainian activity in 1848 can be divided into three phases, which were played out in Galicia, Prague, and Vienna, and which in some cases chronologically overlapped. In their Galician homeland, the Ukrainians organized themselves on May 2 into a political body, the Supreme Ruthenian Council, which, with its several branches throughout eastern Galicia, argued effectively

6 Marta Bohachevsky-Chomiak, *The Spring of a Nation: The Ukrainians in Eastern Galicia in 1848* (Philadephia, 1967).
7 For full references, see Magocsi, *Galicia*, pp. 125–128, notes 33–46.

that Ukrainians were to be considered not Poles but rather a separate national-ity. The council argued further that, because Ukrainians were a distinct nation-ality, it had not only the right but also the duty to demand from the emperor certain corporate or group privileges. Another phase of 1848 activity took place in Prague, where in June representatives of Austria's Slavic peoples met at a Slav Congress. At that congress, the Ukrainians reiterated their demands to be recognized as a distinct nationality, which distinctness, they argued, was suffi-cient justification for the administrative division of Galicia along nationality lines. The third phase of Ukrainian activity occurred at Austria's parliament (Reichstag), which met first in Vienna between July 10 and November 1, 1848, and then in Kroměříž (German: Kremsier) between November 2, 1848, and March 7, 1849. Of the ninety-six parliamentary deputies elected from Galicia, thirty-five were Ukrainians, and of these as many as twenty-three were peas-ants. At the parliamentary sessions, some Galician Ukrainians took a promi-nent role in the debates despite their minimal knowledge of German. Their primary concern was the question of indemnity to the landlords, who were demanding compensation for the loss of their serf labor. Indemnity was some-thing the Ukrainian peasant deputies fervently opposed.

Turning specifically to the Ukrainian reaction to events in Vienna, which meant the Ukrainian view of the Habsburg emperor, that view was consistently and unequivocally positive throughout the revolutionary period. The very first issue of the newspaper *Zoria halytska* (May 15, 1848) began with these words: "We inform you that our most enlightened Austrian Emperor and King has graciously given to all the peoples of his state, including us Ukrainians in the land of Galicia, a constitution according to a patent dated March 25, 1848; this means a funda-mental code which legally permits the existence of elected and trustworthy per-sons and in that way guarantees our own freedom and welfare."[8]

This gratitude for the existence of a constitution was further expressed in a Ukrainian declaration of loyalty to the emperor, dated April 19, and in a de-scription of the Ukrainian reaction from the town of Berezhany as reported on March 23 by a local official:

> The events themselves in Vienna and the most gracious promises of His Royal Highness have created an exceptional sensation, especially the most important point in the patent which gives a constitution to all provinces regardless of lan-guage or nationality .... All people to whom I have spoken about this have be-come flushed in the face, their eyes are filled with tears, and they expressed their deepest support for those good-hearted, understanding, and loyal Austrians who

8 *Zoria halytska* (L'viv), no. 1, May 15, 1848, p. 1.

with their own unswerving faith in the dynasty recognize no ill will towards it [their ruler], and who are happy to live with their brothers under the protection of this deeply loved dynasty; these Austrians voluntarily showed love and respect for all peoples of the dynasty, whom they would like to see united in one, complete, loving family around a common father.[9]

The message is clear. The emperor is good. The emperor has granted his peoples a constitution.

Even more impressive for Galicia's Ukrainians was the imperial decree of April 17 calling for the abolition—beginning May 15—of serfdom. Specifically, this meant the abolition of all dues connected with the serf's condition. In actual fact, the responsibility for the emancipation in Galicia, which occurred two months before the act was declared throughout the rest of the empire, rests with the politically astute governor of Galicia, Franz Stadion, himself under the pressure of local revolutionary events.[10] Yet, ironically, it was not the governor—like all local officials, generally suspect in the eyes of the peasantry—who was given credit, but rather the emperor. After all, such an act of graciousness was "natural" and truly worthy of the benevolent imperial father. Perhaps the best example of the Ukrainian reaction is contained in a letter, dated June 7, from the local Ruthenian Council in Kalush to the Supreme Ruthenian Council in L'viv. Although this document was specifically concerned with the elections to the new Vienna parliament, the very first point evoked the broader context: "All subjects living in the Kalush deanery express their most heartfelt praise to his Royal and Benevolent Highness, Emperor Ferdinand I, for his grace in freeing us from servitude and in raising us to the level of equality with other citizens of the land, for which we promise our loyalty and support to his enlightened throne."[11] Again the message is clear. The emperor is good. The emperor has liberated us from serfdom.

The above descriptions and documentary evidence are not meant to imply that the Ukrainians in Galicia were content with everything that was occurring in 1848. They were not. Not surprisingly, the strongest complaint concerned the question of idemnity that the serfs were expected to repay their former landlords. In that regard, as early as May 22, one local Galician-Ukrainian activist (Oleksander Hitskevych) expressed his indignation to another (Ivan Fedorovych): "Treason, shameful treason! The government has issued a manifesto in which it announced from its side the abolition of serfdom after May 15 with compensa-

---

9 Document 208, in Serhiienko, *Klasova borot'ba*, p. 385.
10 Stadion acted precipitously as part of an ultimately successful effort to undermine the influence of the Polish National Committee, which had called for emancipation.
11 Document 215, in Serhiienko, *Klasova borot'ba*, p. 393.

tion to the landlords via the government. This shameful step of the constitutional government has evoked here among all of us the greatest discontent."[12]

Perhaps what is most interesting from this document is not the attack against indemnification, which was to be expected, but rather that the blame is placed on the government. Even the most famous declaration on this subject by a parliamentary peasant deputy, Ivan Kapushchak, himself a Galician Ukrainian, is careful to draw a clear distinction between the wicked designs of policy makers, who have willfully distorted the good intentions of the emperor, and the emperor himself. After outlining how the peasants had been paying their dues for the past several centuries and asserting that, if anybody owed anything, it was the lords who owed indemnity to the peasants, Kapushchak reflected on the role of the emperor:

> Finally, it is said that the landlords annulled the *robot* [labor dues] as a gift to the peasant. Now they want compensation for that gift. When was this gift granted, exactly? In 1846? Or early in 1848? No, only on April 17, after the sons of the [Austro-] German people had offered up their lives for our rights. To them we should be grateful and to the good emperor.[13]

It seemed, for the Ukrainians at least, that the emperor and the Austria he represented could do no wrong. Several other Ukrainian descriptions from the 1848 period confirm this view. For instance, whenever reports of disturbances in Vienna appeared in the Galician-Ukrainian press or in protocols of national councils, the blame was placed sqarely on what is considered a small minority of "evilly intent people" who were generally not even the Viennese themselves but who were, to use a more modern euphemism, "outside agitators."[14] Thus, the message is again clear. The Ukrainians did have complaints in 1848. They were not content with the way all things were working out. The fault, however, was not that of the good emperor, but of either reactionary Polish landlords, evil administrators, or revolutionary rabble.

Ukrainian loyalty was not limited to words alone. Ukrainians proved ready to fight for their emperor and for the benevolent new order he wanted to give his people. In Ukrainian eyes, the worst "outside agitators" were the Magyars, who were fomenting revolution against the Habsburgs. Moreover, because the

---

12   Cited in Ivan Franko, "Prychynky do istorii 1848 r.," *Zapysky Naukovoho tovarystva im. Shevchenka*, LXXXVIII (L'viv, 1909), p. 106.

13   *Verhandlungen des österreichischen Reichstages nach der stenographischen Aufnahme*, Vol. I (Vienna, 1848–49), p. 586.

14   See, for instance, a report on the emperor's departure from Vienna in *Zoria halytska*, no. 2, May 23, 1848, p. 10; the May 26 petition to the emperor from the Supreme Ruthenian

Magyars and the Poles were more than anxious to cooperate with each other, and since the Poles did not even recognize the existence of Ukrainians in Galicia,[15] the success of the Magyars might lead to success for the Poles—an eventuality that for Ukrainians had to be prevented at all costs. It is therefore not surprising that the imperial call for the creation of provincial national guards (first issued in March and then again in the fall) was greeted enthusiastically by the Ukrainians. Although a more general Ukrainian national guard never really emerged, two other units did: a peasant frontier defense unit (November 1848) and the Ruthenian Sharpshooters (Ruthenische Bergschützen, January 1849). The more important of these units was the Sharpshooters, and it is interesting to see the justification presented by its organizers to prospective volunteers in the following excerpt from the long proclamation issued by the Supreme Ruthenian Council in L'viv on January 1, 1849:

> The revolutionary Magyars, gathering up once again their self-pride and arrogance, now desire to revolt at the expense of destroying the Slavic peoples living in unity with them. They were not pleased when the benevolent monarch proclaimed that all the people in his state would enjoy the same rights and freedoms and that no one would be allowed to advance at the expense of another. Despite these just acts, the Magyars egotistically continued their own self-serving ends and they acted even over the ruins of the Austrian monarchy; they raised a revolt against their monarch, our emperor, forcing him to employ arms in order to defend the weak, preserve justice, and to back up his own imperial promise with all the weight necessary to maintain and defend the integrity and glory of the Austrian state.[16]

Council in *Zoria halytska*, no. 4, June 6, 1848, p. 1; and the November 15 protocol of the Brody branch of the Supreme Ruthenian Council in Ivan Sozans'kyi, "Kil'ka dokumentiv do istoriï 1848–1849 rr.," *Zapysky Naukovoho tovarystva im. Shevchenka*, XC (L'viv, 1909), p. 160.

15 When news of the March revolution reached Galicia, the local Poles immediately organized their own National Committee (Rada Narodowa), which claimed to represent all the inhabitants of Galicia. After the Ukrainians refused to accept such a situation and formed (at the suggestion of the Austrian governor, Franz Stadion) their own Supreme Ruthenian Council in May, the Poles encouraged local "Ruthenians of the Polish nation" to set up a rival Ruthenian Council (Rus'kyi Sobor), which lasted throughout the revolutionary period and supported Polish views on the political and cultural future of Galicia. On the Ruthenian Council, see N.M. Pashaeva, "Otrazhenia natsional'nykh i sotsial'nykh protivorechii v Vostochnoi Galichine v 1848 g. v listovkakh Russkogo Sobora," in Sergei A. Nikitin et al., eds., *Slavianskoe vozrozhdenie* (Moscow, 1966), pp. 48–62.

16 Cited in Ivan Krevets'kyi, "Bataliön rus'kykh hïrs'kykh stril'tsïv 1849–1850," *Zapysky Naukovoho tovarystva im. Shevchenka*, CVII (L'viv, 1912), pp. 52–53.

The Ukrainian willingness to fight and even to die for the emperor was to be put to a test, albeit in a limited way. For instance, the peasant frontier defense unit did encounter minor clashes with Hungarian revolutionary forces along the slopes of the Carpathians in early 1849. As for the Ruthenian Sharpshooters, they accompanied the Austrian imperial army into Hungary to participate in the final drive against the revolutionary Magyars. They arrived after the decisive Battle of Világos (August 13, 1849), however, and thus never saw action.[17]

Indeed, it would be possible to provide further expressions of loyalty, in both word and deed, on the part of Ukrainians toward the Austrian Habsburgs in 1848, but these would only confirm further the picture that has already been provided. What is perhaps more interesting is to ask why Ukrainians chose to show such unswerving loyalty to the Habsburg state in 1848.

One explanation is political. As the news of the March events in Vienna reached Galicia, the local Poles formulated plans to transform Galicia into a constitutional and autonomous Polish province. Within such a configuration, the Ukrainians of Galicia would have no role to play, other than remaining loyal "Ruthenians of Polish nationality" (*gente Rutheni natione Poloni*) who, as was said, merely spoke a dialect of Polish. With few exceptions, Ukrainians were not prepared to accept such a subordinate status.[18] As a result, Ukrainians opposed both the Poles and the latter's political allies, the Magyars, and instead supported the Habsburgs; in other words, the enemy of their enemies. While such an explanation is plausible, it is rather simplistic. A better explanation of why Ukrainians were *Habsburgtreu* (Habsburg loyalists), or more precisely *Kaisertreu* (loyal to the emperor), can be found in what may be called long-term cultural or psychosociological reasons. This subject will be taken up in the next chapter.

---

17 The most comprehensive discussion of these Ukrainian military formations is found in ibid. and in two other studies by Ivan Krevets'kyi, "Oboronna organïzatsiia rus'kykh selian na halyts'ko-uhors'kim pohranychu v 1848–1849 rr.," *Zapysky Naukovoho tovarystva im. Shevchenka*, LXIII–LXIV (L'viv, 1905), pp. 125–142, and "Proby organïzovania rus'kykh natsional'nykh gvardii u Halychynï 1848–1849," *Zapysky Naukovoho tovarystva im. Shevchenka*, CXIII (1913), pp. 77–146.

18 The exception were supporters of the Ruthenian Council (Rus'kyi Sobor). See above, note 15.

chapter five

Ukrainians and the Habsburgs

The era of Austrian Habsburg rule in Galicia and Bukovina that lasted from 1772 to 1918 represents one of the few instances of direct and long-term interaction between the Germanic world and territories inhabited by Ukrainians. Whether subsequent writers describe the Habsburg presence in western-Ukrainian lands in an impartial manner as the "Austrian era" or in negative terms as the Austrian Habsburg "occupation," there is no denying that the new imperial government in Vienna created in Galicia and Bukovina a civil society governed by the rule of law in which, at least by the second half of the nineteenth century, an increasing number of Ukrainians came to play an active role in the local and provincial administration. As a result, it was not long before a significant percentage of the articulate elements in western-Ukrainian society, and perhaps even a larger proportion of the peasant masses, accepted Habsburg rule and considered Austria to be their legitimate homeland.

What were the basic parameters of the Habsburg-Ukrainian relationship, and what was the attitude of Ukrainians toward the Austrian authorities? More importantly, if those attitudes were positive, did the reasons have to do with Austrian governing practices or with basic elements in western-Ukrainian society that predisposed it to the kind of rule offered by the Habsburgs? These are some of the issues to be addressed here.

The Habsburg Empire acquired the bulk of its Ukrainian-inhabited territory in 1772. Before then, only Transcarpathia (Subcarpathian Rus') was under the Habsburg scepter. With the first partition of Poland in 1772, the Habsburgs acquired what they officially called the Kingdom of Galicia and Lodomeria, or Galicia for short. Three years later, in 1775, they acquired from the Ottoman Empire the small mountainous land of Bukovina. Of the three Habsburg-ruled Ukrainian lands—Galicia, Bukovina, and Transcarpathia—Galicia was by far the largest and most important. Therefore, the following discussion will refer primarily to developments there.

The fate of Galicia's Ukrainians (or *Ruthenen*/Ruthenians, as they were officially known) was affected significantly by what could be considered the three phases of Austrian rule, as well as the short but exceptional revolutionary hiatus of 1848–1849. Those three phases were (1) 1772–1847, the Josephinian and pre-March eras, when Austrian rule was characterized first by liberal reforms initiated from above and then by reactionary efforts to return to the political and socioeconomic status quo before the Josephinian reforms; (2) 1849–1860, a decade of neoabsolutism in which many of the radical changes of 1848 were reversed; and (3) 1861–1918, the era of constitutional experimentation and then parliamentary rule, which witnessed changes in the political and to a lesser degree socioeconomic spheres that were implemented gradually as a result of compromise between the central authorities and the population's representatives.

Throughout each of these phases, it was obviously in the interests of Austria's Habsburg rulers to integrate as much as possible the many nationalities living within its vast borders. In practice, however, the central government's efforts at integration were often counterbalanced and even negated by the disintegrative effects of the activity of the empire's diverse nationalities, as each strove in varying degrees to attain cultural and political autonomy or even independence. Throughout the integrative/disintegrative or centripetal/centrifugal cycles that marked the internal history of the last century of the Habsburg Empire, the Ukrainians of Galicia were among the most consistent of Austria's many nationalities. From the very beginning of their association with the Habsburgs in 1772 until and even after the demise of the empire in October 1918, the Ukrainians generally remained *Habsburgtreu*. Indeed, there were many and repeated instances of their loyalty to the Habsburgs, enough to warrant the epithet of endearment by which they came to be known—the "Tyroleans of the East."[1]

Ukrainian loyalty was a function of the concrete advantages given the group by Austrian rule. At the time of its annexation in 1772, Galicia was administered by a Polish aristocratic elite and an urban bureaucracy. The heretofore dominant role of Poles in Galician society was to be replaced by an Austrian bureaucracy under the direct control of the central government in Vienna. Knowing that the former leading Polish echelons would hardly be content with their political, social, and legal demotion, the Habsburg authorities looked to assuage and, they hoped, to gain the support of the other major population element in Galicia, the Ukrainians (who at the time of the first reliable census of

---

1 See above, chapter 4.

1849 comprised a plurality of 46.8 percent of the province's inhabitants). Whether one prefers to describe Austrian policy as some kind of nefarious *divide et impera* or simply as the normal practice of a state acting in its own interests for self-preservation, the practical result was that in comparison to what existed before, the status of Ukrainians in Galicia under Habsburg rule between 1772 and 1918 was to improve in both relative and absolute terms.

Those improvements took place within both the cultural/religious and the socioeconomic spheres, and they began almost immediately in 1772 as part of the general Josephian reform era. Since the Josephian reforms have been described many times before, they will be recalled here only in barest outline. Besides the legal equality accorded the Uniate or newly renamed Greek Catholic church vis-à-vis the Roman Catholic church, and the eventual reestablishment of the Greek Catholic metropolitanate in L'viv (1806), Ukrainian education and national life in general were given a decisive boost with the establishment of new seminaries (in L'viv and Vienna), a university-level program (Studium Ruthenum in L'viv), and elementary education in the vernacular. Nor was the existent and future intelligentsia the only stratum of the Ukrainian population to feel the benevolent (or politically opportunistic) aspects of Austrian rule. In 1785, Emperor Joseph II's government abolished personal serfdom (*Leibeigenschaft*), issued decrees to protect peasants from the annexation of their land by the landlord's manorial estates (demesnes), and separated the local judicial system from its previous dependence on the manor. Although some of these reforms were repealed soon after Joseph's death in 1790, the "good emperor" was immortalized in the Galician-Ukrainian peasant psyche. "The emperor," generations upon generations of the peasantry continued to feel, "was all for us, only the landlords don't allow him to do all that he wants."[2] Many Ukrainian peasants were convinced that Joseph II was still alive, imprisoned by feudal nobles, but would one day free himself and then liberate the people.[3]

Thus, already before the end of the eighteenth century, Habsburg Austria had won over the two basic strata of Galician-Ukrainian society, the proverbial *khlopy i popy*—the peasant masses and the clerical intelligentsia.[4] With respect to the *khlopy*, or peasants, they embodied a kind of naive monarchism in which the *tsisar*, or Habsburg emperor, ostensibly had the welfare of his people in mind and could do no wrong. The persistence of such attitudes is generally

---

2 A common peasant attitude cited in Iuliian Okhrymovych, *Rozvytok ukraïns'koï natsional'no-politychnoï dumky* (L'viv and Kiev, 1922), p. 26.

3 See the tales as related by Ivan Franko, "Panshcyna ta ïï skasuvannia 1848 r. v Halychyni," 2nd rev. ed. (1913), reprinted in his *Tvory*, Vol. XIX (Kiev, 1956), pp. 584ff.

4 A good discussion of the relationship of the clergy and peasantry to Austrian rule is found in the introductory chapters of Jan Kozik, *The Ukrainian National Movement in Galicia, 1815–1849* (Edmonton, 1986), pp. 15–28.

attributed to the low level of political and cultural development of the Ukrainian peasantry. As for the *popy*, their *Weltanschauung* was later described in the following terms: "Polish or German in language and conservative or aristocratic in attitude, the Ukrainian clergy in Austria strove with all its might to please the central authorities ... Such a manner of thinking ... later came to be dubbed aptly by the term: *rutenstvo* (Ruthenianism)."[5]

Given this state of affairs, it would seem easy to predict how Ukrainians would react to the upheavals that wracked the Austrian Empire in 1848–1849. As discussed in the previous chapter, the Ukrainian view of contemporary political events was based almost exclusively on the actions of the Habsburg emperor, and that view was consistently and unequivocally positive throughout the revolutionary period. Commenting on this period, the late-nineteenth-century Galician-Ukrainian proponent of independent statehood Iuliian Bachyns'kyi asked, "What was this so-called 'national revival among the Rusyns [Ukrainians]'?," in order that he could provide an ironic response: "The national movement among the 'Rusyns' in 1848 was exclusively the activity of the Austrian absolutist government—an artificial and tactical maneuver of the Austrian government in its struggle with the Polish revolutionary bourgeoisie in eastern Galicia."[6]

The views of latter-day commentators notwithstanding, the second half of the nineteenth century began with Ukrainian loyalty to the Habsburgs being as strong as if not stronger than it had been even during the liberal days of the Josephinian era. Indeed, the third phase of Austrian rule that began in 1861 coincided with a growth of national consciousness among a broader segment of the Galician-Ukrainian population. The entry of secular leaders (lawyers, teachers, doctors, etc.) into the intellectual and political elite broadened the spectrum of political thought. As a result, the budding ideas of national exclusivism which they promoted sometimes clashed with the older clerical-oriented ideology of Ruthenianism and its commitment to the Habsburgs.

This new ideological dichotomy took the following form during the second half of the nineteenth century. Some of the Ukrainian intelligentsia (the Old Ruthenians/*starorusyny*)—even those of an Austrophile clerical bent—began to express a desire for cultural and even political unity with some vague East Slavic world. Others were more specific, proclaiming their nationality as being either Ukrainian (the populists or Ukrainophiles) or Russian (the Russophiles) and hoping for a political solution that would result in an independent Ukrainian state or in unification with "Holy Rus' " (*Sviatia Rus'*, i.e.,

5 Okhrymovych, *Rozvytok*, pp. 2–29.
6 Iuliian Bachyns'kyi, *Ukraina irredenta*, 3rd ed. (Berlin, 1924), pp. 50–51.

the Russian Empire). While such independentist and irredentist attitudes were in the air (and in relatively liberal Habsburg Austria they could be expressed more or less openly), and while today they are given much attention by the crisis mentality that forms the basis of much historical research, at the time the loyalist Habsburg attitude of the Ukrainian population remained for the most part unchanged. The rural masses, despite their sometimes unenviable socio-economic conditions, continued their staunch loyalty to the Habsburg monarchy. The image of the Habsburgs was embodied in Emperor Franz Joseph, who, like a fine wine improving with age, took on the mantle of a benevolent father figure above the fray of day-to-day political and social realities.

Nor was the intellectual and political leadership as a whole less loyal. To be sure, from time to time Ukrainian activists sent out signals in order that "Austrian politicians understand that we Tyroleans of the East will be forced to entertain other feelings in our hearts if we are not permitted the rights due to us."[7] In retrospect, however, these turned out be little more than efforts at obtaining political leverage in the ongoing struggle of Ukrainians to improve their status vis-à-vis the Poles in Galicia.

More indicative were the acts and expressions of pro-Austrian loyalties, as expressed during Vienna's conflict with the Vatican in 1874, in the platforms of new political groupings (the National Congress, 1880; the National Council, 1885; the Russophile National Congress, 1882), and on the eve of World War I, when Ukrainian politicians united to express their unswerving support for Austria (December 1912 and August 1914).[8] All such verbal declarations, moreover, were backed by deeds. Consequently, during the war Ukrainians fought bravely for Austria in distinct units (Ukrainian Sich Riflemen) as well as in various divisions of the imperial army. In marked contrast to other Slavic units, Ukrainian units experienced no large-scale or even noticeable numbers of desertions. Finally, when it was clear to almost everyone else that the Habsburgs and their empire were a thing of the past, the stubborn "Tyroleans of the East" still somehow hoped beyond hope that a distinct Ukrainian province of eastern Galicia would come into being under the gracious scepter of the Habsburgs.[9] In this sense, the very proclamation of West Ukrainian statehood on November 1, 1918, came about by political default. This is because Ukrainian political leaders justified their preparations for self-rule not on some in-

---

7 An attitude expressed at the dawn of the so-called New Era in 1890, as related by the parliamentary deputy Kost'Levyts'kyi, *Istoriia politychnoï dumky halyts'kykh ukraïntsiv, 1848–1914,* Vol. 1 (L'viv, 1926), pp. 235–236.

8 For details on these and other similar events, see ibid, pp. 138–723 *passim.*

9 Michael Lozynskyj, *Wiederherstellung des Königreiches Halytsch-Wolodymyr Galizien und das ukrainische Problem in Österreich* (L'viv, 1918).

alienable universal right but rather on the guidelines of the October 16 Habsburg imperial manifesto. In short, Galician Ukrainians declared independence only after the emperor had renounced any further participation in the affairs of Austria–Hungary. Although this left them bereft of their monarch, some Ukrainian leaders nevertheless still hoped that the Habsburg empire would survive or, like some mystical phoenix, experience a reincarnation.[10]

But what were the reasons for this unswerving Ukrainian loyalty to the Habsburgs? Was it simply the result of opportunistic maneuvering on the part of generations of Austrian politicans and government officials, as some defenders of the national cause would have us believe? Was it simply the particular circumstances in Austrian Galicia that made it politically wise and inevitable that the Ukrainians be solicited as a counterweight to the more dangerous Poles, as most accounts of this era suggest? Or, was it the result of something more endemic to Ukrainian society?

The end of the previous chapter suggested that the explanation why Ukrainians were *Habsburgtreu*, or more precisely *Kaiserstreu*, can be found in what may be called long-term cultural or psychological reasons. Like all Ukrainians (and for that matter all eastern Slavs), Ukrainians living in eastern Galicia came from an eastern Christian/Orthodox and traditionally patriarchal society characterized by its clearly defined hierarchical structure. In its purest form, that structure comprised three elements: a large mass of peasant serfs, a smaller stratum of lords or hereditary nobles, and the king or emperor at the apex. The only other significant element was the eastern Christian clergy, which acted as an intercessor or kind of transition belt between each of the secular hierarchy's components and the religious world beyond. As Christ was the ruler, protector, and father of the spiritual world, so the earthly emperor appointed by divine right—and therefore the only source of political legitimacy—was the ruler, protector, and father of the temporal world.[11]

10 During the last two weeks of October 1918, Galician-Ukrainian leaders welcomed the continuance of their relation to Austria–Hungary, as long as Polish domination of the eastern half of Galicia ended. At the same time, the Galicians decided against union with their brethren in eastern Ukraine. They were afraid of alienating the Entente, which they thought might still somehow favor the preservation of all or part of the Habsburg monarchy. For a critical view of Galician-Ukrainian policy during these crucial days, see Mykhailo Lozyns'kyi, *Halychyna v 1918–1920* (Vienna, 1922), pp. 28–40. For a more positive appraisal by the head of the Ukrainian National Council in L'viv and later first head of the West Ukrainian People's Republic, see Kost' Levyts'kyi, *Velykyi zryv* (L'viv, 1931), pp. 108–142.

11 On the sources for the divine nature of the secular ruler as perceived in the eastern Christian/Orthodox world, see Ernst Benz, *The Eastern Orthodox Church: Its Thought and Life,* (Garden City, N.Y., 1963), pp. 163–167.

Even after the outset of the eighteenth century, when the last Galician Ukrainians gave up Orthodoxy and became Uniate/Greek Catholics, traditional patriarchal or authoritarian attitudes prevailed. In that context, it would be interesting to test in part the validity of this hypothesis by seeing, at least through published sermons from the late-eighteenth and nineteenth centuries, how often texts of submission to temporal powers—Christ's precept to render unto Caesar and Paul's admonition to the Romans to submit to existing governments—were used as the basis for homilies at the local Galician-Ukrainian parish level.[12]

For their part, the Habsburgs were not at all reluctant to emphasize on every possible occasion their role as protectors of the realm's various peoples, an ideological position made easier to uphold because of the tacit approval and encouragement of the Catholic church of whatever rite. Thus, as the above discussion of loyalty has revealed, the tone was set by the Ukrainians' first Habsburg ruler, Joseph II. He and his successors, culminating with Emperor Franz Joseph, simply could do no wrong.

Indeed, submission to temporal authorities or naive monarchism was characteristic of much of Christian Europe and was hardly unique to Galician-Ukrainian society.[13] In the course of the nineteenth century, however, secularization and industrialization helped to challenge and eventually undermine traditional modes of belief in many European societies. Galicia, at least before 1914, did not yet effectively pass through these processes, and Ukrainian society there continued to lack other social strata whose interests might have counterbalanced the traditional patriarchal outlook. In the absence of a Ukrainian secular elite (polonized centuries before) and a Ukrainian urbanized middle class (industrialization began in Galicia—very slowly—only at the very end of the nineteenth century), all that remained were small clerical elite and a mass of semiliterate peasants. These two groups, each for its own reasons, had a vested material and/or psychological interest in maintaining a patriarchal monarchist outlook.

Nor did the situation change in any significant way during the last phase of

12 The biblical texts in question are: "Render therefore unto Caesar the things that are Caesar's; and unto God the things that are God's," repeated in slightly varied form in Matthew 22:21, Mark 12:17, and Luke 20:25; and Paul's "Let every soul be subject unto the higher powers...that are ordained of God. Whosoever resisteth power, resisteth the ordinance of God: and they that resist shall receive to themselves damnation." Romans 13:1, 2.

13 Some Galician Ukrainians did not look for salvation from their own *tsisar* in Austria, but rather from the tsar in Russia. See John-Paul Himka, "Hope in the Tsar: Displaced Naive Monarchism among the Ukrainian Peasants of the Habsburg Empire," *Russian History*, VII, 1–2 (Tempe, Ariz., 1980), pp. 125–138.

Austrian rule after 1861, when a Ukrainian secular intelligentsia made up of teachers, lawyers, journalists, and other professionals came onto the scene and were given the opportunity to participate in a parliamentary and multiparty political system. Even this so-called "new" Ukrainian elite was (with few exceptions) unable to shed its patriarchal cultural baggage, forcing its members to remain, as we have seen, loyal to the Habsburgs until the very end. As for the rural masses who stayed in their native villages, their monarchist loyalties remained firm and, as the results of recent research have shown, those loyalties may even have been buttressed because of satisfaction with a generally improving economic situation in certain areas of Galicia during the empire's last decades.[14]

Besides the patriarchal character of Galician-Ukrainian society, there is another aspect of Ukrainian intellectual development that in its Galician form made it compatible with Habsburg Austria. This aspect is related to the Ukrainian national revival. A dichotomy existed within the movement, regardless of whether it took place in the Russian or the Austrian Empire. That dichotomy can be seen in the contrast between what may be called the concept of the hierarchy of multiple loyalties and that of mutually exclusive identities.[15]

Because the era of Habsburg rule coincided with the Ukrainian national revival, which is commonly thought to have reached its foremost evolution in Galicia, the question of Ukrainian loyalty to the Habsburgs should also be explored from the standpoint of the national movement. If one accepts the premise that the Ukrainian national revival was ideologically marked by tension between the concept of a hierarchy of multiple loyalties and that of mutually exclusive identities, then it could be argued that Habsburg Austrian rule provided an ideal compromise between the two attitudes.

For the most part, the Polonophile or Russophile Ukrainian elite gave up its native Ruthenian identity for a Polish or a Russian identity. The process began first with a loss of Ukrainian vernacular speech followed by conversion from Greek Catholicism to either Roman Catholicism or Orthodoxy. Although the Greek Catholic clergy espoused the pro-Austrian ideology of Ruthenianism (*rutenstvo*), it did not have potential as a national ideology in large part be-

14   The traditional "doom and gloom" view of Galicia's economically downtrodden rural masses—an attitude that had formed the basis of Soviet and still much non-Soviet Ukrainian writing on the subject—has with much convincing contemporary documentation been challenged with regard to five of eastern Galicia's provinces, where the economic situation at the village level actually is shown to have been improving in the last decades of the nineteenth century. See Stella Hryniuk, *Peasants with Promise: Ukrainians in Southeastern Galicia, 1880–900* (Edmonton, 1991).

15   See above, chapter 2.

cause its propagators (the Old Ruthenians/*starorusyny*) never really developed a clear program. Consequently, by the end of the century, the Old Ruthenians were superseded by people who identified themselves unequivocally as Russians and who often promoted a political orientation that expected assistance from, and even annexation by, tsarist Russia.

Not surprisingly, Austria's governing circles were greatly concerned with what was described as "Ruthenian irredentism" directed toward Russia.[16] Such "irredentism" was limited, however, to the Russophile intelligentsia and to a few villages that had come under the influence of an Orthodox revival. Moreover, by the late nineteenth century, the Russophile orientation was eclipsed by that of the more numerous and influential Galician-Ukrainian Austrophiles.

There were also eastern-oriented irredentists among Galician Ukrainians, such as Iuliian Bachyns'kyi, who called for independent Ukrainian statehood and anticipated legal constitutional changes in Russia that would eventually encourage Galicians to join their brethren farther east.[17] In practical terms, however, the possibility of liberalization in pre-World War I tsarist Russia was as remote as a victory of the Russian national orientation among Ukrainians in Galicia. Finally, there were Galician Ukrainophile activists, going back to Iakiv Holovats'kyi in the 1840s, who saw their homeland as a piedmont that would attract their fellow Ukrainians in the Russian Empire to join them to create a unified Ukrainian entity under the benevolent scepter of the Habsburgs.[18]

Despite such political speculation, most Galician Ukrainians had limited horizons that remained within the bounds of Austria–Hungary. In cultural terms, the Ukrainian orientation was based on the use of the vernacular as a literary language and the belief in mutually exclusive national identities. In other words, the "Ruthenians" of Galicia were part of a distinct Ukrainian nationality; they were not Poles or Russians. For their part, the Habsburg authorities were pleased to encourage a group of people within Austria's borders whose exclusivist Ukrainian identity would, by definition, shield them simultaneously from external Russian as well as internal Polish irredentism. And since the Habsburgs were operating within a Germanic world, there was no fear that Ukrainians would become Austro-Germans. Therefore, the patriarchal tradition so dear to the hearts and minds of Galician Ukrainians could remain in place at the same time that both trends in the national revival—multiple loyalties and mutually exclusive identities—could function and mutually reinforce each other. Put

16 See note 13 above, Himka, "Hope in the Tsar"; and Stanislaus Smolka, *Die reussische Welt: historisch-politische Studien Vergangenheit und Gegenwart* (Vienna, 1916).
17 Bachyns'kyi, *Ukraina irredenta*, p. 80.
18 See Okhrymovych, *Rozvytok*, p. 36.

another way, one could be simultaneously a Ukrainian patriot and a loyal Habsburg subject. The combination turned out to be mutually advantageous to both parties.

In summary, then, Ukrainian-Habsburg relations from 1772 to 1918 were characterized by the mutual benefits that accrued to each side. Expressions of Ukrainian loyalty were not mere political or opportunistic rhetoric. They reflected, instead, a real appreciation for the political and cultural achievements Ukrainians attained in Austria, and they fitted in as well with the historical context of Ukrainian society. That context reflected on the one hand a patriarchal system and, on the other, a compromise between the principles of a hierarchy of multiple loyalties and a framework of mutually exclusive identities that in general was characteristic of the Ukrainian national revival.

The real problem—some would say tragedy—was that for all their participation in a modern political and parliamentary system, most of Galicia's Ukrainian leaders intrinsically expected that the Habsburg Empire would last forever. When it was no longer there, they were forced to face the postwar world alone. In that new world, however, they no longer had the "good and benevolent emperor" and his imperial Austrian system to cushion the blows of the harsh realities of Europe after World War I.

chapter six

The Language Question as a Factor
in the National Movement in Eastern Galicia*

Reflecting in comparative terms on the nature of nationalism, a well-known student of the subject, Hans Kohn, wrote, "In Western Europe, modern nationalism was the work of statesmen and political leaders. ... In Central and Eastern Europe it was the poet, the philologist, and the historian who created the nationalities."[1] Indeed, local nationalist leaders who represented stateless peoples were well aware of the importance of language for the movements they were propagating. Most had looked toward the German experience for ideological inspiration. Already in the late eighteenth century the historian-philosopher Johann Gottfried Herder (1744–1803) posed the now oft-quoted rhetorical question "Has a people anything dearer than the speech of its fathers? In its speech resides its whole thought domain, its tradition, history, religion, and basis of life, all its heart and soul. To deprive a people of its speech is to deprive it of its one eternal good."[2] Contemporary German writers such as Johann Gottlieb Fichte (1762–1814), Ernst Moritz Arndt (1769–1860), Friedrich Jahn (1778–1852), and the Grimm brothers, Jacob (1785–1863) and Wilhelm (1786–1859), adhered to the precepts of Herder, and, soon after, national awakeners in the Slavic lands followed their lead. It is no coincidence

---

* This study first appeared under the same title in Andrei S. Markovits and Frank E. Sysyn, eds., *Nationbuilding and the Politics of Nationalism: Essays on Austrian Galicia* (Cambridge, Mass.: Harvard University Press/Harvard Ukrainian Research Institute, 1982), pp. 220–238; and in a slightly revised form under the title "The Language Question in Nineteenth-Century Galicia," in Riccardo Picchio and Harvey Goldblatt, eds., *Aspects of the Slavic Language Question*, Vol. II: *East Slavic* (New Haven: Yale Concilium on International and Area Studies, 1984), pp. 49–64.

1 Cited in Peter Brock, *The Slovak National Awakening* (Toronto and Buffalo, 1976), front papers.

2 J.G. Herder, *Briefe zu Beförderung der Humanität* (1783), cited in Carlton J.H. Hayes, *Essays on Nationalism* (New York, 1928), p. 3.

that, during the first half of the nineteenth century, national revivals in east-central Europe were led by individuals who were linguists either by profession or by avocation—Dobrovský and Jungmann among the Czechs, Štúr among the Slovaks, Kopitar among the Slovenes, Karadžić among the Serbs, and Gaj among the Croats. Commenting on the language factor from the standpoint of the Habsburg ruling establishment, Austria's minister of education, Count Leo Thun, remarked that "The language of a people is itself the people, it is its ego and its essence; it is with the most profound and sacred interests integrally linked to [a people's] spiritual and moral development."[3]

The principle espoused by Count Thun was known in Galicia, and Iakiv Holovats'kyi used it as an introductory epigram in his 1849 pamphlet about the relation of eastern-Galician dialects to other Ukrainian and East Slavic languages. At the same time, Holovats'kyi published a theoretical discussion on the role of language in Galician-Ukrainian national life in which he argued that "The vernacular language, [which] is the word of God given to mankind for the expression and edification of the human spirit, best expresses the particular life of a people."[4] These statements summed up the importance that Galician-Ukrainian leaders gave to language as a factor in the national movement throughout the course of the nineteenth century.

In comparison to other Slavic nationalities in the empire, the Ukrainians were latecomers in the process of national consolidation. Although the Czechs, Serbs, Croats, and Slovaks had worked out most of the elements of a national ideology by the 1850s, this process was only just beginning among Galician Ukrainians. Until the 1890s, members of the Galician-Ukrainian intelligentsia struggled with one another in an attempt to work out a common national identity. By the end of the nineteenth century, the two most influential factions were the Russophiles, who considered the Slavic population of eastern Galicia to be part of a unified eastern Slavic Rus' people, subsequently referred to as the one and undivided (*edinaia i nedelimnaia*) Russian people; and the Ukrainophiles, who saw themselves as part of a distinct Ukrainian people living not only in the southern part of the Russian Empire (Dnieper Ukraine) but also in the Austro-Hungarian territories of eastern Galicia, northern Bukovina, and north-eastern Hungary. There were also some polonized Galician Ukrainians, who felt that the fate of their people must remain closely linked to that of the Poles. By the second half of the nineteenth century, however, such Polonophiles re-

3 Cited as an introductory epigram in Iakov Holovatskyi, *Rozprava o iazytsî iuzhnorous-kômî y eho narîchiiakh* (L'viv, 1849), p. 1.

4 Iakov Holovatskyi, *Try vstupytel'niy predopodavaniia o ruskôi slovesnosty* (L'viv, 1849), pp. 3–4.

mained decidedly in the minority.

The major factions were the Russophiles and the Ukrainophiles, and although they made some attempts at reconciliation, they never reached an accord. Instead, they engaged in an ideological battle for the allegiance of the local population. By the 1890s, the Ukrainophiles had won, although the Russophiles continued to attract adherents, albeit at a diminishing level, down to and even after World War I. Among the ideological weapons brandished in the Russophile-Ukrainophile struggle, language played a significant role.

The language problem in Galicia was not very different from that faced by other national groups. Sociolinguists such as Joshua Fishman, Einar Haugen, and Robert Auty have found similar patterns in formulating a national language.[5] According to these scholars, language builders may attempt to implement one or a combination of the following alternatives: (1) the revival of a traditional language, usually one found in religious texts; (2) the creation of a new standard based on a single dialect or a fusion of closely related dialects; or (3) the adoption of an already established language used by neighboring or related peoples. The intelligentsia in eastern Galicia tried each of these alternatives, singly and in combination.

Studies covering the entire development of the language question in Galicia are limited to an introductory survey by Vasyl' Lev and to several sections from histories of the Ukrainian literary language and press by Pavlo P. Pliushch and Mykhailo Zhovtobriukh.[6] Most of the literature concentrates on certain aspects of the problem or on specific periods. The early alphabet disputes of the 1830s have received detailed attention in the work of Ivan Franko, Osyp

---

5 Joshua A. Fishman, *Language and Nationalism: Two Integrative Essays* (Rowley, Mass., 1972), pp. 40ff; Einar Haugen, *Language Conflict and Language Planning: The Case of Modern Norwegian* (Cambridge, Mass., 1966), pp. 3–26; Robert Auty, "The Linguistic Revival among the Slavs of the Austrian Empire, 1780–1850: The Role of Individuals in the Codification and Acceptance of New Literary Languages," *The Modern Language Review*, LIII, 3 (London, 1958), pp. 392–404.

6 Vasyl' Lev, "Borot'ba za ukraïns'ku literaturnu movu v Halychyni ta kharakter ïi," *Zbirnyk na poshanu Ivana Mirchuka*, in *Naukovyi zbirnyk Ukraïns'koho naukovoho universytetu*, VIII (Munich, New York, Paris, Winnipeg, 1974), pp. 67–86; P.P. Pliushch, *Istoriia ukraïns'koï literaturnoï movy* (Kiev, 1971), pp. 333–350; M.A. Zhovtobriukh, *Mova ukraïns'koï presy (do seredyny dev"-ianostykh rokiv XIX st.)* (Kiev, 1963), pp. 113ff; and Zhovtobriukh, *Mova ukraïns'koï periodychnoï presy (kinets' XIX-pochatok XX st.)* (Kiev, 1970), especially pp. 19–56. The language question, in particular from the standpoint of the alphabet, figures in a study by Kost' Kysilevs'kyi, "Istoriia ukraïns'koho pravopysnoho pytannia: sproba syntezy," *Zapysky Naukovoho tovarystva im. Shevchenka*, CLXV (New York and Paris, 1956), pp. 74–114.

Makovei, Mykhailo Vozniak, and Vasyl' Shchurat;[7] the postrevolutionary period of the 1850s has been analyzed by Kyrylo Studyns'kyi, Ostap Terlets'kyi, and Pylyp Svystun.[8] The abortive attempts at alphabet reform undertaken by Galicia's Polish governor in 1859 have received much attention in the collection of materials and accounts by Ivan Franko, Ivan Filevich, and Ilarion Svientsits'kyi.[9] Finally, the problem of late- nineteenth-century relations between Galician Ukrainians and Dnieper Ukrainians concerning the formation of a Ukrainian literary standard has been treated in detail by George Shevelov.[10]

In their analyses of language and of nationalism in general in nineteenth-century eastern Galicia, most authors view the language question as a political phenomenon. Their descriptions inevitably sympathize with one of the main contending national factions—either the Ukrainophiles or the Russophiles. The Russophile interpretation is best represented by the work of Pylyp Svystun and Ivan Filevich. They consider all attempts to employ local vernacular as an effort by the Austrian government, in cooperation with Ukrainian "separatists," to undermine both politically and culturally the supposed unity and strength of Russian civilization. Non-Marxist Ukrainian authors, such as Ostap

7 All in *Zapysky Naukovoho tovarystva im. Shevchenka* are the following: Ivan Franko, "Azbuchna viina v Halychyni 1859 r.," CXIV–CXVI (L'viv, 1913), pp. 81–116, 131–153, 87–125; Osyp Makovei, "Try halyts'ki hramatyky," LI and LIV (L'viv, 1903), pp.1–96; Mykhailo Vozniak, "Studiï nad halyts'ko-ukraïns'kymy hramatykamy XIX v.," LXXXIX–XCI (L'viv, 1909), pp. 111–143, 33–118, 126–150, and XCIII–XCV (1910), pp. 90–131, 107–161, 83–106, and XCVIII (1910), pp. 77–146; Mykhailo Vozniak, "Avtorstvo azbuchnoï statti z 1834 r.," CXXXVII (L'viv 1925), pp. 107–118, and Vozniak, "Apologiia kyrylytsi Denysa Zubryts'koho," CL (L'viv, 1929), pp. 122–142; Vasyl' Shchurat, "Azbuchna statia Mykoly Kmytsykevycha z 1834 r.," LXXXI (L'viv, 1908), pp. 134–144.

8 Ostap Terlets'kyi, *Halyts'ko-rus'ke pys'menstvo 1848–1865 rr.* (L'viv, 1903); Kyrylo Studyns'kyi, introduction to *Korespondentsyia Iakova Holovats'koho v lïtax 1850–62,* in *Zbirnyk fil'ol'ogichnoï sektsyi Naukovoho tovarystva im. Shevchenka,* VIII–IX (L'viv, 1905), pp. i–clxi; F. Svistun, "Kril. o. Nikita Izhak iako tsenzor galitsko-russkikh izdanii v 1852–1857 gg.," *Viestnik 'Narodnogo Doma',* XXV (III), 5 and 6 (L'viv, 1907), pp. 70–76 and 90–94, and Svistun, "Materialy dlia istorii iazykovoi bor'by u russkikh galichan," *Viestnik 'Narodnogo Doma,'* XXXI (IX), 3–4 (L'viv, 1913), pp. 67–80.

9 Ivan Franko, "Azbuchna viina," *Zapysky Naukovoho tovarystva im. Shevchenka,* CXIV–CXVI (L'viv, 1913), pp. 87–125; and Franko's compilation, *Azbuchna viina v Halychyni 1859 r.: novi materiialy,* in *Ukraïns'ko-rus'kyi arkhyv,* Vol. VIII (L'viv, 1912); Ivan Filevich, *Iz istorii Karpatskoi Rusi: ocherki galitsko-russkoi zhizni s 1772 g. (1848–1866)* (Warsaw, 1907), esp. pp. 137–162; and Ilarion Svientsitskii, ed., *Materialy po istorii vozrozhdeniia Karpatskoi Rusi,* Vol. II, in *Nauchno-literaturnyi sbornik Galitsko-russkoi Matitsy,* VI, 3–4 (L'viv, 1909), pp. 21–38.

10 George Y. Shevelov, *Die ukrainische Schriftsprache 1798–1965* (Wiesbaden, 1966). See also Paul Wexler, *Purism and Language,* Indiana University Publications, Language Science Monographs, Vol. 11 (Bloomington, Indiana, 1974), pp. 39–109.

Terlets'kyi, Ivan Franko, Osyp Makovei, Kyrylo Studyns'kyi, Mykhailo Vozniak, and Vasyl' Lev, view the gradual introduction of the vernacular, which resulted in the codification of a Ukrainian literary language, as a healthy alternative to the antiquated and artificial language (described pejoratively as the *iazychiie*) of the Russophiles. The Marxist authors Pavlo Pliushch and Mykhailo Zhovtobriukh also adopt the Ukrainophile interpretation, although they are critical of bourgeois-nationalist Ukrainian leaders in Galicia (which means practically everyone but Franko and Pavlyk) for their supposedly overriding concern with class interests and their all-too-often "demagogic" anti-Russian stance.

It could also be argued that the debates over the language question were but a symbolic reflection of deeper socioeconomic changes within Galician society. In March 1848, the Habsburg government liberated the serfs, and as a result the peasant masses, which comprised 95 percent of Galician-Ukrainian society, had for the first time to be considered a real force in political, economic, and cultural life. Some moved to towns and cities, where a Ukrainian middle class came into existence. Within three decades, the intelligentsia, previously composed almost exclusively of priests, soon found more lawyers, journalists, tradesmen, and other secular elements (many of whom were of peasant background) within their ranks. The Ukrainian peasantry, middle classes, and secular intelligentsia had needs that the old social and cultural framework could not meet.

One of those needs was language, that is, a language used not solely for religious purposes and other esoteric pursuits but as a living means of communication in all sectors (educational, political, administrative, or commercial) of the gradually modernizing Galician society. It is no coincidence, as we shall see below, that within one generation after the 1848 revolution—that is, during the 1870s—the first split occurred in Galician-Ukrainian cultural life. And the issue that prompted the split was language.

Although politics played a role in the linguistic debates, an exclusively political analysis of the polemics about language tends to distort the elements involved. Viewing the issue as a simple dichotomy between Russophiles and Ukrainophiles does not reflect the reality of the situation. At least until 1870, the Galician-Ukrainian intelligentsia consisted only of Old Ruthenians (*starorusyny*), traditionalists whose national horizons did not extend beyond the borders of Austrian Galicia.[11] Earlier, a few Polonophiles may have favored the adoption of the Latin alphabet (in Polish form) and perhaps political

---

11 Generally, the traditionalist Old Ruthenians are lumped together with the Russophiles. The first author to criticize this incorrect view was Mykhailo Drahomanov, *Halyts'ko-rus'ke pys'menstva* (L'viv, 1876), esp. pp. 14–33. See also the excellent appraisal of the

accommodation with the Poles, but they never supported linguistic or national assimilation.

Two groups evolved from the Old Ruthenians: first, in the 1870s, the populists, later known as Ukrainophiles; then, in the 1890s, the Russophiles. These chronological divisions were never very clear, and some individuals may have changed their orientation several times. Moreover, there were still some Old Ruthenians left even after the younger Russophiles, and most especially the Ukrainophiles, dominated the scene. Consequently, by the end of the nineteenth century, Galician-Ukrainian society had intellectual leaders representing at least three national orientations: the ever-dwindling traditionalist Old Ruthenians and the younger, more modernist Ukrainophiles and Russophiles.

But what was originally at issue among the intelligentsia of eastern Galicia was not whether one was an Old Ruthenian, a Ukrainophile, a Russophile, or even a Polonophile, but whether or not one was a traditionalist or a modernizer. Adopting the framework established by modern sociolinguists, one can observe in eastern Galicia basically two factions: the traditionalists, who wanted to maintain the Slaveno-Rusyn book language, written in etymological script; and the modernizers, who saw in the vernacular (Galician Ukrainian) or in a foreign medium (Russian) a language that could effectively represent and strengthen the national movement. The underlying theme in the debates, both between the traditionalists and modernizers and within the two groups, was the question of dignity. In other words, which linguistic form—a traditional language, some local vernacular, or even a neighboring literary language— had the dignity and the power to command respect that would entitle it to represent the East Slavic culture of Galicia? In a real sense, the Old Ruthenians, the Ukrainophiles, the Russophiles, and even the Polonophiles were all loyal to their homeland and nationality. Each, however, had a different perception of which linguistic medium would be most appropriate for achieving respect both in their own eyes and in the eyes of others.

That the language question became an issue at all is integrally related to the policies of the Austrian government. During the reigns of Maria Theresa (1740–1780) and her son, Joseph II (1780–1790), the Habsburg administration expressed an interest in establishing a comprehensive educational system for all citizens of the empire. It felt that a properly educated populace would be the best guarantee for a strong and integrated society and state. The principles established in the late eighteenth century remained in force until the end of the empire's existence; that is, schools at the primary level were to instruct their

Old Ruthenians in Mykola Andrusiak, *Narysy z istoriï halyts'koho moskvofil'stva* (L'viv, 1935), esp. pp. 15–45, and chapter 7, below.

pupils in the local national tongue. As for the Slavic inhabitants of eastern Galicia, Austrian officials realized from the beginning that their language was not Polish, but rather Ruthenian (*ruthenisch*). They were uncertain, however, as to what *ruthenisch* actually meant. Similarly, the local intelligentsia were faced with the same problem when they were called upon to prepare textbooks and to teach in this Ruthenian language (*ruthenische Sprache*). Just what was this language? The answer to that question varied from one leader to another and from one generation to the next.

The language question in eastern Galicia can be approached from three aspects or stages: (1) the war between the Latin and Cyrillic alphabets; (2) the theories and programs of the traditionalists; and (3) the theories and programs of the modernizers. The first extensive controversy revolved around the external form of the language, its alphabet. Like the Serbs and Croats, the Galician Ukrainians also had an alphabet war, although of lesser proportions. As Eastern-rite Christians, Galician Ukrainians had for centuries used the Old Slavonic alphabet (*kyrylytsia*) in their religious publications. Because religion and ethnonational identity were basically synonymous, the Old Slavonic alphabet became, in essence, an external symbol of Galician-Ukrainian nationality.

The first threat to this symbol appeared during the first decades of the nineteenth century, when Austrian officials, fearful of tsarist Russia, became suspicious of what they suspected to be linguistic and cultural similarities between Austria's own Ruthenians (that is, Ukrainians) and the Russians. In 1816, Galicia's provincial administration, supported by the local Polish Roman Catholic hierarchy, called for the introduction of Polish texbooks in Ruthenian schools, but this attempt was adamantly rejected by the Greek Catholic metropolitan in L'viv, Mykhailo Levyts'kyi (1774–1858), who at the same time argued that the local Ruthenian speech was a full-fledged language quite distinct from Russian.[12] During the 1820s and 1830s, the metropolitan and writers like Ivan Mohyl'nyts'kyi (1811–1873) and Iosyf Levyts'kyi (1801–1860) argued in their grammars and essays that Ruthenian was not Russian, but rather a separate language related to the speech spoken both in Galicia and in the southern part of Russia.[13] Although such opinions were expressed from time to time in publications, the Galician intelligentsia did not have the organized strength to press the issue until 1848.

More representative was Iosyf Lozyns'kyi (1807–1889). While defending the status of Ruthenian as a language, he proposed that its publication appear

---

12 The metropolitan's 1821 tract is reprinted in Filevich, *Iz istorii*, p. 24.

13 Ioann Mohyl'nytskii, "O języku ruskim," *Czasopism Naukowy Księgozbioru Publicznego im. Ossolińskich*, II (L'viv, 1829), republished in Russian translation: "O russkoi iazykie," *Zhurnal Ministerstva narodnago prosvieshcheniia*, no. 1 (St. Petersburg, 1838),

in Latin script.[14] To illustrate his point, Lozyns'kyi published in 1835 an ethnographic study and in 1846 a Ruthenian grammar, both in a Polish-based Latin alphabet.[15] At the same time, Ivan Vahylevych (1811–1866) published a Ruthenian grammar and pointed out the advantages for Galician Ukrainians if they were to use the Latin alphabet.[16] Neither Lozyns'kyi nor Vahylevych were assimilationists, however. Rather, following the precepts of the influential Slovenian philologist Jernej Kopitar, they felt that Galician-Ukrainian literature and culture could best enter the realm of western Slavic and therefore general European culture by employing a Latin alphabet. In a sense, Lozyns'kyi and Vahylevych were modernists wanting to develop the Galician-Ukrainian vernacular, albeit in Latin script, as a legitimate medium of written communication.

Not surprisingly, the efforts to employ the Latin alphabet were supported by several Polish writers, including Wacław Załeski, August Bielowski, and Anton Dąbczański.[17] Unlike Lozyns'kyi and Vahylevych, however, these men considered Galician Ukrainian to be a dialect of Polish and felt that Ukrainians could survive only if they assimilated with the Poles. It was precisely the danger of national assimilation that in 1834 prompted Iosyf Levyts'kyi and a young seminary student, Markiian Shashkevych (1811–1843), to refute the use by their countryman, Lozyns'kyi, of the Latin alphabet for Galician-Ukrainian writings.[18] Another attempt at using a Polish-based Latin alphabet came during the revolutionary events of 1848, when the Polonophile Ruthenian Council (Ruskij Sobor), which supported the idea of political accommodation with the Poles, published nine issues of a newspaper, *Dnewnyk ruskij*, edited by Ivan Vahylevych. But the more influential Supreme Ruthenian Council (Holovna

pp. 17–43; [Iosyf Levyts'kyi], "Das Schicksal der gallizisch-russischen Sprache und Literatur," *Jahrbücher für slawische Literatur, Kunst und Wissenschaft*, II (Leipzig, 1844), pp. 183–185 and 206–210.

    For a detailed analysis of these grammars, see Vozniak, "Studii," LXXXIX, pp.115–143 and XC, pp. 33–79, 92–109.

14   J. Loziński, "O wprowadzeniu abecadła polskiego do piśmiennictwa ruskiego," *Rozmaitości*, no. 29 (L'viv, 1834).

15   J. Loziński, *Ruskoje wesile* (Przemyśl, 1835) and *Gramatyka języka ruskiego (małoruskiego)* (Przemyśl, 1846). On Lozyns'kyi's grammar, see Vozniak, "Studii," XC, pp. 109–118, and XCI, pp. 126–144.

16   J. Wagilewicz, *Gramatyka języka maloruskiego w Galicyi* (L'viv, 1845). For an analysis of this grammar, see Vozniak, "Studiï," XCII, pp. 90–120.

17   Załeski published 574 Galician-Ukrainian folk songs (using a Polish-based Latin alphabet) in his *Pieśni polskie i ruskie ludu galicyjskiego* (L'viv, 1833). See also Anton Dąbczański, *Die Ruthenische Frage in Galizien* (L'viv, 1848), pp. 20–22, and the discussion in Franko, "Azbuchna viina," pp. 95–99.

18   J. Lewicki, "Odpowiedź na zdanie o zaprowadzenie abecadła polskiego do piśmiennictwa ruskiego," supplement to *Rozmaitości*, no. 52 (L'viv, 1834); [M. Shashkevych], *Azbuka i*

Rus'ka Rada) came out unequivocally against the Latin alphabet, and in the decade that followed, the Cyrillic alphabet, in both the traditional Old Slavonic (*kyrylytsia*) and the more modern civil (*hrazhdanka*) scripts, was used in Galician-Ukrainian publications.[19]

Unlike previous developments, the last stage in the alphabet war did not originate with the Galician-Ukrainian intelligentsia. Rather, it was the Austrian Ministry of Religion and Education in Vienna, together with the support of the Polish governor of Galicia, Agenor Gołuchowski, who in 1859 requested the Czech linguist Josef Jireček (1825–1888) to study the problem of language among Galician Ukrainians. The result was a detailed report in which Jireček proposed introducing a Czech-based Latin alphabet for Galician Ukrainians.[20] In May 1859, Gołuchowski convoked a meeting of Ukrainian leaders with the intention to have Jireček's proposal adopted. When those present resisted, the government was forced to end its interference in the Galician-Ukrainian language question.[21] Thus, beginning in the 1860s, it became clear that Galician-Ukrainian writings would appear only in the Cyrillic alphabet and for the most part in the civil script.[22]

Although the question of basic external form had been settled, the problem of content still remained. In short, what was the Ruthenian language? While attempting to answer that question, Galician-Ukrainian theorists were largely

abecadło (Przemyśl, 1836). Cf. the text and discussion of an unpublished anti-Polish alphabet tract written in 1834 and attributed variously to Mykola Kmytsykevych and Denys Zubryts'kyi: Shchurat, "Azbuchna statia"; Vozniak, "Avtorstvo azbuchnoï statti," and his "Apologiia kyrylytsi"; and the discussion by Makovei, "Try halyts'ki hramatyky," LI, pp. 31–44 and LIV, pp. 77–96; and Franko, "Azbuchna viina," CXIV, pp. 102–116.

19 Franko, "Azbuchna viina," CXV, pp. 131–153; Kysilevs'kyi, "Istoriia," pp. 86–89; Mykhailo Vozniak, "Projekt pravopysy Ivana Zhukivs'koho na z''ïzdï 'rus'kykh uchenykh'," *Zapysky Naukovoho tovarystva im. Shevchenka*, LXXXII, 2 (L'viv, 1908), pp. 53–86.

20 Joseph Jireček, *Ueber den Vorschlag das Ruthenische mit lateinischen Schriftzeichen zu schreiben* (Vienna, 1859). Jireček's proposal is analyzed in great detail by Franko, "Azbuchna viina," CXVI, pp. 87–96. See also Vasyl' Simovych, "Iosyf Iirechek i ukraïns'ka mova," *Pratsi Ukraïns'koho vysokoho pedahohichnoho instytutu im. M. Drahomanova: Naukovyj zbirnyk*, II (Prague, 1934).

21 The protocols of the four meetings in 1859 as well as related documents appear in *Die ruthenische Sprach- und Schriftfrage in Galizien* (L'viv, 1861). See also the contemporary pamphlets of Bohdan Dîditskii: *O nieudobnosty latynskoi azbuky v pys'mennosty ruskoi* (Vienna, 1859) and *Spor o ruskuiu azbuku* (L'viv, 1859); the correspondence from 1859 reproduced in Franko, *Azbuchna viina ... novi materiialy*; and the Polish perspective on this period in K. Ostaszewski-Barański, *Agenor Gołuchowski i Rusini w roku 1859* (L'viv, 1910).

22 Certain details regarding the alphabet still remained to be worked out. The Old Ruthenians and Russophiles preferred the etymological civil script, while the populist Ukrainophiles

influenced by the conflicting opinions of two influential Slavic scholars, the Czech leader and patron saint of Pan-Slavism, Josef Dobrovský (1753–1829), and the Slovenian philologist Jernej Kopitar (1780–1844). Dobrovský believed that there should be a difference between the book or written language and the spoken language of a people, while Kopitar argued that the written language should as closely as possible reflect the spoken vernacular.[23]

The traditionalists in eastern Galicia started from the premise that the language of old chronicles and religious texts ought to be the basis for an acceptable literary language. This so-called Slaveno-Rusyn book language took as its departure the Old Slavonic grammar of Meletii Smotryts'kyi (1578–1633), published in four editions between 1619 and 1721. By the early nineteenth century, the Galician variety of Slaveno-Rusyn had acquired a substantial number of dialectal influences. The important point, however, was that this language, in one form or another, appeared in old books, whether of secular or religious nature. In short, it had a tradition; it had prestige!

Already in the 1820s, Ivan Mohyl'nyts'kyi composed a Slaveno-Rusyn grammar, never published, in which he argued that there should be a special book language for the educated classes and a vernacular-oriented language for the people.[24] The two-language theory was maintained throughout the nineteenth century by a group of traditionalists, best represented by Denys Zubryts'kyi (1777–1862), Ivan Hushalevych (1823–1903), Ivan Naumovych (1826–1891), Bohdan Didyts'kyi (1827–1908), and Antin Petrushevych (1821–1913). In subsequent historical writings, these writers have been described as Russophiles, or Muscophiles, a description implicitly suggesting that they identified themselves as Russians and wanted to introduce the Russian language for use in Galician publications. This may be true, but only if we understand what these

adopted a phonetic civil script. Moreover, until the 1890s, the Ukrainophiles first used an alphabet devised in the Dnieper Ukraine by Mykhailo Maksymovych, and then switched to the alphabet of the Galician linguist Ievhen Zhelekhivs'kyi. Kysilevs'kyi, "Istoriia," pp. 91–96, 102–105.

23 For the impact of these two Slavists on Galician Ukrainians, see Makovei, "Try halyts'ki hramatyky," LI, pp. 1–31, and LIV, pp. 59–76; Ivan Bryk, "Iosyf Dobrovs'kyi i ukraïnoznavstvo," *Zapysky Naukovoho tovarystva im. Shevchenka*, CXLI–CXLIII (L'viv, 1925), p. 35; Mykhailo Tershakovets', "Vidnosyny Vartolomeia Kopitara do halyts'ko-ukraïns'koho pys'menstva," *Zapysky Naukovoho tovarystva im. Shevchenka*, XCIV–XCV (L'viv, 1910), pp. 84–106 and 107–154; Kyrylo Studyns'kyi, "Kopitar i Zubryts'kyi,"*Zapysky Naukovoho tovarystva im. Shevchenka*, CXXV (L'viv, 1918), pp. 115– 164; and Vasyl' Shchurat, "V. Kopitar i ep. Iv. Snihurs'kyi," *Zapysky Naukovoho tovarystva im. Shevchenka*, CXXV (L'viv, 1918), pp. 165–200.

24 For a description of Mohyl'nyts'kyi's grammar, see Vozniak, "Studiï," LXXXIV, pp. 115–143, and XCI, pp. 33–79.

writers meant when they used the term *Russian*. Their interpretation of language was perhaps most concisely summed up in a speech by Ivan Naumovych delivered before the Galician Diet in December 1866:

> Our language has a thousand-year-old history. Some state that our language is Muscovite. We don't know the Muscovite language, just as we don't know the Muscovite people. That there are similarities between the languages of all Slavs; that our language is similar to the written language used in Moscow is not our fault. ... The Great Russian book language (*knizhnyi velikorusskii iazyk*) is basically Little Russian, created by Little Russians. By accepting the Great Russian book language, we are taking back only what is properly ours. The similarity of our language with that of all Rus' cannot be destroyed by anyone in the world, neither by laws, by diets, or by ministers.[25]

The argument here is clear: all the East Slavs are closely related and should be culturally united by one written language. In the past, that language was allegedly Church Slavonic; the modern version was now described as "Russian," or the so-called Slaveno-Rusyn developed by Ukrainian scholars who worked in Moscow during the seventeenth and eighteenth centuries. With this in mind, Bohdan Didyts'kyi proposed that "Great" and "Little" Russians should have a common written language that would be pronounced in different ways.[26] In the hands of the Galician traditionalists, this language was Slaveno-Rusyn, with varying degrees of Great Russian borrowings and local dialectisms—an uncodified conglomerate referred to by its populist antagonists as the *iazychiie*. What did this language have to do with the Great Russian writings of Pushkin, Turgenev, and Tolstoy? Not much. As the contemporary Russian literary scholar Aleksandr Pypin commented, the Galicians write in a language similar to Lomonosov and Sumarokov, that is, of the eighteenth century when Great Russian had not yet fully liberated itself from the Old Slavonic tradition.[27]

The traditionalists made use of their version of "Russian" in the newspaper *Slovo* (1861–87) and in the official publications of the national organizations they controlled: the *Vremennyk* (1864–1915) of the Stauropegial Institute; the *Naukovŷi* (later *Lyteraturnŷi*) *sbornyk* (1865–73, 1885–90, 1896–97) of the Galician-Rus' Matytsia; and the *Vistnyk* (1882–1914) of the National Home. Whenever these and other publications proved unpopular, however, they switched to the two-language principle, as in Naumovych's *Nauka* (1871–1914),

25 Cited in Filipp I. Svistun, *Prikarpatskaia Rus' pod vladeniem Avstrii* (1897; 2nd ed. Trumbull, Conn., 1970), pp. 267–268.

26 B. Dîditskii, *Svoezhyt'evŷy zapysky*, Vol. I (L'viv, 1906), pp. 10–14, and 64–65.

27 A. Pypin, "Osobyi russkii iazyk," *Viestnik Evropy*, XXIII, 11 (St. Petersburg, 1888), p. 357.

which used the vernacular for the masses as opposed to book "Russian" for the educated elite. The two-language principle had been outlined as early as 1849 at the inaugural session of the first Ruthenian cultural organization, the Galician-Ruthenian Cultural Society. Despite the fact that the majority present opted for using a vernacular-based language (*prostyi iazyk*), the Old Ruthenian Antin Petrushevych pushed through a resolution embodying the following principle:

> Everything intended for the general education of the people should be published and printed as much as is possible in that language which is living at the time in the mouths of the people; on the other hand, matters of more developed scholarship, which are intended for circles of literate people, should be published in that written language, which has the beginnings in the distant past and which is erroneously called Great Russian (*chisto-rossiiskii*).[28]

Thus, the Old Ruthenian traditionalists maintained the two-language principle in their writings. They were convinced that the respect and prestige needed for a national language could not be evoked by the local vernacular, but would accrue to an already established Slaveno-Rusyn book language, which they described as "Russian," but which in fact was an uncodified Galician recension of Church Slavonic. They allowed the use of the vernacular only when dealing with the unlettered masses, whom they hoped would eventually acquire enough education to employ only the Slaveno-Rusyn language when dealing with serious matters.

While the traditionalists followed the precepts of Dobrovský, the modernizers or the populist Ukrainophiles, as they were known, heeded Kopitar's call to develop the local vernacular as a medium for written communication. Generally, the vernacular principle was favored by the Austrian government. This happened when Vienna finally realized that the people in question were in fact not Russian, in the sense of Great Russian. Therefore, it lent its support to the populist-Ukrainophile movement, which it viewed as a stopgap to the threat of infiltration from the tsarist east.

A vernacular-based language first began to appear in publications during the 1830s. The most important of these was the first book of secular literature, *Rusalka dnistrovaia*, published in 1837 by Markiian Shashkevych, Iakiv Holovats'kyi, and Ivan Vahylevych, a group of writers known as the Ruthenian Triad. *Rusalka dnistrovaia* was based on Galician-Ukrainian dialects, but even more revolutionary was the fact that it was printed in a phonetic variety of the civil script. For this reason, it was refused for publication by the Galician censor and had to be printed in Budapest. The use of vernacular and a phonetic alphabet, instead of the traditional Old Slavonic or etymological civil scripts, were to be the hallmarks of the populist-Ukrainophile movement.

The vernacular principle was given a further boost during the revolutionary period of 1848-1849. Both the Congress of Rusyn Scholars (Sobor Rus'kykh Uchenykh) and the political body, the Supreme Ruthenian Council, called for the introduction of "that language, which our people speak" (*toho iazyka, iakym nash narod hovoryt'*).[29] Moreover, the Supreme Ruthenian Council made a clear distinction between Ruthenians and Russians, stating that the 2.5 million Galician Ruthenians were part of the 15-million-strong Ruthenian (that is, Ukrainian) nationality that inhabits not only Galicia but southern Russia, Bukovina, and northeastern Hungary as well.

Despite such declarations, however, the leading newspaper of the time, *Zoria halytska* (L'viv, 1848–57), as well as other publications, were for the most part written in the traditional Slaveno-Rusyn book language, now supplemented with an increasing number of Great Russian borrowings.[30] It was not until the 1860s, and under the influence of the Ukrainian- and Russian-language journal *Osnova* (1861–62) published in St. Petersburg, that the Galician populists began to publish several periodicals in the local vernacular: *Vechernytsî* (1862–63), *Meta* (1863–65), *Nyva* (1865), *Rusalka* (1866), and *Pravda* (1867–96). Attempts to standardize this vernacular were first put forward in a grammar (1863) by Mykhailo Osadtsa (1836–1865) and in a German-Ruthenian dictionary (1867) by Omelian Partyts'kyi (1840–1895). These were followed by grammars (1880, 1889) of Omelian Ohonovs'kyi (1833–1894) and, more importantly, by the two-volume Ruthenian-German dictionary (1886) of Ievhen Zhelekhivs'kyi (1844–1885).[31] The latter work set a standard popularly known as the *zhelekhivka*, which was to be approved by the Austrian government and employed in the four editions of the widely used grammar coauthored by Stepan

29 Cited in Lev, "Borot'ba," p. 73.
30 During its first two years of existence, *Zoria halyts'ka* appeared in the vernacular, but changed to the traditional Slaveno-Rusyn book language under the Old Ruthenian editors I. Hushalevych (1851–1853), B. Didyts'kyi (1853–1854), and S. Shekhovych (1854–1857). Studyns'kyi, *Korespondentsyia*, pp. xivff.
31 Mykhayl Osadtsa, *Hramatyka ruskoho iazyka* (L'viv, 1862), 2nd ed. (1864), 3rd ed. (1876); Emil Partytskii, *Deutsch-ruthenisches Handwörterbuch—Nimetsko-ruskyi slovar*, 2 vols. (L'viv, 1867); Emil Ogonowski, *Studien auf dem Gebiete der ruthenischen Sprache* (L'viv, 1880); O. Ohonovskii, *Hramatyka rus'koho iazýka* (L'viv, 1889); Ievhenyi Zhelekhovskyi, *Malorusko-nimetskyi slovar—Ruthenishch-deutsches Wörterbuch*, 2 vols. (L'viv, 1886)—the second volume in collaboration with Sofronii Nedil's'kii.

Smal'-Stots'kyi (1859–1938) and Fedor Gartner (1843–1925).[32] In the last decades of the nineteenth century, the circulation of vernacular publications expanded, especially as a result of the widespread network of reading rooms and libraries under the auspices of the Prosvita Society (est. 1868) and the scholarly Shevchenko Scientific Society (est. 1873). The movement was so successful that in 1893 the Austrian school administration in both Galicia and Bukovina accepted the vernacular, according to the model of Zhelekhivs'kyi, for use in schools and for official purposes.

Finally, the Ukrainophiles had on their side the force of literary genius. The greatest author in late-nineteenth-century Galicia, Ivan Franko (1856–1916), chose to write in a vernacular-based medium. Through his incredibly large corpus of prose, poetry, plays, translations, essays, social criticism, and historical works, he was able to show that the Ukrainian language was a viable instrument of expression for all aspects of intellectual endeavor. Thus, by the 1890s, it became evident that the Ukrainophile faction was going to win the struggle for the allegiance of the population, and that a vernacular-based Ukrainian language would become the predominant form of communication in the cultural life of eastern Galicia.

It was precisely the imminent success of the Ukrainophiles that led some traditionalist Old Ruthenians to protest against what they believed was the Austrian government's unwarranted support of the Ukrainian language in eastern Galicia.[33] Some members from the traditionalist camp—Pylyp Svystun (1884–1916), Osyp A. Markov (1849–1909), Osyp Monchalovs'kyi (1858–1906), Iuliian Iavors'kyi (1873–1937), and Semen Bendasiuk (1877–1965)—felt that such protests to Vienna were useless and that a more dynamic approach to the language question should be adopted. These Russophile modernizers rejected the traditionalist Slaveno-Rusyn book language and preferred to adopt instead standard literary Great Russian. They put into practice their linguistic preferences by starting new organs such as *Besieda* (1887–97), *Golos naroda* (1909–15), and *Prikarpatskaia Rus'* (1909–15), or by russifying the publications of the traditionalist Old Ruthenian national organizations.[34] These Russophiles (referred to pejoratively as Muscophiles by their Ukrainophile

32 S. Smal'-Stots'kyi and F. Gartner, *Rus'ka hramatyka* (L'viv, 1893), 2nd ed. (1907), 3rd ed. (1914), 4th ed. (1925).

33 *Vorstellung der Repräsentanten des ruthenischen Matica-Vereines gegen die, der ruthenischen Litteratur zugedachte phonetische Orthographie an das Hohe k. und k Ministerium für Kultus und Unterricht* (L'viv, 1892).

34 In 1901, the Russophiles revived the scholarly journal of the Galician-Rus' Matytsia under a Russian title, *Nauchno-literaturnyi sbornik*, and it appeared irregularly until 1934. In 1905, the Russophiles changed the format of the Stauropegial Institute's *Vremennik* and

rivals) not only used the Great Russian language, they also rejected the very idea of a Ukrainian nationality. Instead, they felt themselves and all of eastern Galicia's Slavs to be part of one Russian nationality, and they hoped that one day their Galician homeland would become part of the Russian Empire. Despite their linguistically modern and aggressive approach, the Russophiles had arrived too late on the Galician cultural scene and continued to be overshadowed by the Ukrainophile movement.

Yet even if the populist Ukrainophiles dominated the cultural scene in eastern Galicia at the beginning of the twentieth century, the language question was still not settled. Although the general principle favoring the use of the vernacular was accepted, there was still the problem of *which* vernacular to recognize as authoritative. The Galician Ukrainophiles, who had for decades seen themselves as part of one people living not only in the Habsburg Empire but also in the steppes along the lower Dnieper River, generally had only limited contact with their eastern brethren in the Russian Empire. After 1876, however, they began to have firsthand exposure to Dnieper Ukrainians.

As a result of tsarist Russia's increasingly intolerant attitude toward its national minorities, the Ukrainian language was generally outlawed in publications between 1876 and 1905, and many leading Dnieper-Ukrainian writers turned to Galicia to publish their works. The Galicians both welcomed them and accepted their own new role as defenders of the Ukrainian language and nationality. There were obvious dialectal differences between Galicia and the Dnieper Ukraine, which were reflected in publications from both areas. The increased contact did not smooth out the differences, nor did it lead to a merger of the two versions of the language. Virtually the opposite occurred.

Both the Galician Ukrainians and the Dnieper Ukrainians continued to write in their own manner, and each group attacked the other in a series of fierce polemics initiated in 1891 with a scathing attack by the Dnieper Ukrainian Borys Hrinchenko (1863–1910) against the language used by the Galician writers Ivan Franko and Osyp Makovei (1867–1925). Hrinchenko characterized the language of the Galician Ukrainians as little more than another *iazychiie*, not much better than the traditionalist Galician-Ruthenian variety.[35] Hrinchenko was later joined by Ivan Nechui-Levyts'kyi (1838–1918), Ahatanhel Kryms'kyi (1871–1941), and Musii Kononenko (1864–1922), who were pitted against the Galician defenders Ivan Franko, Illia Kokorudz (1857–1933), Ivan Verkhrats'kyi (1846–1919), Oleksander Borkovs'kyi (1841–1921), and Osyp

published it in standard Russian; and the following year it did the same with the National Home's *Viestnik*.

35 V. Chaichenko [B. Hrinchenko], "Halyts'ki virshi," *Pravda*, III, 9 (L'viv, 1891), pp. 15–158.

Makovei. The Dnieper-Ukrainian writers felt that the Ukrainian language, which their own countrymen—writers such as Shevchenko, Kvitka, Hulak-Artemovs'kyi, Kulish, and Vovchok—had created, was being woefully corrupted in Galician writings by foreign influences, including Polish and German borrowings, and by the archaic dialectisms. For their part, the Galicians retorted that a viable literary language must include all dialects and not be limited to the narrow provincial region of the Psel and Sula rivers (Dnieper tributaries) of the Poltava region.[36]

By 1905, when publications in Ukrainian were again permitted in the Russian Empire and the focus of Ukrainian intellectual life shifted from L'viv to Kiev, extremists in both camps compromised. This was reflected in Hrinchenko's four-volume Ukrainian-Russian dictionary (1907–09), which had a broad dialectal base and included many Galicianisms.[37] But polemics, especially when they concern a medium as sacred as language, do not die easily. As late as 1911, Ivan Nechui-Levyts'kyi wrote, "In general one must say that the Galicians should not write any books, neither for the Ukrainian people, nor for children."[38]

By the first decade of the twentieth century, the leading Galician-Ukrainian writers began to accept the idea of a literary language that was based mainly on the Poltava region of the Dnieper Ukraine but that also contained Galician elements, especially in its scientific and administrative vocabulary. As a result, Galician Ukrainians could now call as their own a standard language used by a population almost ten times larger than themselves. This gain in prestige was obtained in part, however, at the expense of the vernacular principle that at home they had used so effectively in the fight against Galicia's traditionalist Old Ruthenians and modernist Russophiles. In the end, the Galician Ukrainians accepted a literary norm that was substantially different from their own local standard, although it had the prestige of being used by 32 million Ukrainians from the Carpathians to the Caucasus.

36 Details of the Galician–Dnieper-Ukrainian polemic are found in Shevelov, *Die ukrainische Schriftsprache*, pp. 37–77, and Wexler, *Purism and Language*, pp. 47–139.
37 B.D. Hrinchenko, *Slovar' ukraïns'koï movy*, 4 vols. (Kiev, 1907–09).
38 I. Nechui-Levyts'kyi, "Kryve dzerkalo ukraïns'koï movy," in his *Novi povisti i opovidannia*, Vol. VIII (Kiev, 1912), p. 82.

chapter seven

Old Ruthenianism and Russophilism: A New Conceptual Framework for Analyzing National Ideologies in Late-Nineteenth-Century Eastern Galicia*

Like other nationalities within the Habsburg Empire, as well as within eastern and western Europe as a whole, the Ukrainians of Galicia experienced a national revival in the course of the nineteenth century. This meant that people who before had been content with identifying themselves in terms of religious affiliation or territory of habitation (whether a province, smaller region, river valley, or village) were now being called upon to identify themselves in terms of nationality, that is, as belonging to a larger group of people because of similar cultural and linguistic characteristics.

For Ukrainians as well as other nationalities, or national minorities, living within the Habsburg Empire, the year 1848 was an important turning point. The revolutionary events of that year brought recognition to Ukrainians as a national group within Austria. Ukrainian leaders were unprepared, however, for the new status thrust upon them. Influenced by external events, they created new political and cultural institutions, but they did so in the name of a group whose precise identity had not yet been defined either to their own satisfaction or to the satisfaction of others. In other words, Galicia's Ukrainians had an organizational superstructure without an ideological infrastructure. Therefore, during at least the next half-century, the history of eastern Galicia was marked by a quest to create an ideological infrastructure during which the group's leaders struggled among themselves in an effort to find an acceptable national ideology. Their quest began largely in the negative mode, however. While most leaders had a clear perception of who they were not—they knew they were not Poles—they had more difficulty in defining precisely who they were. Were they members of a separate East Slavic Ruthenian nationality which

---

* This is a revised version of an article that first appeared in Paul Debreczeny, ed., *American Contributions to the Ninth International Congress of Slavists, Kiev 1983*, Vol. II (Columbus, Ohio: Slavica, 1983), pp. 305–324.

lived only in Austria? Were they, together with Ukrainians in the Russian Empire, part of a distinct Ukrainian nationality? Or were they, together with Ukrainians, Belorusans, and Great Russians in the Russian Empire, part of one, united, common-Russian (*obshcherusskii*) nationality? In their efforts to find an answer to that question and at the same time gain the allegiance of the peasant masses in eastern Galicia, the local intelligentsia eventually coalesced into three rival groups or national orientations known as Old Ruthenians (*starorusyny*), populist Ukrainophiles, and Russophiles. These groups did not come into existence immediately in 1848. Rather, they gradually evolved at various times during the following decades, especially beginning in the 1860s.

The advantage of historical hindsight allows us to know in advance the outcome of the rivalry between these three nationalist orientations. By about 1900, the Ukrainophile orientation was clearly in the ascendant, and, despite the continued existence of the Old Ruthenians and especially Russophiles, the vast majority of the East Slavic inhabitants of eastern Galicia had accepted a Ukrainian national identity by the first decades of the twentieth century. Yet, the same hindsight which provides us with the advantage of knowing in advance the outcome of a particular historical process also contains disadvantages. We often become prisoners of our own historical perspective and consequently present distorted descriptions of certain phenomena that may not seem important for future developments. Despite our skepticism toward the cliché that history is written by the winners, we often do little to correct that approach. In the constellation under discussion, the winners were the Ukrainophiles and the Ukrainian national orientations; therefore, it is not surprising that most of the existing literature on the national movement in eastern Galicia tends to emphasize the achievements of that orientation and to downplay and even denigrate the activity of the losers—the Old Ruthenians and Russophiles. Moreover, because so little serious analysis of the Old Ruthenian and Russophile position has been undertaken, both orientations tend to be lumped together and described by the opprobrious term *Muscophile*.

This study hopes to initiate a reversal in the historiographical trend that until now has dominated our understanding of the national movement in late-nineteenth-century eastern Galicia. The approach employed here is not motivated by a nostalgic interest in lost causes or by a particular sympathy for fringe groups or small nationalities who have of late become attractive in certain intellectual circles.[1] Rather, this study is motivated by the belief that to understand

1 See, for instance, the burgeoning literature on "little peoples": Walker Conner, "Nation-Building or Nation-Destroying?," *World Politics*, XXIV, 3 (Princeton, N.J., 1972), pp. 319–355; Meiç Stephens, *Linguistic Minorities in Western Europe* (Llandysul, Wales, 1976); Milton J. Esman, ed., *Ethnic Conflict in the Western World* (Ithaca, N.Y., 1977);

any historical period it is necessary to analyze all aspects of a given problem and not simply those which seem to have had more lasting significance. To put it more plainly, in the case of the national movement in late-nineteenth-century eastern Galicia, if one wishes to know why the Ukrainian orientation won, one needs to know why the Old Ruthenians and Russophiles lost.

The problem of nationalism in eastern Galicia is, almost without exception, presented in terms of a dichotomous rivalry between two, not three, national orientations: the Russophile and the Ukrainophile. There is an extensive polemical literature on the subjects, but I shall mention here only the more serious analyses. Even these, which may strive toward scholarly objectivity, are often not much of an improvement, except perhaps in style and form, over the polemical writings. The Russophile viewpoint, best represented in the works of Fedor F. Aristov, Pylyp Svystun, Ivan Filevich, and Ilarion Svientsits'kyi, starts from the premise that there exists one Russian (*russkii*) or common-Russian (*obshcherusskii*) nationality, composed of the three branches of the eastern Slavs—Great Russians (*velikorosy*), Belorussians (*belorosy*), and Little Russians/Ukrainians (*malorosy*). Although proponents of this ideology admit that there are recognizable cultural and linguistic differences among the three components of this supposed "common-Russian people," they argue that members of each of the component branches should identify themselves as Russian and use one literary language, Russian, for intellectual discourse. The Slavic inhabitants of eastern Galicia are considered part of the Little Russian branch of the common Russian people. Thus, in analyzing the national movement in eastern Galicia, the Russophiles view as heros all those who in any way expressed sympathy for the idea of unity with Russia (whether cultural or political), and in turn they consider as national traitors any Galicians who sympathized with what is considered "Ukrainian separatism." As a corollary to this view, cooperation with Galician Poles is considered an anathema, and the Austrian government is castigated for having supported Ukrainianism as part of its own efforts to undermine its international rival, tsarist Russia.[2]

The Ukrainophile viewpoint has a much more extensive literature, whether by individuals who were themselves participants in the late-nineteenth-cen-

and the award-winning biography of Thomas Hutchinson, the loyalist governor of Massachusetts who opposed the American Revolution: Bernard Bailyn, *The Ordeal of Thomas Hutchinson* (Cambridge, Mass., 1974).

2 F.F. Aristov, "Istoriia Karpatskoi Rusi," in his *Karpatorusskie pisateli*, Vol. I (Moscow, 1916; 2nd rev. ed.: Bridgeport, Conn., 1977), pp. 1–32; Filipp I. Svistun, *Prikarpatskaia Rus' pod vladieniem Avstrii*, 2 vols. (L'viv, 1896; reprinted Trumbull, Conn., 1970); Ivan P. Filevich, *Iz istorii Karpatskoi Rusi: ocherki galitsko-russkoi zhizni s. 1772 g.* (Warsaw,

tury nationality controversies (Omelian Ohonovs'kyi, Ivan Franko, Mykhailo Pavlyk, Ostap Terlets'kyi, Mykhailo Lozyns'kyi, L'ongyn Tsehel's'kyi, Volodymyr Hnatiuk, Kost' Levyts'kyi),[3] by latter-day historians of non-Soviet Ukrainian (Mykhailo Vozniak, Matvii Stakhiv, Stepan Baran, Stepan Ripets'kyi, Ivan L. Rudnytsky)[4] and Soviet Ukrainian[5] persuasion, or by Soviet Russian (Viktor Malkin)[6] and Polish (Leon Wasilewski, Stanisław Smolka, Jan Kozik, Mieczysław Tanty)[7] writers on the subject. All these authors start from the premise that the idea of one common-Russian nationality is an ideological fantasy, and that instead there exist three distinct East Slavic peoples—Russians, Belorusans, and Ukrainians. The inhabitants of eastern Galicia, there-

1907); I.S. Svientsitskii, "Obzor snoshenii Karpatskoi Rusi s Rossiei v 1-uiu polovinu XIX v.," *Izviestiia otdieleniia russkago iazyka i slovesnosti Imperatorskoi akademii nauk*, XI, 3 (St. Petersburg, 1906), pp. 259–367.

3 Omelian Ohonovskii, *Ystoriia lyteratury ruskoy*, 4 vols. (L'viv, 1887–94); Ivan Franko, "Iz istoriï 'moskvofil's'koho' pys'menstva v Halychyni" (1899), in *Ivan Franko: zibrannia tvoriv*, Vol. XXXI (Kiev, 1981), pp. 458–480; Franko, "Formal'nyi i real'nyi natsionalizm," in Ivan Franko, *Tvory*, Vol. XVI (Kiev, 1955), pp. 132–140; and Franko, "Shchyrist' tonu i shchyrist' perekonan'" (1905), in *Tvory*, XVI, pp. 345–355; M. Pavlyk, *Moskvofil'stvo ta ukraïnofil'stvo sered avstro-rus'koho narodu* (L'viv, 1906); Ostap Terlets'kyi, *Moskvofily i narodovtsï v 70-ykh rr.* (L'viv, 1902); Mykhailo Lozyns'kyi, "Suchasne moskvofil'stvo," *Literaturno-naukovyi vistnyk*, XII [XLVI], 4 (L'viv and Kiev, 1909), pp. 190–197; L'ongyn Tsehel's'kyi, "Halyts'ke moskvofil'stvo v ostanïi ioho fazï," *Literaturno-naukovyi vistnyk*, XIII [L], 5 (L'viv and Kiev, 1910), pp. 389–406; Volodymyr Hnatiuk, *Natsional'ne vidrodzhennie avstro-uhors'kykh ukraïntsiv (1772–1880 rr.)* (Vienna, 1916); Kost' Levyts'kyi, *Istoriia politychnoï dumky halyts'kykh ukraïntsiv, 1848–1914*, 2 vols. (L'viv, 1926).

4 Mykhailo Vozniak, *Iak probudylosia ukraïns'ke narodnie zhyttia v Halychyni za Avstriï* (L'viv, 1924); M. Mykolaievych [Matvii Stakhiv], *Moskvofil'stvo, ioho bat'ky i dity: istorychnyi narys* (L'viv, 1936); Stepan Baran, *Vesna narodiv v avstro-uhors'kii Ukraïni* (Munich, 1948); S. Ripets'kyi, "Moskvofil'stvo," *Entsyklopediia ukraïnoznavstva: slovnykova chastyna*, Vol. V (Paris and New York, 1966), pp. 1652-1654; Ivan L. Rudnytsky, "The Ukrainians in Galicia under Austrian Rule," *Austrian History Yearbook*, III, pt. 2 (Houston, 1967), pp. 394–429.

5 Soviet Ukrainian historiography has not devoted particular attention to what it calls Muscophilism. See the general history of Ukrainian Galicia: *Torzhestvo istorychnoï spravedlyvosti* (L'viv, 1968) and the brief article "Moskvofily" in *Radians'ka entsyklopediia istoriï Ukraïny*, Vol. III (Kiev, 1971), pp. 175–177.

6 Viktor A. Malkin, *Russkaia literatura v Galitsii* (L'viv, 1957). This effort to "rehabilitate" certain Old Ruthenians and Russophiles was strongly criticized by seven Soviet-Ukrainian reviewers in an extensive article: "Domysly i perekruchennia pid vyhliadom nauky," *Zhovten'*, IX, 2 (L'viv, 1959), pp. 132–145.

7 Leon Wasilewski, *Ukraina i sprawa ukraińska* (Cracow, [1911]), esp. pp. 88–184; Stanislas Smolka, *Les ruthènes et les problèmes religieux du monde russien* (Berne, 1917), esp. pp. 86–140; Jan Kozik, *Między reakcją a rewolucją: studia z dziejów ukraińskiego ruchu narodowego w Galicji w latach 1848–1849*, Zeszyty Naukowe Uniwersytetu

fore, belong to a distinct Ukrainian nationality that inhabits a compact ethnographic territory from the Carpathian Mountains to the foothills of the Caucasus Mountains.

If one accepts such a premise, the Ukrainian viewpoint becomes the obverse of the Russophile. Therefore, all those in eastern Galicia who strove to propagate national feeling through the medium of the vernacular language and who felt a sense of unity with Ukrainians living in the Russian Empire are described in positive terms. On the other hand, those Galicians who spoke about the unity of one eastern Slavic Rus' or Russian civilization are—regardless of whether they call themselves Old Ruthenians or Russians—lumped together under the opprobrious term *Muscophiles* and described in a generally denigrating manner. Some Ukrainian authors (Levyts'kyi, Rudnytsky) do make an attempt to distinguish between Old Ruthenians and Russophiles within the Muscophile camp, although they tend to see both groups not as distinct orientations but rather as part of a chronologically and ideologically evolving continuum. Hence, during the 1850s and 1860s, most "Muscophiles" are described as Old Ruthenians who are loyal to Austria. But after Austria's defeat by Prussia in 1866 and its acquiescence in Polish domination over the Galician provincial administration after 1868, the Old Ruthenians ostensibly lost faith in Austria and looked henceforth for salvation to Russia, with which they felt a cultural and spiritual affinity. Thus, in most of the existing literature on the subject—which happens to represent the Ukrainian viewpoint—the terms *Old Ruthenians*, *Russophiles*, and *Muscophiles* are used interchangeably as if they mean the same thing. They do not, however, and to use them in such a manner tends to distort a proper understanding of the national movement in late-nineteenth-century Galician society.

I therefore propose to draw distinctions among these various terms and to suggest a new conceptual framework for future analyses of the subject. Before the 1870s, there were only Old Ruthenians among the Galician-Ukrainian intelligentsia. Beginning in the late 1860s and early 1870s, one group, known as populists, split off. They eventually accepted the idea of identification with a distinct Ukrainian nationality. The Old Ruthenians, however, continued to exist. In the late 1890s, another group split off, known as Russophiles, who from the very beginning identified unequivocally with the Great Russian nationality. It should be remembered that, despite this second split, the Old Ruthenians continued to survive, albeit in ever-decreasing numbers.

Jagiellońskiego, CCCLXXXI: Prace Historyczne, pt. 52 (Warsaw and Cracow, 1975); Mieczysław Tanty, "Kontakty rosyjskich komitetów slowiańskich ze slowianami z Austro-Węgier (1868–1875)," *Kwartalnik Historyczny*, LXXI, 1 (Warsaw, 1964), pp. 59–77.

The point is that, by the end of the nineteenth century, there were three, not two, orientations among the nationalist intelligentsia of eastern Galicia—those of Old Ruthenians, Ukrainophiles, and Russophiles. Such a framework rejects the simplistic Ukrainophile–Russophile dichotomy. It also rejects the term *Muscophile*, which is basically a latter-day reflection of attitudes held by Galician-Ukrainophile polemicists, who applied this term indiscriminately to all their self-designated local enemies (both Old Ruthenians and Russophiles) and intended it to suggest political as well as cultural subjection to that so-called wicked enemy of Ukrainians—Muscovite Russia. Terms like these should have no place in serious scholarly discourse.

My suggested framework for analyzing the nationality movement in eastern Galicia does not affect the traditional view concerning the Ukrainian orientation. The concept of Ukrainianism started in the 1860s among populists favoring the use of a vernacular language and then progressed into broader cultural and political spheres until it came to mean a distinct nationality and culture represented by inhabitants within both the Austro-Hungarian Empire (northern Bukovina and Hungarian Transcarpathia as well as eastern Galicia) and the Russian Empire (the Dnieper Ukraine). I do propose, however, that it is necessary to reevaluate the non-Ukrainian options in eastern Galicia (namely, the Old Ruthenian and Russophile orientations), to describe their ideologies, and to suggest how they were distinct from each other.

I am not the first to propose that such distinctions existed. As early as 1873, a perceptive political thinker from the Dnieper Ukraine, Mykhailo Drahomanov, stressed that the Old Ruthenians were not calling for national and linguistic subordination to Russia.[8] Subsequently, during the twentieth century, in what are still the best essays on Galician Old Ruthenianism and Russophilism, the Ukrainian historian Mykola Andrusiak briefly traced the careers of several Old Ruthenians who until then had been incorrectly described and unjustly castigated as Muscophile renegades.[9] Unfortunately, in most subsequent writings on the subject, the approach of Drahomanov and Andrusiak has not been adopted. This is perhaps because the only primary source material used to analyze the Old Ruthenian and Russophile movements are the writings of Ivan

---

8 Mykhailo Drahomanov, *Halyts'ko-rus'ke pys'menstvo* (L'viv, 1876), esp. pp. 14-22; and Drahomanov, "Halyts'korus'ke pys'menstvo (Perednie slovo do 'Povistei' Osypa Fed'kovycha [1876])," reprinted in Mykhailo P. Drahomanov, *Literaturno-publistychni pratsi*, Vol. I (Kiev, 1970), pp. 309–348.

9 Mykola Andrusiak, *Narysy z istoriï halyts'koho moskvofil'stva* (L'viv, 1935); and his *Geneza i kharakter halyts'koho rusofil'stva v XIX-XX st.* (Prague, 1941).

Franko, Mykhailo Pavlyk, and other contemporary Ukrainophiles who were actively engaged at the time with ideological opponents about whom they could not be expected to write in favorable, let alone objective, terms.[10] Therefore, to obtain an insight into the ideologies of the Old Ruthenians and Russophiles, I have reviewed what they themselves wrote in their contemporary press organs.[11]

Surveying the writings by members of the groups in question seems a self-evident and basic prerequisite for understanding the problem under considera-tion. Nevertheless, with the exception of citing *Slovo*, most researchers have heretofore not used contemporary publications by group spokespersons (or have at least not cited them) when describing the Old Ruthenian and Russophile orientations.

What, therefore, were Old Ruthenianism and Russophilism as understood by proponents of those views? Stated most succinctly, the proponents of Old Ruthenianism were first and foremost local Galician patriots who had a vague sense of cultural unity with other Rus' people then living in the Russian Em-pire (Russians, Belorusans, and especially Ukrainians), but whose national, political, and religious loyalties did not extend beyond the boundaries of the Austrian Empire. In a sense, they were analogous to the Swiss Germans (Schwyzerdütsch) and northern Tyroleans who were of Germanic culture, but who considered (and still consider) themselves to be distinct groups whose primary political loyalty is Swiss or Austrian. It is no coincidence that the Old Ruthenians often described themselves—and were described by others—as the Tyroleans of the East.

---

10 It is interesting to note that the Ukrainophile Ivan Franko, who had no hesitation in criticizing his "Muscophile" opponents in Galicia, did warn against using terms such as *smittia* (trash), *renegaty* (renegades), and *zaprodantsi* (sell-outs or traitors). He even went so far as to admit that "some of our 'renegades' from among our trash (for instance, Naumovych, Didyts'kyi, and others) did ten times more for the development of Galician-Rusyn society and its masses than hundreds and thousands of our best unrenegade-like purists put together." Franko, "Formal'nyi i real'nyi natsionalizm," p. 137.

11 These include *Slovo* (1861–87), *Russkaia rada* (1871–1912), *Druh* (1874–77), *Russkoe slovo* (1890–1914), and *Halychanyn* (1893–1913) for the Old Ruthenians; and *Besieda* (1887–97), *Zhivaia mysl'* (1902–05), *Prikarpatskaia Rus'* (1909–15), and *Golos naroda* (1909–15) for the Russophiles. All were published in L'viv.

In citing titles from the Cyrillic alphabet, I employ the Library of Congress transliteration system for Ukrainian for works by Old Ruthenian authors, with the following additions: ѣ=î ; ы = ŷ. The Russian system is employed for works by Russophiles. In both instances, the original etymological script (so dear to both orientations) has been maintained in the transliterations. Final hard signs (so dear especially to the Old Ruthenians) have not been indicated.

As the oldest of the three national orientations in eastern Galicia, the Old Ruthenians played a leading role in the revolutionary events of 1848–1849. At that time they founded and continued to control until the end of the century the oldest cultural and political organizations—the Stauropegial Institute, the Galician-Rus' Matytsia (est. 1848), the National Home (est. 1864), and the Kachkovs'kyi Society (est. 1874); as well as the first newspapers and journals—*Zoria halytska* (1848–57), *Pchola* (1849), *Vîstnyk posviashchennoie Rusynov avstriiskoi derzhavŷ* (1850–66), *Otechestvennŷi sbornyk* (1853–66), and *Slovo* (1861–87). Also, because the socioeconomic structure of Galician society before 1848 was such that only two classes were represented among Ukrainians—peasants and a small group of Greek Catholic priests—the earliest intelligentsia and spokesmen for Old Ruthenianism were almost all Greek Catholic priests. Among the more influential of these were Mykola Ustiianovych (1811–1885), Antin Petrushevych (1821–1913), Ivan Naumovych (1826–1891), and Bohdan Didyts'kyi (1827–1908), who along with other clerics formed the center of Old Ruthenian strength in the consistory of the Greek Catholic metropolitanate at the St. George Cathedral in L'viv—from which the group obtained the epithet St. George Circle (*sviatoiurtsi*). This does not mean that all Old Ruthenians were priests, and among the more influential nonclerical representatives were the jurist Mykhailo Kachkovs'kyi (1802–1872), the university professor Izydor Sharanevych (1829–1901), and the insurance clerk Ivan E. Levyts'kyi (1850–1913).

In terms of national ideology, the Old Ruthenians were slow to resolve (and perhaps never really got over) the problem of identity by negation. They would continually proclaim themselves to be sons of Rus', but they were often uncertain in defining what Rus' actually meant. They seemed much better at responding to the encroachments of Polish politicians and administrators in Galician affairs or at denying suggestions by some Polish writers that the East Slavic inhabitants of Galicia spoke only dialects of Polish and were therefore Poles of the Greek Catholic faith, or Greek Catholic Ruthenians of the Polish nation (*gente Rutheni natione Poloni*). Thus, much of the material in Old Ruthenian newspapers consisted of anti-Polish diatribes. In a sense, it could be said that the only unifying hallmark of Old Ruthenianism in Galicia was its anti-Polish stance, an attitude that was summed up in the newspaper *Slovo* by the observation that "our Ruthenian has more hatred for Poland than love for Rus'."[12]

As for more positive attitudes on national identity, the Old Ruthenians always seemed to want to stress the fact that they were distinct. The very first

12 "Ystorycheskaia Nemezys y mŷ," *Slovo*, no. 41–42, April 13 (25), 1883.

article in *Slovo* (1861) began with the formulation, "We live in God's world as Ruthenians [*rusyny*] and as Ruthenians we have our own stock [*rod*], customs, language, and faith."[13] Indeed, one might ask what the Old Ruthenians had in mind when they spoke of Ruthenians (*rusyny*). Did they mean just themselves in eastern Galicia, or they together with Ukrainians in the Russian Empire, or they together with all the Rus' people—Great Russians, Belorusans, and Ukrainians? In fact, at different times they seemed to have in mind each of these alternatives, often expressed in terms of three numbers—3 million, 15 million, and 60 million—figures which symbolically represented, respectively, the Galician-Ruthenian, Galician-Ruthenian and Dnieper-Ukrainian, and common-Russian (Galician-Ruthenian, Dnieper-Ukrainian, Belorusan, and Great Russian) populations.

For instance, in 1848, the leaders of the Supreme Ruthenian Council, the group's first political body, expressed a clear sense of unity with the 15 million other Ruthenian (i.e., Ukrainian) people living in the Russian Empire.[14] Similarly, in the anti-Polish vein so typical of the Old Ruthenians, Ivan Naumovych stated in the Galician Diet in 1866 that "just as we cannot be Poles, so are we not Great Russians [*Velykorusamy*]; we always were, are, and will be Little Russians [*Malorusamy*]."[15] On the other hand, that same year, a seemingly frustrated Galician peasant declared in a letter to *Slovo* that "we are brothers to a great 60-million strong people and therefore are not bastards or some kind of unfortunate neutral or non-descript race; rather we are known to all as the sons of Rus', a one, great Rus'."[16] Still later, in 1870, the Greek Catholic church strove to bring the increasingly divergent populist Ukrainophiles and the Old Ruthenians together by proposing that Galicians recognize themselves as a

13 "Nash program," no. 1, January 25 (February 7), 1861. The term *Rusyn* was the self-designation employed by the East Slavic inhabitants of Galicia. The official Austro-German designation for the group was *Ruthenen* (Ruthenians). As for the varying national orientations, all three orientations recognized that the term *Rusyn*, which derived from the substantive *Rus'*, was the term the people used to describe themselves. In the writings, however, the Old Ruthenians used either the substantive *ruteny*, or the adjectives *ruskyi* and later *russkyi*. The populist Ukrainophiles used *rusyny* and *rus'kyi*; then, on the eve of World War I, *ukraïntsi* and *ukraïns'kyi*. The Russophiles used *russkie* and *russkii*. For translations of the various forms of the same word into English, it seems appropriate for purposes of distinction to render the Old Ruthenian usage as Ruthenian, the Ukrainophile usage as Rusyn, and the Russophile usage as Russian.

14 "We Galician Ruthenians (*rusyny*) belong to the great Ruthenian people (*ruskoho narodu*) who speak one language and number 15 million, of which 2 1/3 million live in the Galician land." "Ôdozva do ruskoho narodu," *Zoria halytska*, I, 1 (L'viv, 1848), p. 1.

15 "Besîda posla Naumovycha v spravî zapomohy dlia ruskoho teatra skazana na 65. zasîdaniiu soimovom, dnia 12. tsvîtnia s.h.," *Slovo*, no. 27, April 6 (18), 1866.

16 "Z vostoka (Rusynŷ-Moskalî)," *Slovo*, no. 24, March 23 (April 5), 1866.

separate people of three million inhabitants.[17] Thus, the Old Ruthenians had different views at varying times about their national relationship to Eastern Slavs in the Russian Empire. But as the polemics regarding this issue increased during the nineteenth century, those individuals who wanted to have a clearer position left the Old Ruthenian camp and joined the populist Ukrainophiles (such as Ivan Franko and Mykhailo Pavlyk) or the Russophiles (such as Osyp Monchalovs'kyi and Iuliian Iavors'kyi). Actually, as time went on, those who remained Old Ruthenians were forced by the increasing populist-Ukrainophile and Russophile challenge to define more precisely what they meant by Galician-Ruthenian particularism or distinctiveness.

The most obvious distinctive traits that Old Ruthenians could propose in juxtaposition to Slavs living in the Russian Empire were that they were Greek Catholics and subjects of Austria's Habsburg monarchy. Not surprisingly, the Greek Catholic hierarchy, from which many Old Ruthenians derived, was anxious to justify its middle-of-the-road distinctiveness vis-à-vis both the Orthodox, with whom they shared a common liturgy, and the Roman Catholics, with whom they shared a common hierarchical structure and papal authority. Thus, being a Greek Catholic Galician meant that one was by definition different from both the Roman Catholic Poles to the west and the Orthodox Dnieper Ukrainians and Russians to the east.[18]

Together with Greek Catholic distinctiveness came loyalty to the Austrian state or, more precisely, to the ruling Habsburg monarch. This tradition of loyalty went back to the days of Emperor Joseph II, whose attempts to liberate the serfs in the eighteenth century were still being praised in Galician folklore a century later. Loyalist views were further enhanced by the revolution of 1848, in which the Austrian emperor was cast as the person responsible for the final liberation of peasants from serfdom and the guiding force behind a system that brought education, cultural enlightenment, and, by the 1860s, political freedoms in the form of parliamentarism at the provincial and imperial levels. Old Ruthenian publications depicted the Ruthenian population as being thankful for such gifts of "Austrian civilization," which were presented as a stark contrast to the autocratic system in the neighboring Russian Empire. A quarter of a century later, one Old Ruthenian writer recalled how, in 1848, "we Ruthenians

17 This was part of a list of theses proposed at the metropolitan's request by Canon Malynovs'kyi and presented to representatives of the Ukrainophile Prosvita Society and the Old Ruthenian Ruskaia Rada. See Levyts'kyi, *Istoriia politychnoï dumky*, p. 117.

18 Old Ruthenian clerical leaders were particularly sensitive to any trends that seemed to "Latinize" their rite. Thus, many of their religious and secular publications were filled with articles about the Catholic "Jesuit danger" in Galicia and the need to maintain traditional practices such as the Julian calendar.

truly appreciated such freedom given to us, and leading our people were intelligent and responsible leaders who told our people: 'Don't act crazy, don't
rattle your swords, don't get mixed up in military units as some fickle Poles
do, but be instead loyal to your monarch.' "[19]

But neither religious affiliation nor political loyalties were sufficient to create a sense of national distinctiveness. Most especially in the intelligentsia-
inspired variety of nationalism, it was language that seemed to be the most
important criterion of national identity. The Galician experience was no exception, so that most of the discussion about national identity was couched in
discussions about language. In effect, the contemporary Galician-Ukrainophile
writer Ostap Terlets'kyi was describing all three orientations when he wrote:
"Not having the capacity to create a national renaissance by itself, the intelligentsia made from the national problem an exclusively language question. ...."[20]

The Old Ruthenians never really argued that their Galician people spoke a
distinct language or that their written language should be unique to the region.
In practice, however, they unintentionally did create a written language that
was used only by themselves and that seemed strange both to their ideological
rivals in Galicia and to contemporary observers in the Russian Empire.[21] In
theoretical terms, the Old Ruthenians adopted the two-language principle proposed earlier in the century by the Czech national leader and patron saint of
Pan-Slavism, Josef Dobrovský. According to this theory, publications intended
for the masses should be in a language that approximated the spoken vernacular,[22] while more serious works (literature, scholarship, theology, politics) should
be in the so-called book language. This book language, which we will call
Ruthenian, was referred to by its users with various adjectives derived from
the noun Rus'—whether *slaveno-ruskyi*, *ruskyi*, or *russkyi*. It was basically the

19 "O pershom zahal'nom zasîdaniiu chlenôv russkoho 'Narodnoho Doma' v L'vovî,"
    Russkaia rada, II, 23 (L'viv, 1872), p. 174.
20 Terlets'kyi, *Moskvofîly i narodovtsî*, p. 38. For details, see above, chapter 6.
21 Galician Ukrainophiles referred to the Old Ruthenian language as the macaronic jargon
    (*iazychie*). The Dnieper-Ukrainian Drahomanov called it "some kind of dead Church-
    Rusyn language": Drahomanov, *Halyts'ko-rus'ke pys'menstvo*, p. 20; while the Russian
    scholar Pypin and the radical thinker Chernyshevskii were unfavorably struck by this
    seemingly "unique Russian language," which reminded them of the eighteenth-century
    writings of Lomonosov and Sumarokov: A. Pypin, "Osobyi russkii iazyk," *Viestnik
    Evropy*, XXIII, 11 (St. Petersburg, 1888), p. 357; N. Chernyshevskii, "Natsional'naia
    beztaktnost' (Slovo. Rochnik pervyi. Chisla 1, 2. L'vov 1861 g.)," *Sovremennik* (St.
    Petersburg, 1861)—reprinted in N.G. Chernyshevskii, *Polnoe sobranie sochenenii*, Vol.
    VII, pt. 3 (Moscow, 1950), pp. 775–793.
22 Some Old Ruthenians did publish works in the Galician vernacular, such as Ivan
    Naumovych's enormously popular *Nauka* (1871–1914), the journal of the Kachkovs'kyi
    Society.

Galician recension of Church Slavonic, traditionally known as Slaveno-Rusyn and distinguished by its unstandardized form and varying degrees of influence whether from the local dialects or from standard Great Russian. This language was used by the Old Ruthenians because it had prestige, and the source of that prestige was a publication tradition of several centuries and assumed use at the present in the Russian Empire. Because of the latter assumption, the enemies of the Old Ruthenians, whether Poles or populist Ukrainophiles, accused them of being Russophiles or Muscophiles.

Since language and national identity tended to be perceived in synonymous terms, it is important to understand what the Old Ruthenians themselves felt about their Slaveno-Rusyn or Ruthenian language. On the one hand, the Old Ruthenians were fully aware that the language spoken by Galicia's East Slavs was similar to that spoken by Dnieper Ukrainians and yet decidedly different from that spoken by Great Russians. On the other hand, written language was most important, and the Old Ruthenians had a rather strange understanding of what that language was. In the words of Ivan Naumovych,

> Our language has a thousand year old history. Some state that our language is Muscovite. We don't know the Muscovite language, just as we don't know the Muscovite people. That there are similarities between the languages of all Slavic peoples, and that our language is similar to the written language used in Moscow is not our fault. ... The Great Russian book language [*knizhnyi velikorusskii iazyk*] is basically Little Russian, created by Little Russians. By accepting the Great Russian book language, we are taking back only what is properly ours.[23]

Another Old Ruthenian, Antin Petrushevych, even went so far as to conclude that this so-called Great Russian book language cannot be understood by the uneducated Great Russian (*rosiianin*), while a Ruthenian from Galicia (*rodovytŷi Rusyn*) "even without the help of grammatical training can understand it."[24]

Petrushevych and other Old Ruthenians were correct in assuming that Great Russians (educated or uneducated) would have difficulty understanding the Galician-Ruthenian written language. The reason had nothing to do with the contemporary status of spoken and literary Russian, however. Rather, as Ukrainian and Russian critics from the Russian Empire pointed out, the

23 From a speech delivered in the Galician Diet, on December 27, 1866, cited in Svistun, *Prikarpatskaia Rus'*, pp. 267–268.
24 From a speech delivered by Antin Petrushevych at the founding meeting of the Galician-Rus' Matytsia, as related by Mykola Ustiianovych in "Nîskol'ko slov v otvît na statiu H. Kostetskoho," *Slovo*, no. 6, February 11 (23), 1861. The Old Ruthenian views on their written language continued to be propagated (Cf. "Lyteraturnŷi iazŷk," *Slovo*, nos. 144–

Galicians (despite what they may have called it or believed about its origin) had created a written language that was unique to the time and region from which it derived.[25]

Much of what has been said here about the Old Ruthenians is accepted in previous studies for the period until the 1860s. Those same studies argue, however, that in subsequent decades there was supposedly a rise in pro-Russian attitudes, so that before long the Old Ruthenian orientation became indistinguishable from Russophilism. As proof of such an evolution from Old Ruthenianism into Russophilism, writers point to the decline of Austria's international prestige following the empire's defeat by Prussia in 1866, as well as to Vienna's decision after 1868 to permit an increase in Polish administrative control over Galicia at the expense of the Ukrainians. As a result, there allegedly was an increase in pro-Russian sympathy among the Old Ruthenians as evidenced by greater Russian language usage in Galician publications, by tsarist Russian subsidies to the newspaper *Slovo*, and by the ultimate compromise of the Old Ruthenian orientation following a treason trial held in 1882. It is true that some individuals did become more Russophile in orientation: the first head of the Department of Ruthenian Studies at the University of L'viv, Iakiv Holovats'kyi, emigrated to Russia in 1867, and the influential Old Ruthenian leader Ivan Naumovych followed him in 1884. Nevertheless, the Old Ruthenian movement continued to exist until the end of the century and even, although in a substantially reduced form, until the outbreak of World War I. Moreover, as the populist-Ukrainophile and later Russophile orientations grew in strength, the Old Ruthenians were forced to define their position more clearly than they had ever done before.

By the 1870s, Old Ruthenian publications were indeed using more and more Russian words, although we have already seen how by using those forms Galician writers presumed, albeit erroneously, that they were simply partaking of their own literary tradition—one which they argued was not "natural" to the Russian/Muscovite environment. At about the same time, a group of students representing the Old Ruthenian position (including Ivan Franko, who later became the foremost spokesman of the Ukrainophile orientation) founded a journal called *Druh*. In a spirited exchange of polemics with the Dnieper-Ukrainian national activist Mykhailo Drahomanov, the editors of *Druh* responded categorically: "Leave us alone with Ukrainianism and Great Russianism, we

146, December 20, 1883 [January 1, 1884]– December 24, 1883 [January 5, 1884]) and were elaborated in great detail in the memoirs of Bohdan Dîdytskii, *Svoezhyt'evŷy zapysky*, 2 vols. (L'viv, 1907–08).

25 See above, note 21.

have our own language!"[26] "The fact is," they continued, "that the greater part of our people ... now consider that some kind of literary union of 60 million [Russians] or 15 million [Ukrainians] would be utopian and would be the equivalent of the gradual death of our people and nationality, [who instead] have set out toward unity on a third path, one which is organically based on the people living within the political boundaries of Austria."[27] This sense of distinctiveness from both Ukrainians and Russians continued among Old Ruthenians and led Drahomanov to quip in ironic wonderment, "You Galician intellectuals really do think of creating some kind of Uniate Paraguay, with some kind of hierarchical, bureaucratic aristocracy, just like you have already created an Austro-Ruthenian literary language!"[28]

Supporters of the view that the Old Ruthenians merged into Russophiles are fond of pointing out that (1) in 1866, Ivan Naumovych described himself as a "genuine Russian" and demanded the removal of barriers to the East; (2) at the same time, Bohdan Didyts'kyi called upon Galicians to learn Great Russian (which they ostensibly could do in one hour); and (3) beginning in the 1870s, the tsarist government supposedly increased its subsidy to russify Old Ruthenians. Each of these points requires analysis.

Naumovych's call for cultural unity with the rest of the Rus' world was nothing particularly new. While his statement that "we are not Ruthenians [ruteny] of the 1848 variety but rather staunch Russians [nastoiashchii russkii]," may have indicated a change of emphasis in his own views, this was not necessarily indicative of the Old Ruthenian orientation as a whole.[29] As for Didyts'kyi, his little brochure, quaintly entitled *In One Hour a Little Rusyn Can Learn Great Russian* (*V odyn chas nauchyt'sia Malorusynu velykorussky*), was never meant for Galicians, but rather for Greek Catholic priests sent to the neighboring

26 "Ôtpovîd' na pys'mo h. Ukrayntsa v ch. 11 nashoy chasopysy," *Druh*, II, 12 (L'viv, 1875), p. 292.

27 "Otpovîd' na 'vtoroe pys'mo' h. Ukrayntsia," *Druh*, III, 7 (L'viv, 1876), p. 110.

28 Ukraynets [M. Drahomanov], "Ukraynshchyna yly Rutenshchyna," *Druh*, III, 5 (L'viv, 1876), p. 80.

29 Naumovych's statement actually appeared as a lengthy letter entitled "Pohliad v buduchnost'," *Slovo*, no. 59, July 27 (August 8), 1866, signed by One in the Name of Many *Odyn ymenem mnohykh*). Although O. Ohonovs'kyi claimed that the letter was probably not written by Naumovych—*Ystoriia lyteratury ruskoy*, Vol. III, p. 1307—the editor of *Slovo* at the time, Bohdan Didyts'kyi, confirmed that Naumovych was indeed the author—"Yz svoezhyt'evŷkh zapysok," *Vîstnyk 'Narodnoho Doma'*, XXIV, 2 (L'viv, 1906), pp. 29–30. By the end of the century, the Russophiles praised Naumovych for having made such a "bold statment" in 1866—O.A. Monchalovskii, *Zhit'e i dieiatel'nost' Ivana Naumovicha* (L'viv, 1899). The Old Ruthenian Didyts'kyi claimed the letter-article was misconstrued at the time by the Polish press (thereby wrongly associating their movement with anti-Austrianism), and he regretted the pro-Russian implications of the

Russian-controlled Chełm region.[30] And finally, with regard to tsarist aid to the Old Ruthenians, the phenomenon of the so-called rolling ruble has been overstated. Even the contemporary Ukrainophile Mykhailo Pavlyk denied that Russian infiltration was present in Galicia.[31] Although it is true that officials in the tsarist political police (the notorious Third Department) did follow events in Galicia and in 1875 decided to provide financial assistance to Venedykt Ploshchans'kyi (1834–1902), then editor of *Slovo*, the promised annual subsidy (20,000 Austrian crowns) was realized only once, in 1876. Why was the tsarist government reluctant to provide further sums? The answer is simple: after fifteen years of observing the situation in Galicia, it saw clearly that "there was far from full agreement between the Old Ruthenian party and the tasks and goals of the Russian government."[32]

There is also the treason trial of 1882 in L'viv, which is held up as an example to show that the Old Ruthenians were really crypto-Russians. Their loyalties toward Austria proclaimed during the trial are described as empty phrases, which allegedly explains why the Old Ruthenian orientation became compromised in the eyes of the Galician public. Actually, the trial was directed primarily not at Galicians but rather at staunch Russophiles from Hungary, Adol'f Dobrians'kyi (then living in L'viv) and his daughter, Ol'ga Grabar (then on a visit from Moscow), in whose names the suit was brought. Several of Galicia's Old Ruthenian leaders (including Ivan Naumovych, Venedykt Ploshchans'kyi, and Osyp Markov) were accused of maintaining contacts with Dobrians'kyi's son, Miroslav (a tsarist official), with the intention of detaching Galicia, Bukovina, and northern Hungary from Austria and provoking "internal disorder," that is, promoting Orthodoxy.

After thirty-five days of testimony (lasting from June to August 1882), the

article that were later adopted by the new Russophile movement—"Svoezhyt'evŷy zapysky Bohdana A. Dîdytskoho," *Vîstnyk 'Narodnoho Doma'*, XXVI, 3 (L'viv, 1908), p. 54.

30 More than forty Galician priests were sent to the Chełm region to replace Greek Catholic priests suspected by the Russian government of having supported the 1863 Polish uprising. By 1875, the Russian government had liquidated this last Greek Catholic eparchy on its territory. Cf. Bohdan A. Dîdytskii, "Yz svoezhyt'evŷkh zapysok," *Vîstnyk 'Narodnoho Doma'*, XXIV, 2 (L'viv, 1906), pp. 28–29.

31 Pavlyk, *Moskovofîl'stvo ta ukraïnofîl'stvo*, p. 10. This is not to deny that there was grassroots sentiment among Galician peasants for Russia, but this arose out of indigenous cultural conditions, not propaganda from abroad. See John-Paul Himka, "Hope in the Tsar: Displaced Naive Monarchism among the Ukrainian Peasants of the Habsburg Empire," *Russian History*, VII, 1–2 (Tucson, Ariz., 1980), pp. 125–138.

32 Dispatch by the governor general of the Warsaw district to the Third Department in St. Petersburg, cited in Fedir Savchenko, "Sprava pro shchorichnu, taiemnu subsydiiu l'vivs'komu 'Slovu'," *Zapysky Naukovoho tovarystva im. Shevchenka*, CL (L'viv, 1929), p. 400.

accused were acquitted of any treasonous activity against Austria, although Naumovych and Ploshchans'kyi, together with two peasants, received brief prison terms on the grounds that they had disturbed the public order by promoting Orthodoxy against the will of the inhabitants in one Greek Catholic village (Hnylychky). Not surprisingly, the Old Ruthenian press viewed the 1882 trial as just another Polish plot to discredit their national movement in Galicia.[33] More interesting were the opinions of the foreign press, which followed the trial closely. The leading Budapest daily, *Pester Lloyd*, argued that "the trial was not against Naumovych and company, but against the Russian government, whose machinations are well-known throughout all of Europe."[34] In other words, the Old Ruthenians were simply convenient scapegoats in an attempt to uncover an anti-Austrian Russian intrigue. The effort failed, however, and, in the words of Berlin's *Deutsche Zeitung,* the trial had the opposite effect: it proved once again the staunch loyalty of the Old Ruthenians toward Austria.[35]

Thus, it is difficult to see how the Old Ruthenian movement either abandoned its traditional views or became Russophile in orientation during the 1870s and 1880s. To be sure, the movement did decline. Most of its cultural organizations had limited impact on the masses, and its leadership ranks were depleted by death, emigration abroad, or defection to the more vibrant populist-Ukrainophile and later Russophile movements. Nonetheless, Old Ruthenians continued to function at least until World War I and to proclaim their distinctiveness in terms of their Greek Catholicism, loyalty to Austria, and use of the traditional Ruthenian language. During the 1890s and early 1900s, the Old Ruthenian position was argued on the pages of two new newspapers, *Halychanyn* and *Russkoe slovo*, which criticized both the Ukrainophiles and the Russophiles. Characteristically, it was once again the language question that served as the excuse for polemics against their ideological rivals. The Ukrainophiles were attacked not so much because they used the vernacular but because they denied the unity of all East Slavs and used the phonetic

---

33   The supposed plot was based on cooperation between Polish activists and Ukrainophiles in Galicia (as well as the Dnieper-Ukrainian Panteleimon Kulish, who hoped to reach an accord with Poles) in order to discredit the Old Ruthenians as anti-Austrian Muscovites. "Halytsko-russkii vopros y h-n Kulysh v varshavskoi pol'skoi pechaty," *Slovo*, no. 40, April 15 (27), 1882. Cf. also the account of one of the defendants: Venedikt Ploshchanskii, *Iz istorii galitskoi Rusi s 1882 goda: politicheskii protsiess russkikh galichan voobshche riedaktora Slova v osobiennosti* (Vilnius, 1892).

34   Cited in "Epylog protsessu Ol'hy Hrabar' y tovaryshchei," *Slovo*, no. 80, July 27 (August 8), 1882.

35   Ibid.

alphabet.[36] The Russophiles were attacked because they refused to write and speak in the traditional Galician-Ruthenian language, because they adopted modern Russian, and because they became increasingly critical of the Austrian government.[37]

If Old Ruthenianism continued to exist as a movement, who, then, were the Russophiles, and when did they come into existence? If one adopts the definition proposed earlier, that Russophilism accepts the existence of a single or common-Russian people (*obshcherusskii narod*) of which East Slavs in Galicia are an integral part, and that this people should use Russian as their literary language and promote cultural and perhaps even political unity with Russia, then Russophilism as a national movement in eastern Galicia really came into existence only in the 1890s.

This does not mean that there were no Russophiles in Galicia before the 1890s. There were. Intellectual history, of which the development of national ideologies forms a branch, defies any effort to place strict chronological limits upon when a movement might begin or end. Hence, following the definitions set forth above, Denys Zubryts'kyi could be considered a Russophile who was active in Galicia already during the 1840s. Also Iakiv Holovats'kyi, whose early writings suggest that he was an incipient populist Ukrainophile, ended his career in Galicia during the 1860s as a Russophile. Others (Naumovych, Ploshchans'kyi, Severyn Shekhovych, Ksenofont Klymkovych) seemed to waver in the 1870s and 1880s between Old Ruthenianism and Russophilism.

A real change did not take place until the 1890s, however, when a second wave of defections took place within the Old Ruthenian orientation. The first split that occurred during the 1860s and early 1870s led to the beginnings of the populist-Ukrainophile orientation. In essence, it was the success of that orientation that caused the second defection in the 1890s. The Ukrainophiles had by then obtained the backing of the Austrian Ministry of Education, and in 1893 a vernacular-based language in the phonetic script was accepted as the government-recognized national language for eastern Galicia's Slavic population. The following year, another university department, this time in Ukrainian

---

36 Orfoloh, "Znachenie fonetyky," *Halychanyn*, no. 166, July 28 (August 9), 1893. The Old Ruthenians actually were displeased with the etymological civil alphabet (*hrazhdanka*) they were using and would have preferred to return to the pre-Petrine Slavonic alphabet (*kyrylytsia*).

37 The elderly Didyts'kyi expressed a mood of profound sadness when the young Russophiles decided to take over the Galician-Rus' Matytsia and adopted standard Russian for its publications. "Svoezhyt'evŷy zapysky Bohdana A. Dîdytskoho," pt. 2, *Vistnyk `Narodnoho Doma'*, XXVI, 3 (L'viv, 1908), pp. 50–54.

history, was established in L'viv. Seeing these achievements and frustrated by what seemed to be the stagnant political and cultural attitudes of the Old Ruthenians, several individuals, led by Osyp Monchalovs'kyi (1858–1906), Pylyp Svystun (1844–1916), Ilarion Svientsits'kyi (1876–1956), Dmitrii Vergun (1871–1951), and especially Iuliian Iavors'kyi (1873–1937), set out on a new course. At first, these "followers of a new line" (*novokursnyky*, as they were known) seemed to be simply redirecting the Old Ruthenian orientation into a more modern and activist cultural and political approach. But when their positions seemed too "radical," the Old Ruthenians parted ideological company with the Russophiles.

The Russophiles were able to take over some Old Ruthenian organizations and publications (the Stauropegial Institute and its *Vremennik*, the Galician-Rus' Matytsia and its *Sbornik*, and the National Home and its *Viestnik*). They also started new organs (*Zhivoe slovo*, 1899; *Zhivaia mysl'*, 1902–05; *Prikarpatskaia Rus'*, 1909–15; *Golos naroda*, 1909–14) and joined a new political organization, the Russian National party (Russko-narodnaia partiia, est. 1900). It was not long before the Russophiles put forth views that not only distinguished but alienated them from the Old Ruthenians.

Like their Old Ruthenian and Ukrainophile rivals, the Russophiles formulated the issue of national identity in terms of language, which was considered the "most important foundation and the very essence of the national being."[38] The Ukrainophiles were rejected outright because of their linguistic "separatism" (both in terms of vernacular content and phonetic form). As for the Old Ruthenians, even though they may have believed in linguistic unity with the other Rus' lands (albeit on their own terms), their uncodified and antiquated Galician-Ruthenian language was no longer acceptable to the generation of the 1890s.[39] The Russophiles argued that there was only one language created by the "southern and northern, by the Great, Little, and Belo-Russians, and by Novgorod, Vilnius, Moscow, and Halych," and that it was transformed "into one harmonious, beautiful, great symphony whose name is the Russian language."[40] Moreover, no part of this symbolic orchestra had the right to consider its own language as a valid instrument for cultural use. For the Old Ruthenians, as the aging Bohdan Didyts'kyi related in his memoirs, views such as these represented a totally unacceptable denial of the Galician tradition.[41]

38   Iu. Iavorskii, "Russkii iazyk," *Zhivaia mysl'*, I, 2 (L'viv, 1902), p. 25.
39   Dm. Vergun, "Nieskol'ko azbuchnykh istin i odin proekt," *Zhivaia mysl'*, I, 1 (L'viv, 1902), pp. 4-6.
40   Iavorskii, "Russkii iazyk," p. 26.
41   See above, note 37.

Dogmatic claims about the necessity for linguistic unity were only a step away from acceptance of the idea of full cultural and political unity with Russia. In this regard, the Russophiles argued unequivocally that Galicia represented the so-called *Pod"iaremnaia Rus'* (Rus' under the [Austrian] yoke) as opposed to *Derzhavnaia Rus'* (the tsarist Russian Empire), and that the "plans of Austrian politicians ... to separate the Russians of Galicia from the other 100-million strong Russian people" would not succeed.[42] Russophile political leaders Dmytro Markov (1864–1938), Mykola Hlibovyts'kyi (1876–1918), and Volodymyr Dudykevych (1861–1922) put forth similar views in both the imperial parliament in Vienna and the Galician Diet in L'viv. They criticized the Austrian government for its support of "Ukrainian separatism," for not recognizing Galicians as Russians, and for not allowing them to address their elected colleagues in literary Russian. They also tried to buttress their relatively weak political position within Galicia by cooperating with the local Poles and by accepting funds from the St. Petersburg-based Galician-Russian Benevolent Society. Thus, rejection of the traditional Galician-Ruthenian language, a desire for cultural and political unity with Russia, strong criticism of Austria, and finally cooperation with local Poles characterized the Russophile orientation in Galicia and both distinguished and alienated its representatives from the Old Ruthenians.[43]

It would seem that discussions which treat Old Ruthenianism and Russophilism in eastern Galicia as similar phenomena—a view that until now has dominated most literature on the subject—represent an approach not warranted by the historical evidence. The new conceptual framework proposed here takes into account the existence of three distinct orientations. The first of these was the Old Ruthenian, which dominated the Galician-Ukrainian national revival during the first decades after 1848. From this orientation arose the populist Ukrainophiles beginning in the late 1860s and then the Russophiles beginning in the 1890s. Despite these defections, the Old Ruthenian orientation continued to survive alongside the younger orientations at least until the outbreak of World War I.

To be sure, this study does not pretend to exhaust either the purely ideological or the many other aspects (socioeconomic, administrative, legal, political) of the Ukrainian national movement in late-nineteenth-century Galicia. More-

---

42 "Est' russkii v Galichinie!," *Golos naroda*, no. 8, February 28 (March 10), 1911.
43 In 1908, the Old Ruthenian politicians Mykhailo Korol' and Vasyl Davydiak broke with the Russophiles because they refused to identify as Russians and deplored the Russophiles, anti-Austrian statements, cooperation with the Poles, and acceptance of aid from tsarist Russia.

over, future research may revise or refine the chronological framework suggested here, especially if detailed statistical and sociological analyses of the Old Ruthenian and Russophile organizations, anthologies of literature by both groups, and scholarly biographies of their leaders are completed. More than eighty years ago, the Galician Ukrainophile Ivan Franko stated that the "cultural historian, for whom every spiritual deviation is equally interesting, ... must also turn his diligent attention to ... Muscophilism" (i.e., Old Ruthenianism and Russophilism) in Galicia.[44] Unfortunately, Franko's call has yet to be answered. Let us hope that scholars will become interested in this subject and consider Old Ruthenianism and Russophilism not simply, to quote the polemicist Franko, as "a symptom of a disease," but rather as legitimate intellectual phenomena within the Ukrainian cultural tradition. Only after serious work on this subject is undertaken will we be able to obtain a better understanding of the national movement among the Ukrainians of eastern Galicia during the second half of the nineteenth century.[45]

44 Franko, "Iz istoriï 'moskovofil's'koho pys'menstva," p. 458.
45 Since the appearance of this essay, several scholars have indeed contributed important studies on various aspects of Old Ruthenianism and Russophilism, including John-Paul Himka, *Religion and Nationality in Western Ukraine* (Montreal, London, and Ithaca, 1999) and Himka, "The Construction of Nationality in Galician Rus'," in Ronald Grigor Suny and Michael D. Kennedy, eds., *Intellectuals and the Articulation of the Nation* (Ann Arbor, 1999), pp. 109–164; Peter Galadza, "Tyt Myshkovsky: The Esteemed Russophile of the Lviv Greco-Catholic Theological Academy," *Journal of Ukrainian Studies*, XVIII, 1–2 (Edmonton, 1993), pp. 93–122; Jarosław Moklak, *Łemkowszczyzna w Drugiej Rzeczypospolitej* (Cracow, 1997), esp. pp. 17–100; and Olena Arkusha and Mar'ian Mudryi, "Rusofil'stvo v Halychyni v seredyni XIX-na pochatku XX st.," in *Visnyk L'vivs'koho universytetu: Seriia istorychna*, No. 34 (L'viv, 1999), pp. 231–268. The most comprehensive work on the subject is by the German Ukrainianist Anna Veronika Wendland: *Die Russophilen in Galizien: ukrainische Konservative zwischen Österreich und Russland, 1848–1915* (Vienna, 2001) and "Die Rückkehr der Russophilen in die ukrainische Geschichte: Neue Aspekte der ukrainischen Nationsbildung in Galizien, 1848–1914," *Jahrbücher fur Geschichte Osteuropas*, XLIX (Stuttgart, 2001), pp. 389–421.

chapter eight

The Kachkovs'kyi Society and the National Revival in Nineteenth-Century East Galicia*

The nineteenth century was the era when most Slavic peoples, including Ukrainians, experienced a national revival. At the time, the vast majority of Ukrainians (approximately 85 percent) lived in the tsarist Russian Empire, with the remainder living within the neighboring Austro-Hungarian Empire. Although numerically fewer than their brethren in the Russian Empire, Ukrainians in politically more liberal Austria–Hungary had much greater opportunities to develop a national revival. This began seriously during the revolutionary years of 1848–1849, then blossomed during the 1880s and 1890s, and finally culminated in the first decade and a half of the twentieth century. Of the Ukrainian-inhabited lands in the Austro-Hungarian Empire, it was most especially in the largest region—roughly the eastern half of the Austrian province of Galicia—that the national revival was played out in full force.

In the course of the national revival, cultural organizations played a crucial role in transmitting cultural and national awareness from the educated elite—the intelligentsia—to the peasantry, who comprised nearly 90 percent of Galicia's Ukrainian population. The first modern Ukrainian cultural organizations came into being in 1848. During the next half-century, several other Ukrainian cultural organizations came into being, including university departments, numerous publishing houses, and an unofficial academy of sciences known as the Shevchenko Scientific Society.

Among the various cultural organizations, the most influential for the national revival were those which reached directly into the villages, where they had an impact on the daily lives of peasants. In Ukrainian-inhabited eastern

---

* First published in *Harvard Ukrainian Studies*, XV, 1–2 (Cambridge, Mass., 1991), pp. 48–87; and in an abridged Russian translation in V.I. Zlydnev, ed., *Slavianskie i balkanskie kul'tury XVIIIBXIX vv.: sovetsko-amerikanskii simpozium* (Moscow: Akademiia nauk SSR, Institut slavianovedeniia i balkanistiki, 1990), pp. 132–143.

Galicia there were two such popular-education societies, the Prosvita Society (Tovarystvo 'Prosita') established in 1868 and the Kachkovs'kyi Society (Obshchestvo Kachkovskoho) established in 1874. Each lasted through World War I and even beyond, and therefore both were active throughout the whole era of the Galician-Ukrainian national revival.

Despite the importance of both the Prosvita Society and the Kachkovs'kyi Society for the development of a national consciousness in Ukrainian Galicia, only the Prosvita Society has been analyzed with any seriousness.[1] In an attempt to correct the imbalance, this essay will provide at least the broad outlines of the history of the Kachkovs'kyi Society from its establishment in 1874 down to the outbreak of World War I in 1914, that is, during the period which coincides with the height of the Ukrainian national revival in East Galicia. Following a review of existing literature on the subject, attention will be given to the establishment and structure of the Kachkovs'kyi Society, its activity, and its historical evolution and ideology.

Secondary Literature and Sources

The secondary literature on the Kachkovs'kyi Society is scant and limited primarily to works published before 1910. Of this material, the most extensive include a memorial book published on the twenty-fifth anniversary of the society's activity (1899) and a very rare history published in the Russian Empire at the outset of the twentieth century by P.O. Goptsus.[2] Aside from these early works, there are only a few short articles and encyclopedia entries on Mykhailo Kachkovs'kyi in which the society named after him is mentioned,[3] some comments on the society in more general studies that deal with the Russophile

---

1 For a review of the literature on the Prosvita Society, see Paul Robert Magocsi, *Galicia: A Historical Survey and Bibliographic Guide*, 2nd ed. (Toronto, 1985), pp. 37 and 144.

2 O.A. Monchalovskii, *Pamiatnaia knyzhka v 25-litnii iuvylei Obshchestva ymeny Mykhaylo Kachkovskoho, 1874–1899*, Izdanie Obshchestva Mykhayla Kachkovskoho, No. 285 (L'viv, 1899); P.O. Goptsus, *Zarubezhnaia Rus' v bor'bie za svoiu natsional'no-kul'turnuiu samobytnost': narodnoprosvietitel'naia dieiatel'nost' Obshchestva imeni Mikhailo Kachkovskogo v Galitskoi Rusi, osnovannago prosvietitelem ee o. Ioannom Naumovichem* (Poltava, 1909).

3 Afanasii Vasil'ev, "Mikhail Alekseevich Kachkovskii i obshchestvo ego imeni na Galitskoi Rusi," *Izviestiia Sankt-Peterburgskago slavianskago blagotvoritel'nago obshchestva*, V (St. Petersburg, 1888)—reprinted in his *Zarubezhnaia Rus'* (Petrograd, 1905), pp. 1–6, and in *Russkaia besieda*, I, 8 (St. Petersburg, 1895), pp. 99–108; J. Hejret, "Spolek Michaila Kačkovského," *Česka osvěta*, No. 10 (Prague, 1909); and more recently, Jarosław Moklak, "Mychajlo Kaczkowskij i czytelnie jego imienia na Łemkowszczyzne," in *Magury '87* (Warsaw, 1987), pp. 52–64.

movement in Galicia,[4] and passing references to the society in general histories[5] and in memoirs or essays by contemporaries, whether visitors from the Russian Empire such as Mykhailo Drahomanov and Elizaveta de Vitte[6] or local Galician activists such as Mykhailo Pavlyk, Ivan Franko, and Kost' Levyts'kyi.[7]

There are several reasons for the dearth of literature on the Kachkovs'kyi Society. While individual histories of other Old Ruthenian and Russophile cultural organizations in Galicia have been published,[8] the Kachkovs'kyi Society, with its more populist and less "scholarly" concerns seemed less important. For other reasons, the society has been of little concern to both Soviet and non-Soviet Ukrainian historians writing in the period since World War II. The postwar scholars have disregarded the earlier assessment of Franko that the Kachkovs'kyi Society "published a series of books that were important for the practical life of the peasantry";[9] or the conclusion of Mykhailo Hrushevs'kyi regarding the national orientation that the Kachkovs'kyi Society epitomized: "The so-called 'provincial Muscophiles' ... are in no way Muscovites or Russians, despite what their L'viv critics may say; they are simply Old Ruthenians—

The longest encyclopedia entry on Kachkovs'kyi with a description of the society is in the tsarist Russian *Éntsiklopedicheskii slovar'*, Vol. XIVa (St. Petersburg, 1895), pp. 814–815. It is interesting to note that the most important pre-World War I Polish encyclopedia, Samuel Orgelbrand's *Encyklopedja powszechna* (Warsaw, 1898–1912), did not carry any entry on Kachkovs'kyi, but that the analogous Czech encyclopedia did include a brief entry on him by the Prague specialist on Ukrainian affairs František Řehoř, *Ottův slovník naučný*, Vol. XIII (Prague, 1898), p. 729.

4 Mykola Andrusiak, *Narysy z istoriï halyts'koho moskvofil's'tva* (Prague, 1935), pp. 42–45; Stefan A. Fentsik, "Galitsiia," *Karpatskii sviet*, I, 10 (Užhorod, 1928), pp. 380–382.

5 Omelian Ohonovskii, *Ystoriia lyteraturŷ ruskoy*, Vol. II (L'viv, 1889), pp. 89–90; Filipp I. Svistun, *Prikarpatskaia Rus' pod vladieniem Avstrii* (1896), 2nd rev. ed. (Trumbull, Conn., 1970), pp. 417–418.

6 Mykhailo Drahomanov, "Avstro-rus'ki spomyny" (1889–92), in his *Literaturno-publitsystychni pratsi*, Vol. II (Kiev, 1970), esp. pp. 254–257; Elizaveta de Vitte, *Putevyia vpechatlieniia s istoricheskimi ocherkami: lieto 1903 g., Bukovina i Galichina* (1904), 2nd ed. (Bridgeport, Conn., 1977), esp. pp. 226–244.

7 Mykhailo Pavlyk, "Pro rus'ko-ukraïns'ki narodni chytal'ni" (1887), in his *Tvory* (Kiev, 1985), pp. 233–235; Ivan Franko, "Narys istoriï ukraïns'ko-rus'koï literatury do 1890 r." (1910), in his *Zibrannia tvoriv*, Vol. XLI (Kiev, 1984), pp. 331 and 420; Kost' Levyts'kyi, *Istoriia politychnoï dumky halyts'kykh ukraïntsiv 1848–1914*, pt. 1 (L'viv, 1926), pp. 146–147.

8 For instance, the Stauropegial Institute has an extensive literature, while the Galician-Rus' Matytsia and National Home have at least one major study on them. See Magocsi, *Galicia*, pp. 35–36.

9 Franko, "Narys istoriï," p. 420. See also the positive assessment of Andrusiak, *Narysy z istoriï*, pp. 42–45.

that is, Ukrainians also, even if they have old-fashioned and strange views. ... They are a very useful force whether in economic or political activity, and without them one cannot carry on any work in the countryside, because they are the real power among the local intelligentsia."[10] Instead, most Soviet and non-Soviet Ukrainian historians seem intent on dismissing the Kachkovs'kyi Society outright, or at best in criticizing it for its supposed Russophile, conservative, clerical, tsarist, and, worst of all, "anti-revolutionary" tendencies.[11] It is only in the past few years that two Canadian specialists on Ukrainians in Galicia have called for a reassessment of the Kachkovs'kyi Society and for a dispassionate analysis of its historic role.[12]

Unpublished sources on the Kachkovs'kyi Society are held in the Central State Historical Archive in L'viv. Colleagues who have recently reviewed the archival holdings devoted to the organization report that they contain only minutes and reports similar to those available in published sources.[13] The present study is based on materials in the contemporary press from the time of the establishment of the Kachkovs'kyi Society in 1874 until its first demise following the outbreak of World War I in 1914.

Although the society never had its own newspaper or journal, several periodicals provided systematic coverage of its activity. In this regard, the most important were the newspapers *Slovo* (L'viv, 1861–87), *Chervonnaia Rus'* (L'viv, 1888–91), and *Halychanyn* (L'viv, 1893–1913), which carried once each year the full texts of the Kachkovs'kyi Society's annual reports (*otchety*) as well as descriptions throughout the year of the activity of the society's affiliates. Four other periodicals—*Nauka* (1871–99, 1902–14), *Russkaia rada*

10 Mykhailo Hrushevs'kyi, "Konets' rutenstva," *Literaturno-naukovyi vistnyk*, XL (Kiev and L'viv, 1907), p. 139.

11 The Kachkovs'kyi Society is given a negative assessment in a brief entry in the non-Soviet Ukrainian *Entsyklopediia ukraïnoznavstva*, Vol. V (Paris and New York, 1966), p. 1807, while neither the society nor Kachkovs'kyi have any entry in the first or second editions of the *Ukraïns'ka radians'ka entsyklopediia* (Kiev, 1959–65 and 1977–85) and in the *Radians'ka entsyklopediia istoriï Ukraïny* (Kiev, 1969–72).

12 John-Paul Himka, *Socialism in Galicia: The Emergence of Polish Social Democracy and Ukrainian Radicalism (1860-1890)* (Cambridge, Mass., 1983), p. 42, mentions the "progressive qualities" of Russophilism; and Stella M. Hryniuk, "A Peasant Society in Transition: Ukrainian Peasants in Five East Galician Countries, 1880–1900" (Ph.D. diss., University of Manitoba, 1984), esp. pp. 175–179, after discussing in some detail Kachkovs'kyi Society activity at the local level, suggests that "it is possible that its contribution to Ukrainian enlightenment in East Galicia has been underestimated."

13 The L'viv archival material in question is held in *fond* 182: "Materialy ob organizatsionnoi i propagandistskoi dieatel'nosti Obshchestva im. M. Kachkovskogo" (1879–1909). I am grateful to Dr. Stella Hryniuk, who reviewed the holdings at my request.

(1871–1912), *Russkoe slovo* (1890–1914), and *Golos naroda* (1909–15)—were less systematic in reproducing the annual reports, but they did provide detailed descriptions of the society's annual meetings and other activity throughout each year. Thus, the contemporary Galician press provides extensive data to trace the history and development of the Kachkovs'kyi Society.

The Establishment and Structure of the Kachkovs'kyi Society

There is no question that the idea to establish the Kachkovs'kyi Society originated with the Reverend Ivan Naumovych (1826–1891), a Greek Catholic priest in the town of Skalat not far from the Russian border. Naumovych was already well known throughout Ukrainian-inhabited Galicia as the author of several widely read short stories and plays and as the founding editor of *Nauka*, the popular journal for rural domestic affairs. In short, Naumovych's influence and popularity were based on the fact that he knew how to reach the Galician-Ukrainian peasantry, to speak their language, and to respond to their needs. He was a classic populist, whose primary life goal was to raise the cultural level of the Galician-Ukrainian masses by working with them and at their level, or in his words, by going to the people (*k narodam*).[14]

Two other cultural organizations were already in existence: the Galician-Rus' Matytsia (est. 1848) and the more recent Prosvita Society (est. 1868). However, the Matytsia limited itself to publishing an irregular and rather esoteric scholarly journal, while Prosvita, which was established to correct the Matytsia's isolation, did not (at least initially) do much better. For instance, during Prosvita's first eight years of existence, only 564 persons joined the organization, whose high dues and cost of publications closed out the peasant masses, making it just another cultural society "for the intelligentsia."[15]

---

14 Naumovych's role was even acknowledged by his adversaries, such as the socialist and Ukrainophile activist Mykhailo Pavlyk. Although staunchly opposed to the conservative, clerical, Orthodox, and pro-Russian views of Naumovych, Pavlyk could nonetheless write that the priest-activist "rendered a great service toward the enlightenment of the Rus' people of Galicia! ... despite himself he cleared the Galician ground for true Ukrainophilism, even more so than most certified populists, since he readied the masses of our people for Ukrainianism." M. Pavlyk, *Moskvofil'stvo ta ukraïnofil'stvo sered avstro-rus'koho narodu* (L'viv, 1906), p. 45.

On Naumovych's career, see the two biographies by his, respectively, Old Ruthenian and Russophile ideological descendants: O.A. Monchalovskii, *Zhyt'e i dïiatel'nost Ivana Naumovycha* (L'viv, 1899) and Vasilii R. Vavrik, *Prosvititel' Galitskoi Rusi Ivan G. Naumovich* (L'viv and Prague, 1926).

15 Mykhailo Lozyns'kyi, *Sorok lït dïial'nosty 'Pros'vity'* (L'viv, 1908), p. 10.

It was in these circumstances that Ivan Naumovych, the newly elected deputy to the national parliament in Vienna (1873), decided to act. While his new position did not garner for his people any concrete advantages from the Austrian government, it did give him a chance to interact in Vienna with fellow leaders of other Slavic national revivals.

Generally, it is thought that the Galician-Ukrainian national revival looked to Poles, Serbs, and most especially Czechs to point the way. While this is true in general, Naumovych found encouragement among the Slovenes, numerically the smallest Slavic people in the Habsburg Empire, divided geographically and administratively between Carniola and five other Austrian provinces. From Slovene representatives in Vienna, Naumovych learned of their struggle for national survival in the face of Germanization, and he was particularly impressed with the popular Slovene cultural society known as the Society of St. Hermagoras (Družba sv. Mohorja). This was actually a publishing house whose members (23,000 in the mid-1870s) guaranteed through their annual dues the publication of books in Slovene that no commercial publisher would be willing to underwrite.[16] Thus, reasoned Naumovych, if the numerically small Slovenes could survive in the face of German influence, so too could the Rus' people of Galicia stand up to the Poles.[17]

With the Slovene model in mind, Naumovych turned first to the Galician-Rus' Matytsia and the Prosvita Society, recommending that they dissolve themselves, join forces, and create a single publishing house. When his proposal was rejected, he decided instead to form a new cultural organization. On August 20, 1874, he summoned a group of Galician-Rus' patriots, not to the Polish-dominated provincial capital of L'viv, but to the small town of Kolomyia tucked in a Carpathian Mountain valley of southeastern Galicia. About 300 people, half of them peasants from the local countryside, gathered in Kolomyia to form what became known as the Mykhail Kachkovs'kyi Society (Obshchestvo im. Mykhaila Kachkovskoho).

But why was the new society named after Kachkovs'kyi? Mykhail Kachkovs'kyi (1802–1872) was an Austrian civil servant, who from 1848 onward

16 For an introduction to the Hermagoras Society in the context of similar organizations, see Stanley B. Kimball, *The Austro-Slav Revival: A Study of Nineteenth-Century Literary Foundations*, Transactions of the American Philosophical Society, Vol. LXIII, pt. 4 (Philadelphia, 1973), p. 66.

17 On the influence of the Slovenes on Naumovych, see his statements in "O obshchestvî Mykhayla Kachkovskoho," *Russkaia rada*, V, 24 (Kolomyia, 1875), p. 190, and "Poslanie k vsîm nashym chlenam OMK y dobrŷm liudam, shchyrŷm Rusynam!," *Kalendar OMK na hod prostŷi 1885* (L'viv, [1884]), pp. 69–71; as well as O.A. Monchalovskii, "Rîch, proyznesennaia v heneral'nom sobraniy chlenov OMK, 17 (29) sentiabra v Ternopolî," *Slovo*, September 29, 1884, pp. 1–2, and October 2, 1884, pp. 1–2.

had spent a rather uneventful career as a judge at the district court in Sambir, where he acquired a reputation for defending peasants whenever disputes with manorial landlords were brought before him regarding forest and pasture rights.[18] Unmarried and with no other family obligations, he attained a certain amount of wealth, which he used to support a few important publications in the late 1850s. In 1861, he provided funds for the establishment of the newspaper *Slovo*, which for nearly two decades was to serve as the authoritative organ of the Old Ruthenian orientation in Galician-Ukrainian society. In 1871, he provided funds to help Naumovych publish a popular journal (*Nauka*) and a newspaper (*Russkaia rada*), both written in the vernacular. When Kachkovs'kyi died unexpectedly a few months after his retirement in 1872 (while on a trip to the Russian Empire), he left in his estate the sum of 60,000 guldens to the National Center (Narodnyi Dom) in L'viv for the "publication of books for the spiritual welfare of the Rus' people."[19] Two years later, Naumovych thought that naming the new society after Kachkovs'kyi and carrying out the publication goals of the deceased's will would guarantee endowed funding for the fledgling organization. The matter was contested in Austrian courts for more than a decade, and the National Home never released the funds, so that in the end the society named for Kachkovs'kyi never received any income from his estate.[20]

With no funding either from the Kachkovs'kyi estate or, with a few exceptions very much later, from the Austrian central or Galician provincial governments, the Kachkovs'kyi Society had to survive solely on support from its own members. Moreover, since the vast majority of those members consistently came from the peasantry, it could, in fact, be called a national society.

The basic goals of the Kachkovs'kyi Society were outlined in the first paragraph of its statutes, issued at the founding meeting in Kolomyia: "to spread knowledge, morality, industriousness, thriftiness, sobriety, civic awareness, and

18 For further details on Kachkovs'kyi, see the only significant biography, Bohdan A. Dîdytskii, *Mykhayl Kachkovskii y sovremennaia halytsko-russkaia lyteratura: ocherk biohrafycheskii y ystoryko-lyteraturnŷi* (L'viv, 1876); on the background to forming the Kachkovs'kyi Society, see Pavlyk, "Pro ... chytal'ni," pp. 226–233.

19 From a speech by Kachkovs'kyi in Sambir (November 13, 1860), as recorded by B.A. Dîdytskyi, "Vspomynka o M. Kachkovskom," *Slovo*, November 9 (21), 1885, p. 1. For the text of Kachkovs'kyi's will, see "Zavîshchanie Mykhayla Kachkovskoho, ehozhe slavnoe ymia nashe Obshchestvo nosyt," in *Yliustrovannŷi kalendar' OMK na hod prostŷi 1886* (L'viv, [1885]), pp. 155–160.

20 Y. Naumovych, "O obshchestvi Mykhayla Kachkovskoho," *Russkaia rada*, V, 24 (Kolomyia, 1875), p. 190. Several sources still assume incorrectly that the Kachkovs'kyi Society was funded by the Kachkovs'kyi estate. Cf. the editorial note in Franko, *Zibrannia tvoriv*, p. 624.

all aspects of integrity among the Rus' people of Austria" (see Appendix 8.1). These goals were frequently summed up in the slogan "study, pray, work, and prosper" (*uchysia, molysia, pratsiui, statkui*; or *molys', uchys', trudys'i shchady*, depending on the language of the author), which appeared over and over again in the annual reports and speeches of society members. It seemed to Naumovych and to most of his successors that the best way to achieve those goals was through the "diffusion of inexpensive and useful booklets among our Rus' people living in the Austrian state."[21]

The Kachkovs'kyi Society had the following structure. Individual members paid only one Austrian gulden annually, in return for which they received, gratis, a publication each month, including the society's annual almanac.[22] (It is interesting to note that, during the first nine years of its existence, Kachkovs'kyi's older rival, the Prosvita Society, charged two guldens to become a member plus nearly eight guldens in annual dues; moreover, publications had to be purchased separately by Prosvita members.)[23]

According to a revision of the statutes made in 1875, Kachkovs'kyi Society members belonged to local affiliates, which could be formed whenever at least twenty members submitted a petition to the central branch in L'viv for approval. The affiliates were generally based in district centers and were responsible for the territory of the given district (*Bezirk/povit*). Of the fifty-five districts in Ukrainian-inhabited eastern Galicia, the Kachkovs'kyi Society had affiliates at some time or other in thirty-two districts, with a total of thirty-one affiliates in 1913 (see Appendix 8.2). The affiliates carried on their own cultural activity and were entitled to 10 percent of the annual dues of members living within their jurisdiction, the remainder going to the central branch. The founding statutes already made provision for the establishment of reading rooms, which could be set up with a minimum of twelve members (see Appendix 8.1, section VII).

The central branch itself was first located in Kolomyia (on Honchars'ka Street), but as a result of an extraordinary general meeting held in January 1876, it was decided to change its location to L'viv. For nearly the next three decades, the central branch had its offices in the National Center (Narodyni Dom at No. 22 Teatral'na Street) in downtown L'viv, for which it paid rent, until it was finally able to purchase its own building in 1904 at No. 14 on nearby Valova Street.

21 "Zahal'noe sobranie obshchestva Myhayla Kachkovskoho otbudesia v Stryî dnia 22. lat. (10 rus) serpnia seho roku," *Russkaia rada*, VI, 15 (Kolomyia, 1876), p. 110.

22 "Otchet OMK … 1876–1877," *Slovo*, September 27, 1877, pp. 1–2.

23 Lozyns'kyi, *Sorok līt*, p. 10, actually states four crowns membership and 1.4 crowns monthly, which after conversion (one gulden equalled two crowns before 1892) equals the figures given here.

The governing body of the central branch and of the Kachkovs'kyi Society as a whole was its central committee (*tsentral'nyi vydil*), composed of twelve members, of which eight were full members and four were alternates. From among the eight full members there were also four officers—a chairman, a vice-chairman, a secretary, and a treasurer. The central committee was elected at each annual meeting by dues-paying members in attendance, and it was responsible for all policy and financial aspects of the society's activity. Not surprisingly, the first elected chairman was Ivan Naumovych, and in the period down to World War I there were only four other chairmen (see Appendix 8.3), those with the longest tenure being Bohdan Didyts'kyi (1884–1903) and Pylyp Svystun (1903–1914).[24] All work by the officers was done on a voluntary basis, Didyts'kyi gaining his livelihood, for instance, as curator of the National Center and Svystun as a *gymnasium* teacher.

The original statute (see Appendix 8.1) suggested that the Kachkovs'kyi Society was to represent the Rus' people throughout all of Austria, and at its founding and subsequent annual meetings much emphasis appeared in reports about representation from neighboring Bukovina. It was also because of the Bukovinian presence that the religious issue arose. When at the second meeting, held in historic Halych, a local Galician Greek Catholic priest expressed concern that the Orthodox Bukovinian guest and his fellow Galician Rus' were of a different religion, the speaker was criticized "because our members did not meet here for religious speeches but for the purposes of raising the level of education and welfare of the people."[25]

Bukovinian participation at annual meetings was to continue, and by 1876 there were eight Kachkovs'kyi reading rooms in Bukovina. This was in sharp contrast to Subcarpathian Rus' where, during a period of increasing magyarization before World War I, there was no participation in or even awareness of the Kachkovs'kyi Society.[26] This was confirmed during a visit to the area by Mykhailo Drahomanov, who later recalled an interview with Anatolii Kralyts'kyi, the well-known Subcarpathian writer and archimandrite of the

24 For biographies of the first four chairmen, see Monchalovskii, *Pamiatnaia knyzhka*, pp. 6–8, 113–120.
25 "Zahal'noe sobranie OMK v Halychy," *Russkaia rada*, V, 17 (Kolomyia, 1875), p. 132. It is interesting to note that it was also at this meeting that a suggestion of the university student and future radical politician Mykhailo Pavlyk, to have the Gospel "translated into the popular speech," was turned down. "Otchet yz vtoroho heneral'noho sobraniia OMK," *Slovo*, August 19, 1875, p. 1.
26 One commentator suggested that back in the 1880s the Subcarpathian Rusyns were still "with us," but that "since then they have no contacts with us as if they were not of Rus' origin." "O heneral'nôm sobraniiu chlenôv OMK v Kolomŷî," *Russkaia rada*, XXXIV, 17 (Kolomyia, 1905), p. 134.

Mukachevo monastery: "I couldn't believe my ears: the archimandrite of a Rus' monastery, a contributor to *Slovo*, and he never saw a publication of the Kachkovs'kyi Society until [I], a Ukrainophile from Russia, brought some to him."[27] On the other hand, the Kachkovs'kyi Society did make its presence felt among immigrants in the New World (mostly from Subcarpathian Rus' and the Lemko Region) and, beginning in the 1890s, frequently sent its publications to immigrant organizations in the United States, Canada, and Brazil. By 1903, there were 139 Kachkovs'kyi Society members in the United States, most of whom were in branches located in Seymor, Connecticut, and Olyphant and Shamokin, Pennsylvania.[28]

The Activity of the Kachkovs'kyi Society

We have seen how Naumovych's idea for creating the Kachkovs'kyi Society was derived from the success of a Slovene publishing house. While it is true that the Kachkovs'kyi Society with its various affiliates became increasingly involved in other kinds of activity, the "main task of the central committee" remained throughout its history the publication program. Its importance was further underlined by the fact that the chairman of the central committee was simultaneously responsible for publications.

The object of the publication program was accessibility and frequency. This meant small booklets (generally between 75 and 125 pages) published each month and sent gratis to all members. In practice, members received a booklet an average of ten to eleven times a year (some of the summer months were often doubled up), including, after 1885, an annual farmer's almanac (*kalendar*) that was usually large enough to cover the page allotment for two months. The monthly series was officially known as the *Izdaniia Obshchestva ymeny Mykhayla Kachkovskoho* (Publications of the Mykhailo Kachkovs'kyi Society), and between 1875, when the first booklet appeared, and the outbreak of World War I more then 460 numbers were issued.

Taking into consideration the double numbers assigned to certain titles, more than 400 booklets appeared between 1875 and 1914.[29] The size of the printings

On the magyarization process in Subcarpathian Rus' and decreasing contacts with Galicia, see Paul Robert Magocsi, *The Shaping of a National Identity: Subcarpathian Rus', 1848–1948* (Cambridge, Mass., 1978), pp. 55–75.

27 Drahomanov, "Avstro-rus'ki spomyny," p. 276.

28 "OMK: spravozdanoe … za lîta 1894–95 y 1895–96," *Russkoe slovo*, VII, 35 (L'viv, 1896), p. 6; "OMK: otchet o diiatel'nosty tsentr. výdîla," *Halychanyn*, September 8, 1897, pp. 1–2; *Halychanyn*, September 30, 1903, pp. 1–2.

29 I am not aware of any complete list of all Kachkovs'kyi Society publications. The estimate

remained stable for each number within each year (with the exception of the almanac, which was usually printed in an extra 1,500 copies), but they changed from one period to the next depending on the society's membership. The initial four numbers (1875) came out in print runs of 10,000, but quantities thereafter dropped to 6,000 and then, after 1879 (the lowest point in membership), to 5,500 and 5,200. It was not until the 1890s that the printings were again increased, culminating during the first decade of the twentieth century in 8,500 (1900) and then 10,500 (1904).

Since the Kachkovs'kyi Society was so consistent in getting out its monthly publications, during the thirty-eight-year period down to 1914 it printed perhaps over 2.5 million copies. The importance of the publication program was confirmed by the annual budgets, over half of which each year were designated for editorial and printing costs.[30]

Just what were these publications and did they fulfill the intended goal of the society's statute: "to spread knowledge, morality, industriousness, thriftiness, sobriety, [and] civic awareness?" With regard to form, they were all written in the so-called traditional Galician-Rus' book language, that is, basically, Galician-Ukrainian vernacular with a significant number of archaic forms and Church- Slavonic influences and a lesser number of Russian influences. This book language was used in church books and had been taught in elementary schools at least until the 1870s. Moreover, in a semiliterate, conservative, and rural environment that was sensitive to any deviation from traditional forms, the etymological alphabet was used, with its *iery* [ы], *iat* [ѣ], and hard sign [ъ]. Thus, the Kachkovs'kyi Society publications had a familiar look and were perceived by the peasant masses to be "our" Galician- Rus' books.[31]

In terms of content, each booklet included sometimes a single title or, more often, several titles. The subjects included information of a practical nature

given here is based on the annual reports (*otchety*), which indicated the numbers in the series published in a given year and often provided titles as well. The most comprehensive list available (before 1893) is found in Ivan Em. Levytskii, *Halytsko-russkaia bybliohrafiia XIX-ho stolitiia*, Vol. II: *1861–1886* (L'viv, 1895) and the supplements under the title *Materiialy do ukraïns'koï bibliohrafiï: Ukraïns'ka bibliohrafiia Avstro-Uhorshchyny za roky 1887–1893*, 3 vols. (L'viv, 1909–11). See also the discussion of the society's publishing activity and lists of publications (down to 1905) arranged according to subject matter in Goptsus, *Zarubezhnaia Rus'*, pp. 72–82.

30 For instance, looking at a typical budget during an early and later period, we see that the printing, binding, and postage costs represented 51 percent of expenses during the fiscal year 1885–1886 and 50.5 percent during the 1900–1901 fiscal year. *Slovo*, September 3 (15), 1886, p. 3; *Halychanyn*, September 13, 1901, pp. 1–2.

31 This was in sharp contrast to the populist Ukrainophiles. Beginning in the 1870s, they gradually introduced the phonetic alphabet, but its "strangeness" often alienated unsophisticated readers. On the alphabet and related problems, see above, chapter 6.

concerning farming and personal health care, or were devoted to moral (i.e., religious) and civic concerns (Austrian citizenship, Galician-Rus' history), or were aimed at exposing the masses to culture, whether in "high" forms through works by renowned Russian authors such as Gogol and Tolstoy or in more popular forms through plays and short stories by local Galician authors such as Ivan Naumovych, Ievhen Zhars'kyi (1834–1892), Dmytro Vintskovs'kyi (1846–1917), and Orest Avdykovs'kyi (1843–1913). The titles issued during the first year set the tone that was to be followed for the next four decades. Among these were "What Does a Person Need to Know about Health," by Dr. Kornylii Merunovych; "Notes on the Use of Plants for Human Consumption," by P. V.; "Domestic Flocks," by Ignatii Hal'ka; "Vodka—the Ruination of Man and How to Overcome It"; "On the Planting of All Kinds of Trees," "Dwellings for Sheep," and "What Our Houses Should Look Like," all by Mykhail Klemertovych; "God Be with Us," by Ivan Naumovych; "Love for the Fatherland," by V. Ruzhyts'kyi; "On the Rights and Duties of Citizens at the Village, District, Province, and State Level," by Ignatii Hal'ka; "A Conversation between an Illiterate Father and a Learned Son," by I. Sh.; literary works by Orest Avdykovs'kyi, Ievhenii Zhars'kyi, and Dmytro Tretiak; and several reports on the society itself.

Throughout the four decades of the Kachkovs'kyi Society's publication program, one title was singled out as the "crown of our educational work."[32] This was the *Slaviano-russkii bukvar* (*Slaveno-Rus' Primer*) published in 1895 in an initial printing of 20,000. This was the largest print run of any Kachkovs'kyi Society publication, and its seeming popularity led to a second printing—this time of 30,000 copies—in 1905.[33] The primer was not only an elementary educational tool. It also became an element in the society's ideological struggle to preserve the traditional Galician-Rus' book language and etymological alphabet in the face of the phonetically based alphabet of the Ukrainian vernacular, which had been officially recognized by the Austrian provincial school administration in 1893.

Besides the publication program, the other way in which the Kachkovs'kyi Society advertised itself and tried to gain new members was through its annual conventions. Although the founder, Naumovych, quipped that "we could have not made a greater mistake than to designate Kolomyia as the seat of our headquarters,"[34] his own preference for L'viv did not blind him to the necessity

32 Cited from chairman Bohdan Didyts'kyi's opening speech at the twenty-second annual convention in Stanyslaviv, "Narodnyi prazdnyk," *Russkoe slovo*, VII, 35 (L'viv, 1896), p. 1.
33 "OMK v 1905/6 hodu," *Halychanyn*, September 19, 1906, pp. 1–3.
34 From the chairman's speech at the extraordinary third convention in L'viv, "Heneral'noe sobranie chlenov OMK," *Slovo*, January 13, 1876, p. 1.

for the Kachkovs'kyi Society to avoid the example of all other Galician-Rus' societies, which often closed themselves off in the "big city," far from the provincial environment of the smaller towns and countryside.[35] Thus, to avoid the pitfalls of isolation for an organization whose goals were to work among the masses, the Kachkovs'kyi Society used its annual conventions as an instrument for "going to the people." Each year, the annual convention was held in a different Galician town, during the thirty-eight conventions held between 1874 and 1912 rotating among Brody (2 times), Drohobych (3), Halych (1), Jarosław (1), Kalush (1), Kolomyia (4), L'viv (12), Przemyśl (2), Sanok (2), Sambir (2), Stanyslaviv (2), Stryi (2), Ternopil' (3), and Zolochiv (1)—see Appendix 8.4.

According to the founding statute, the annual conventions were to be held each August 20 (August 8, old style), the day of Mykhail Kachkovs'kyi's death. While the founding meeting and some of the early conventions were held on or near that day, the norm soon became the second to third week of September, when the bulk of the harvest was in, allowing more peasant agriculturalists to attend. In a sense, the annual conventions became national holidays, which usually drew a few thousand participants and in some cases as many as 5,000, making them among the largest Rus' manifestations in Galicia and lending some credence to the standard description of a national holiday (*narodnŷi prazdnyk*) given them by the Old Ruthenian and Russophile press.

A typical national convention went something like the one held in Kolomyia in 1905.[36] The participants arrived the day before, and already on the eve of the meeting at 7:30 p.m. there was a parade with choral music, torches, and lanterns that wound its way through the streets of Kolomyia, culminating at the local Kachkovs'kyi Society reading room, where a theatrical performance began at 9:00 p.m. The next day the convention began at 8:00 a.m. with a liturgy and *panakhyda* (memorial service) for Mykhail Kachkovs'kyi and deceased members of the society in the local Greek Catholic church. This was followed at 10:00 a.m. by a parade from the church to the city park, where at 10:30 a.m. the meeting was formally opened by the singing of the hymn of the Slavic patron saints, Cyril and Methodius: *"Slava Vam bratia"* ("Glory unto You, Brothers").

After a break for luncheon, the proceedings resumed outside at 12:00 noon with a welcoming speech by the chairman of the society, Pylyp Svystun. This

35 For instance, the headquarters of the Prosvita Society was in L'viv, and this, combined with other reasons, led to the popular view that Prosvita was *pans'ke*—for the upper echelons; while Kachkovs'kyi was *khlops'ke*—for the peasant masses. Andrusiak, *Narysy*, p. 43.

36 Based on the description in *Russkoe slovo*, August 11, 1905, p. 1.

37 This description, generally applicable to Galician-Ukrainian society (as well as immigrant

was followed by the reading of congratulatory telegrams, the election of a board of comptrollers, a reading of the financial report for the previous fiscal year (1904–1905), a speech by a woman villager, a poetry reading, the report of the board of comptrollers, and the election of the chairman and central committee for the following year. Each of these activities was, of course, accompanied with speeches by—to quote the words of one outside visitor—"Galician orators ... who are incapable of speaking briefly, clearly, and to the point," so that "to survive a Galician meeting is a difficult task even for an educated person, let alone a simple one."[37] When all was finally said and done late in the afternoon, the meeting closed with the singing of *"Khto za namy, Boh za nym"* ("May God Be with Those Who Are with Us").

With formal affairs out of the way, the evening was left to a public festival that included theatrical performances, a concert by a military band and the local Kolomyia choir, a firework display at 8:30 p.m., and, finally, a public ball from 10:00 p.m. until the wee hours of the morning. The following day was reserved for a trip to the Hutsul resort of Iaremche along the Prut River, after which the participants returned home on foot, if they were from nearby villages, or by train if they were part of the central branch's delegation from L'viv or from other branches.

The main object of the annual meetings was to bring Galician Ukrainians together and give them a sense of their national unity through social contact and relaxation at the same time as they were exposed to patriotic speeches and cultural performances. The effort must have been successful, since with only a few exceptions the Kachkovs'kyi Society conventions continued to attract thousands of participants right down to the last meeting (1912) held before World War I. Moreover, the proposal, made a few times in the mid-1880s, to hold meetings only once every three years was never adopted.[38]

The annual meetings also provided the motivation for another important aspect of Kachkovs'kyi Society activity—agricultural work. Already in 1875, just one year after the society was founded, it was agreed to amend the statute "so that at the national conventions exhibits would be set up to display tools and agricultural products."[39] The first of these exhibits accompanied the annual meetings in 1879 (Stanyslaviv) and 1880 (Kolomyia). They were enor-

descendants of that society in North America), actually pertained to the 1876 annual convention. Drahomanov, "Avstro-rus'ki spomyny," p. 255.

38 Actually, a resolution for meetings to take place on a three-year cycle was proposed at the thirteenth annual convention in Sanok (1885), but apparently it was never adopted. "XIII hener. sobranie chlenov OMK v Sianokî," *Slovo*, August 31, 1885, pp. 1–2.

39 "Otchet yz vtoroho heneral'noho sobraniia OMK," *Slovo*, August 14 (26), 1875, p. 1.

mously popular, because they spoke the language known best by the population of a rural area; namely, the visual language of exhibits that included samples of the newest crops—such as American potatoes, "Mamut" beets, kohlrabi, and soybeans—and made available, gratis, sample seeds of these and other agricultural products. The peasants were also able to get concrete ideas from other parts of the exhibit, which displayed the newest tools, milk and meat products, handicrafts, and domestic animals—chickens, geese, et cetera.[40] Whereas agricultural exhibits were held at a few subsequent annual conventions (Sanok, 1900, and bee raising at Kolomyia, 1905), this activity was basically left to the affiliates, which mounted their own exhibits usually in conjunction with their own general meetings.

The central branch was more active in sponsoring courses such as fruit raising and orchard care (1906), local store management (1906–07, 1911–12), production of butter and milk products (1908–09, 1911–12), and animal care (1911–12), all of which were held in or near L'viv.[41] More ambitious was a scholarship program begun in 1906 for five young peasants to spend nearly half a year (April 1–September 15) as guests of the Economic Union (Hospodařský Svaz) in Chrudim, Bohemia. There they worked and learned the more advanced agricultural techniques and cooperative ventures from Czech farmers. The Kachkovs'kyi Society's Bohemian scholarships lasted until 1912.[42]

Perhaps the most successful of the central branch's agricultural activities was the establishment in 1909 of an agricultural office to distribute various farming products, the most popular of which were fertilizers and seeds for feed grains.[43] The demand for agricultural-related activity remained so great that finally, in 1907, the Kachkovs'kyi Society started its own monthly newspaper, *Ekonomychnyi lystok*, devoted almost exclusively to agricultural matters.[44]

40 *Russkaia rada*, IX, 17–18 (Kolomyia, 1879), pp. 125–126 and X, 4 and 7 (1880), pp. 32–33 and 60–61; *Slovo*, February 14, 1880, p. 1, April 24, 1880, p. 2, and September 9, 1880, p. 2.

41 See the reports in *Russkoe slovo*, XVII, 37 (L'viv, 1906), p. 5, and in *Halychanyn*, September 12, 1907, pp.1–2, and September 13, 1907, pp.2–3; October 1, 1909, p. 2; September 30, 1910, p. 1; and September 20, 1912, p. 2.

42 See the report of a participant during the first year of the program in *Russkoe slovo*, XVII, 37 (L'viv, 1906), pp. 1–2.

43 During its first year of operation, August 1909 to April 1910, the agricultural office distributed forty railroad boxcar loads of fertilizer. *Halychanyn*, September 30, 1910, p. 1. Cf. the report in *Halychanyn*, September 20, 1912, p. 2.

44 *Ekonomychnyi lystok* appeared in eight issues in 1907 and, under the title *Lystok,* in eleven issues in 1908 as supplement to the monthly booklets.

Another rural concern was the need for fire companies. In 1904, the central committee decided to issue statutes for volunteer fire companies and to provide instruction to members on how to become effective firefighters at the village level. By 1909, the number of volunteer fire companies had risen to 119.[45]

There were also, of course, the reading rooms, which were proposed in the society's founding statute, provided there was a request by at least twelve members in a given village (see Appendix 8.1, section VII). The central committee issued charters to reading rooms, which were treated as individual members. Such a status entitled them to receive the monthly publication series as well as duplicate copies of books sent out periodically by the central branch. It is interesting to note that Kachkovs'kyi publications were sent to its own as well as to those Prosvita reading rooms which were paid members of the society.

The real growth of the reading rooms took place around the turn of the twentieth century. It is difficult, however, to provide reliable figures regarding their number because of the great fluctuation at the village level (inactivity or permanent or temporary change of allegiance to the Prosvita Society). For instance, on the occasion of the Kachkovs'kyi Society's twenty-fifth anniversary in 1899, the memorial volume listed 559 reading rooms. A decade later, the official annual report for 1911–1912 mentioned 1,225 reading rooms, but at the same time it admitted that most of these existed only on paper and that the actual number was probably closer to 800.[46] Similarly, the number of affiliates increased from 21 in 1899 to 31 in 1913 (see Appendix 8.2). Finally, there were student dormitories, of which the Kachkovs'kyi Society operated eight by 1910. In most cases, poor students from the countryside enrolled in *gymnasia* located in towns were given living accommodations and meals free or at greatly reduced cost.[47]

Thus, by the first decade of the twentieth century, the Kachkovs'kyi Society had a seemingly large number of affiliates (31), reading rooms (1,225), fire companies (119), and student dormitories (8), but this tells us little about its actual assets. Only very few of the buildings used in Kachkovs'kyi-related

45 *Halychanyn*, September 7, 1905, pp. 1–2 and October 1, 1909, p. 2.
46 Monchalovskii, *Pamiatnaia knyzhka*, pp. 105–112; OMK annual report for 1911–1912 in *Halychanyn*, September 21, 1912, p. 2. The Prosvita Society claimed during the same period (1910) 2,376 reading rooms. Volodymyr Doroshenko, *'Prosvita': ïï zasnuvannia i pratsia* (Philadelphia, 1959), p. 24.
47 The student dormitories were operated by Kachkovs'kyi Society affiliates in Brody, Drohobych, Kaminka Strumylova, Rava Rus'ka, Sambir, Stanyslaviv, Zhovkva, and Zolochiv. See the OMK annual report for 1909–1910 in *Halychanyn*, October 2, 1910, p. 2.

activities actually belonged to the society. In fact, the society's largest asset was the building for its central branch in L'viv, bought in 1904 after a decade-long fund-raising campaign and valued in 1912 at 183,170 crowns. The society also owned two houses in Brody, property in Sokal', and minor undeveloped land in a few villages, all of which were bequests to the society by members who had died.[48] Whether or not the Kachkovs'kyi Society actually owned the buildings and settings that used its name, it was nonetheless able through its publication program, annual conventions, agricultural programs, volunteer fire departments, reading rooms, and student dormitories to achieve in large measure its basic goal of raising the cultural level, self-esteem, and, in part, economic capacity of the Ukrainians in Galicia.

The Evolution and Ideology of the Kachkovs'kyi Society

One way to trace the evolution of a self-supporting organization such as the Kachkovs'kyi Society is to look at the growth of its membership. To be sure, figures on membership, such as those recording the number of reading rooms, need to be treated with caution. Nonetheless, they provide at least some idea of the relative fluctuation in the society's fortunes.

The expectations of the society's founder, Naumovych, who used as his model the numerically strong Slovene St. Hermagoras Society, proved to be overly optimistic. The original plan in 1874 (confirmed by the large print runs of the first four publications) was for the Kachkovs'kyi Society to have 10,000 members after the first year.[49] After one year, however, only 1,439 members were registered. In fact, the 10,000 figure for active dues-paying members was not attained until thirty-six years later, when in 1910 the society reached its highest point, recording 10,700 members (see Appendix 8.5). Nonetheless, until the outset of the twentieth century, the Kachkovs'kyi Society was to be the largest Galician-Ukrainian cultural society, having a total of 25,422 members registered at one time or another between 1874 and 1912. Its closest rival, the six-years-older Prosvita Society, caught up in membership numbers for a given year only in 1905–1906, after which it became the

---

48 Figures on all property (valued at 212,234 crowns in 1912) are from the OMK annual report for 1911-1912 in *Halychanyn*, September 24, 1912, p. 2.

    The three-story building with two facades at 14 Valova Street in the center of L'viv was purchased on March 24, 1904, for 166,000 crowns, of which 71,983 were collected during a building-fund campaign, the remainder being paid by two mortgages (20,000 and 94,016). See the OMK annual report for 1903–1904 in *Halychanyn*, September 9, 1904, pp. 1–2.

49 *Slovo*, August 10 (22), 1874, p. 1.

larger of the two both in current members and in total members during the entire history of the organization.[50]

More interesting is the social composition of the Kachkovs'kyi Society. The organization was successful in its goal to reach the rural masses of Galicia, since the majority of its members at any one time was always made up of peasants. Although we do not have access to membership rolls (which may or may not have indicated social status), we do have data on new members from 1884–1885 and 1890–1891 according to social status.[51]

	Total	Priests	Teachers/ Civil Servants	Townspeople	Peasants	Organizations
1884–85	392	20	49	39	180	104
1890–91	858	40	46	–	734	38

It is clear for each of these two representative years that peasants formed by far the largest number of new members. Moreover, the respective percentages of

50 Most of the literature that mentions in passing or that deals specifically with the Prosvita Society claims it had always been much larger (in terms of membership) than the Kachkovs'kyi Society. Such claims are invalid, since they are based on the practice of citing for any given year all members that had ever belonged to Prosvita (including deceased or former members) since its establishment in 1868. For instance, *Ukraine: A Concise Encyclopedia*, Vol. II, ed. Volodymyr Kubijovyč (Toronto, 1971), p. 337, claims 19,000 Prosvita members in 1905, when in fact there were only about half that number, or 8,500. The important distinction between all-time totals and membership in a given year is made in the first important historical survey of the Prosvita Society, which for 1908 shows an all-time total of 23,164 members as well as the "real number of members" in that year—about half, or 12,000. That same year Prosvita claimed 2,043 reading rooms. Lozyns'kyi, *Sorok lit*, pp. 36 and 47. The closest comparative figures for both organizations are from 1906:

	Kachkovs'kyi	Prosvita
Total members	19,710	20,085
Members in 1906	9,229	10,000
Reading rooms	1,261	1,693
Affiliates	26	39

51 The statistics are drawn from the OMK annual reports for 1884–1885, in *Slovo*, November 23, 1885; and for 1890–1891, in *Russkoe slovo*, II, 34 (L'viv, 1891), p. 4.

peasant membership—45.9 percent in 1884–1885 and 87.2 percent in 1890–1891—should be considered the minimum, since most of the new members listed under "organizations" were reading rooms located in villages and made up almost exclusively of peasants.

Although we have no concrete data on women members, we do know that the Kachkovs'kyi Society included them. Already at the second annual convention in 1875 the question of women members was discussed as "a matter of great importance," because "it is from the breast of the mother that the child begins to learn how to love its homeland and Rus' mother tongue."[52] Women were frequent speakers at the annual conventions and affiliate meetings, although it was not until 1910 that a woman (Mariia Koliankivs'ka, the wife of a *gymnasium* director) became a member of the central committee in L'viv. We also know that, during the 1909–1910 campaign to collect funds for the Kachkovs'kyi Society, thirty-three of the forty-four districts in Galicia included women donors, and that in several districts women formed a majority or plurality of those who gave.[53]

The role of the priests and the attitude of the Kachkovs'kyi Society toward them was more problematic. Much of the literature on Galicia in the late nineteenth century frequently describes the Kachkovs'kyi Society as one of many in which priests played a dominant role. In certain affiliates, priests were indeed prominent. Frequently, however, members spoke out against the upper classes and clergy, especially the hierarchy, who unlike "in the good old days" did not participate in or support the Kachkovs'kyi Society.[54]

Beyond the realm of impressions, it should be noted that priests played a very small role in the leadership and operation of the organization. Of the five chairmen between 1874 and 1914 (see Appendix 8.3), two were priests (the founder Ivan Naumovych and the Reverend Feofil Pavlykov), but they headed the organization for only seven of the forty years during this period. Moreover, no priest ever held the influential posts of secretary or treasurer, and at any one

52 Cited from a report on the second annual convention, "Zahal'noe sobranie OMK v Halychy," *Russkaia rada*, V, 16 (Kolomyia, 1875), p. 132.

53 A full list of the names of donors appears as a supplement to issue 207 of *Halychanyn*, September 29, 1910.

54 Cited from the invitation to the eighteenth annual convention in Ternopil', *Russkoe slovo*, I, 30 (L'viv, 1890), pp. 2–3. The good old days referred primarily to 1848–1849, when the head of the Supreme Ruthenian Council was under the leadership of the Greek Catholic metropolitan, Hryhorii Iakhymovych, and Canon Mykhailo Kuzems'kyi. In their concern with the political and cultural needs of the population, they were contrasted to the ostensibly more passive church leadership and clerical rank-and-file of the 1870s and 1880s, who "are indifferent to the important matter of popular culture and education." Cited from a letter from Drohobych in *Slovo*, June 3, 1880, p. 1.

time, out of twelve members on the central committee, only two, at most, were priests. Thus, in terms of its membership and leadership, the Kachkovs'kyi Society remained, from its foundation in 1874 down to World War I, a peasant-based organization led by a secular intelligentsia who for the most part were journalists, teachers, and most especially lawyers or court officers.

A glance at the yearly membership statistics (Appendix 8.5) shows that after getting off to a slow but steady growth pattern, the Kachkovs'kyi Society began to decline in the late 1870s, reaching a low point in 1884. Thereafter, it began slowly to recover until the late 1890s, when it finally reached the level of membership it had had twenty years earlier. From then on there was a steady increase in membership until 1910, after which a leveling-off occurred. The reason for these fluctuations had to do with internal policy of the Kachkovs'kyi Society as well as external events.

After the initial establishment and flush of enthusiasm had passed, members began to criticize the Kachkovs'kyi Society for doing little other than publishing books—which was, of course, one of its main goals.[55] Moreover, continual reports in the late 1870s suggested that the dozen or so affiliates were, with few exceptions, doing little. True, successful agricultural exhibits were organized at the 1879 and 1880 annual conventions, but these, it was argued, had a limited effect on the vast majority of Galician-Ukrainian peasants.

Then, in 1882, came the widely publicized trial in L'viv against eleven Austrian-Rus' leaders suspected of conspiring with the Russian Empire to commit treason against Austria.[56] Among the accused were the founding and second chairmen of the Kachkovs'kyi Society, the Reverend Ivan Naumovych and Viktor M. Ploshchans'kyi (1834–1902). Even though they and the other accused were acquitted, both soon emigrated to the Russian Empire. Back home in Galicia, however, the damage was done. The Kachkovs'kyi Society and its

---

55 The early criticism that "only books were being published," *Russkaia rada*, IX, 1 (Kolomyia, 1879), p. 4, was still being reiterated two decades later: "The booklets, it is true, are with few exceptions quite good, but we consider this to be little more than editorial work which any talented person could accomplish and without, moreover, the need for a central branch and numerous affiliates." From the speech of a member at the twenty-third annual convention in Drohobych, cited in *Russkaia rada*, XXVI, 12 (Kolomyia, 1897), p. 89.

56 Actually, the two main defendants were the Subcarpathian Rusyn political leader Adol'f Dobrians'kyi and his daughter, Ol'ga Grabar (mother of the distinguished twentieth-century Soviet art historian Igor Grabar), who were living in L'viv because of the pressure against them for their political activity in Hungary. "Protses rusynov v sudî karnom v L'vovî: akt obzhalovania," *Russkaia rada*, XII, 12 (Kolomyia, 1882), pp. 34–37.

leaders—in particular its founder, Naumovych, to whom unlimited praise was always given—were suspected of being agents and part of a front organization for the anti-Austrian interests of the Russian Empire in Galicia. Loyal pro-Habsburg peasants stopped paying their dues, and the tenth annual convention held in L'viv after the close of the trial in 1882 was able to attract barely 160 participants.[57]

In short, by the 1880s, the Kachkovs'kyi Society had few friends. The provincial diet and Polish-dominated administration, which had always been reluctant to relinquish any funds to Rus'-Ukrainian organizations, was certainly not about to do so for those suspected of antistate activity. Analogously, the Austrian government in Vienna remained increasingly suspicious of any movement that would enhance the interests of its Russian imperial rival in the East, while the new metropolitan of the Greek Catholic church, Syl'vester Cardinal Sembratovych (1836–1898, consecrated 1885), was not about to make the mistake of his predecessor and tolerate, let alone support, the activity of the "suspicious" Kachkovs'kyi Society.[58] Finally, local populist-Ukrainophile activists (narodovtsi), who had always been opposed to the Kachkovs'kyi Society on ideological grounds, began in the 1880s to step up their attacks.

In such circumstances, the Kachkovs'kyi Society had only a few members in the Galician Diet and in Vienna's imperial parliament of the Old Ruthenian political persuasion who were still willing to speak up on behalf of the organization. But there was never any real hope of government support. For instance, while the Prosvita Society received a subsidy each year from the Galician provincial government (2,000 crowns between 1870–1876 and 1884–1907, then progressively 6,000 and 8,000 crowns),[59] the Kachkovs'kyi Society was refused every time it made a request. Finally, in 1910 it received its first grant of 9,000 crowns, and another in 1911 of 6,000 crowns, specifically for economic-

---

57   *Slovo*, August 21, 1882, p. 1; *Russkaia rada*, XII, 16–17 (Kolomyia, 1882), p. 122. The negative impact of the 1882 trial on the Kachkovs'kyi Society was still being written about years later. N. Holovka, "O obshchestvî Kachkovskoho," *Russkoe slovo*, I, 25 (L'viv, 1890), pp. 4–5. For the contemporary Polish Catholic view, which considered the OMK and its publications dangerous and religiously "schismatic," see "Towarzystwo ruskie imienia Kaczkowskiego," *Przegląd Kościelny*, X, 2 (Poznań, 1888), pp. 786–788.

58   In effect, Cardinal Sembratovych's predecessor (and relative), Metropolitan Iosyf Sembratovych, was forced out of office in 1882 because of the treason trial. For criticism of Metropolitan Syl'vester Cardinal Sembratovych and the Polish viceroy of Galicia, Count Casimir Badeni, as the cause of the sad fate of the Kachkovs'kyi Society at the end of the nineteenth century, see *Russkoe slovo*, September 13, 1901, p. 1.

59   Lozyns'kyi, *Sorok lït*, pp. 62–64.

related activity. Subsequent grants were dependent on the organization's ability to prove its ideological loyalty to Austria.[60]

Friction between the governmental authorities and fellow populist-Ukrainians took several forms. During the so-called New Era of the early 1890s, when efforts were made to bring the Poles and Ukrainians closer together through political compromise, the Galician viceroy singled out in a speech to the diet in 1892 the government's need to be vigilant in the face of the suspect Kachkovs'kyi Society. The viceroy couched his suspicions in terms of concern about the specter of an Orthodox threat from the Russian east: "We cannot be indifferent when a society, in which we see Catholic priests, publishes books which on the first page include well-known figures who have left the faith for the great schism."[61] That same year, the society's annual almanac was confiscated, and two years later the 1894 almanac was threatened with the same fate because a spot was ostensibly found on the eye of a portrait of the emperor that appeared in the volume.[62] Then in 1911, the society was forbidden, in the interests of public order, from holding its thirty-seventh annual convention out of doors in L'viv, while two years later the planned thirty-ninth annual convention was banned entirely (just one week before delegates were to arrive) on the grounds that there was a cholera epidemic in the province.[63]

It is interesting to note that initially there were normal and even friendly relations with the populist Ukrainians. The future socialist politician Mykhailo Pavlyk attended the founding and second annual conventions of the

---

60 The grant figures are taken from the society's annual report for 1910–1911 in *Halychanyn*, September 27, 1911, p. 2. As for proving ideological loyalty, the Kachkovs'kyi Society could receive future publication grants in the amount of 9,000 crowns annually only if its booklets appeared in the local Galician-Ukrainian language, and specifically not in Russian. From the society's 1912–1913 annual report in *Golos naroda*, October 3, 1913, pp. 4–5.

61 The viceroy's reference was obviously to Naumovych and his conversion to Orthodoxy. In response, the Kachkovs'kyi Society's chairman and secretary issued an official statement praising their founder's cultural work but disavowing his "political activity" and Orthodox conversion. B.A. Didytskii and I.N. Pelekh, "Otvît na napast'," *Russkoe slovo*, III, 29 (L'viv, 1892), p. 1–2.

62 The pedantic concern with detail on the part of the local Austrian authorities in this incident has all the makings of a ridiculous plot for a Viennese operetta. The incident was brought to the provincial criminal courts; only seventeen issues were found to have the "spot"; concern was still high for the seventeen peasants who had the "seditious" material; in the end, the court annulled the confiscation order. The details of the saga of the spotted almanacs are provided in "Snesenŷ konfyskatŷ kalendaria OMK," *Russkoe slovo*, V, 20 (L'viv, 1894), pp. 1–2, and "Ôtozva do chlenôv OMK," *Russkoe slovo*, V, 27, pp. 3–4.

63 "Narodnŷi prazdnyk," *Russkoe slovo*, October 5, 1911, p. 1; "Obshchoho sobraniia chlenôv OMK ne bude!," *Golos naroda*, September 24, 1913, p. 1.

Kachkovs'kyi Society, where he proposed that it publish the Bible in the Galician vernacular. Pavlyk's proposal was turned down, and in general he and other younger figures such as Ivan Franko, who once called the Kachkovs'kyi Society "the most important organization for raising the material standards of the people," became alienated from it because they were kept out of leadership roles and because of their own change to a populist-Ukrainian national orientation under the impact of Drahomanov.[64] Nonetheless, the Kachkovs'kyi Society did welcome the creation of the Ukrainian Radical party in 1890, in which Pavlyk and Franko played leading roles.[65]

As for the Ukrainophile Prosvita Society, it was for the longest time considered not a rival but rather a partner in the common goal of educating the Galician-Rus' people. Thus, at its founding in 1874, the influential populist-Ukrainian journal *Pravda* commented that the "newly established [Kachkovs'kyi] Society should attract support among every patriotic Rusyn,"[66] while as late as 1892, the Kachkovs'kyi Society welcomed the creation of Prosvita affiliates which might attract "new members from among those peasants, teachers, and civil servants who—only God knows why—might be afraid to belong to the Kachkovs'kyi Society."[67]

By the first decade of the twentieth century, however, friction replaced mutual tolerance. In 1908, the influential Ukrainian daily newspaper *Dilo* accused the Kachkovs'kyi Society of being an "agent of Moscow,"[68] and from 1906 on, when all but two of its annual conventions were held in L'viv, Ukrainian students tried to disrupt what they called "Muscovite" meetings, either by heckling speakers and throwing stones or by attacking the building of the society's central branch.[69]

---

64 Ivan Franko, "Kil'ka sliv o tim, iak uporiadkuvaty i provadyty nashi liudovi vydavnytstva" (1882), in his *Tvory*, Vol. XIX (Kiev, 1956), p. 24. On the rejection of the younger populists from the Kachkovs'kyi Society, see *Russkaia rada*, V, 17 (Kolomyia, 1875), pp. 131–133; and *Pravda*, IX, 16 (L'viv, 1876), pp. 635–638.
65 "Kol'ko slôv o t.z. 'radykalakh'," *Russkoe slovo*, V, 50 (L'viv, 1894), pp. 2–5.
66 *Pravda*, VII, 13 (L'viv, 1874), p. 568.
67 *Russkoe slovo*, III, 27 (L'viv, 1892), p. 7.
68 "Diial'nist' tovarystva im. Kachkovs'koho," *Dilo*, September 24, 1908, p.1, and September 25, 1908, p. 2. According to a Prosvita Society activist, the populist-Ukrainophile view was that the Kachkovs'kyi Society did positive work, especially in producing popular publications, until the 1890s, after which it began to publish in an artificial language that no one could understand. Cf. Ivan Bryk, "Korotkyi ohliad ukraïns'koï populiarnoï lïteratury v Halychynï," in Ivan Bryk and Mykhailo Kotsiuba, eds., *Pershyi ukraïns'kyi pros'vitno-ekonomichnyi kongres uladzhenyi Tovarystvom 'Pros'vita' u L'vovi ... 1909 roku: protokoly i referaty* (L'viv, 1910), pp. 116–117.
69 See the reports on the 1907, 1911, and 1912 annual conventions in *Russkoe slovo*, XVIII, 36 (L'viv, 1907), pp. 1–2; XXII, 41 (1911), pp. 1–3; and XXIII, 25 (1912), pp. 2–3. The

As a result of the prewar international tension between Russia and Austria and the increasing intolerance of local Ukrainians toward what had become "Muscovite" enemies (Old Ruthenians as well as Russophiles) in their midst, the Kachkovs'kyi Society began what seemed to be a period of new decline. It was reported that as many as five society-sponsored student dormitories (in Chortkiv, Kaminka Strumylova, Rava Rus'ka, Zhovkva, and Zolochiv) had been closed by the Austrian authorities, while "long-standing members were asking the central committee to remove their names, albeit temporarily, from the membership rolls and not to send them publications."[70] Moreover, the talk of war and mobilization made it impossible to send agricultural students to Bohemia or to organize other courses in Galicia as had been done in the past. Thus, even before the outbreak of World War I in August 1914, the future of the Kachkovs'kyi Society seemed in doubt, prompting its central committee to issue a declaration in which it stated flatly that "our society is being threatened with closure."[71]

But why was the society on the decline once again, and why did it become the focus of attack on the part of the Austrian central government, the Polish-dominated provincial Galician administration, and local Ukrainophiles? In large part, the reasons have to do with the group's national ideology.

In essence, the Kachkovs'kyi Society was an ideological child of the so-called Old Ruthenian (*starorusyny*) movement in Galician-Ukrainian society, whose main characteristic could be described as wanting to maintain the status quo. Whereas such a position would seem ideal for the ruling Austrian authorities, it in effect proved to be dangerous in a Galician environment in which both Poles and populist Ukrainians were continually pushing for changes that would enhance their own political status in local affairs and perhaps someday even lead to political independence. The Old Ruthenians, most of whom were in leadership positions in the Kachkovs'kyi Society (Bohdan Didyts'kyi, Pylyp Svystun, Osyp A. Markov, Osyp Monchalovs'kyi), were certainly united on one issue—opposition to what they considered Polish political and cultural infiltration and dominance over historically Rus' (eastern) Galicia.[72]

In that regard, the only seeming ally of the Old Ruthenians was the Austrian Habsburg throne, which in the past had protected them (and ostensibly would

attack on the Kachkovs'kyi Society in L'viv occurred in November 1912 and caused about 300 crowns in damages. See the annual report for 1912–1913 in *Golos naroda*, September 24, 1913, pp. 5–6.

70   Ibid.
71   "Pros'ba k chlenam OMK," *Russkaia rada*, XLI, 2 (Kolomyia, 1912), p. 1.
72   For details on the Old Ruthenian movement, see above, chapter 7.

continue to do so) from the inroads of Polish aristocratic and bureaucratic rule and its corollary the Roman Catholic church. Within such a constellation, it was not difficult to understand why at Kachkovs'kyi Society meetings speakers would with great sincerity refer to the eighteenth-century Empress Maria Theresa (during whose reign Galicia had become part of Austria) as a "second Moses" who had liberated the Galician-Rus' people after 432 years of "Polish-Egyptian" slavery,[73] or would declare that if ever they needed to "send a delegation to the monarch [Franz Joseph], he for certain would not reject our demands and presentations."[74] Thus, pro-Austrian loyalty directed toward the Habsburg emperor, for which Galicia's Rus'-Ukrainians had become proverbially known as the "Tyroleans of the East," was to remain a basic ingredient of Kachkovs'kyi Society political ideology.[75]

The other ingredient of Old Ruthenianism was cultural, although enemies of the Kachkovs'kyi Society would argue that this, too, was political in nature. The issue was the idea of the unity of Rus'. Without going into details, the Old Ruthenian ideology of the Kachkovs'kyi Society argued that all the Rus' (*russkyi*) people—the Great Rus', White Rus', and Little Rus', or to use modern terminology, Russians, Belorusans, and Ukrainians—were equal descendants of the common heritage of medieval Kievan Rus'. Indeed, such a view coincided with the contemporary Russian understanding of Pan-Slavism and with the official policy of the tsarist government, providing the latter with ideological legitimacy for claims to Austro-Hungarian historic Rus' lands (eastern Galicia, northern Bukovina, and Subcarpathian Rus'). The Galician Old Ruthenians did not wish, however, to be ruled by the tsarist Russian Empire. They considered their relationship to the so-called common-Rus' East solely in cultural terms that were analogous to the situation of Austria's German speakers, who were culturally and linguistically related to the Germanic world without being politically subordinate to the German Empire.[76]

The living symbol of Old Ruthenian cultural unity with "Holy Rus' " (*Sviataia Rus'*) was language—not, however, the vernacular of the peasant

---

73 From a speech at a meeting of the Sokal' affiliate, cited in "Zahal'noe sobranie chlenôv fyliy OMK v Sokaly," *Russkaia rada*, IX, 12–13 (Kolomyia, 1879), p. 92.

74 From a speech at the 1892 annual meeting, cited in "Sobranie chlenôv OMK," *Russkoe slovo*, III, 35 (L'viv, 1892), p. 3.

75 On the dominant monarchical tendencies in Galician-Rus' society, see John-Paul Himka, "Hope in the Tsar: Displaced Naive Monarchism among the Ukrainian Peasants of the Habsburg Empire," *Russian History*, VII, 1–2 (Tempe, Ariz., 1980), pp. 125–138; and above, chapters 4 and 5.

76 The best introduction to Old Ruthenian ideology is found in O.A. Monchalovskii, *Sviataia Rus'* (L'viv, 1903).

masses (which they would admit was differentiated into at least three distinct languages or "dialects": Russian, Belorusan, and Ukrainian), but the traditional *russkyi* book language used since time immemorial in church books in Galicia and, of course, in the publications of the Kachkovs'kyi Society. Thus, as is typical of the early stages of many national movements, the medium or form of the language—in this case the etymological alphabet and important-sounding words drawn from Church Slavonic—became more important than the message, especially since the medium somehow conveyed a sense of unity with an eastern Rus' culture that had the prestige of several centuries of history. In the words of one Kachkovs'kyi Society member: "Our people have the greatest respect for the book language in which our church books and Holy Liturgy are written. ... That language, which our patriotic forefathers wrote and still write since time immemorial, is called 'Muscovite' by the Ukrainophile populists. Our people, however, know nothing and do not wish to know anything about such things, because for them there is only one Rus' language. ... The realization of the unity of Rus' has always lived and still lives in the hearts of our people."[77] Indeed, prestige and dignity became in themselves prime commodities for an intelligentsia who had an ingrained sense of inferiority and who felt that they had to stand up to the more "prestigious" Polish culture in the context of an Austrian provincial environment.

It was this sense of looking to the past, of depending upon it as a crutch for existing in the present, that was at the heart of the Kachkovs'kyi Society's national ideology, summed up so well in 1891 by its long-time chairman Bohdan Didyts'kyi (1827–1908):

> We call ourselves Old Rus', and that name comes from the fact that we fervently stand by those beginnings which our ancestors gave to us, in particular our own saint and equal to the apostles, Prince Vladimir, with whom our ancestors accepted sacred Christianity and our Slavonic-Rus' rite and Rus' alphabet as well. We are proud that they call us Old Rus' [*starorusyny*], because we stand by our olden beginnings and wish to remain in union with our church which has existed for a thousand years.[78]

In a late-nineteenth-century environment in which new ideas and movements (nationalism, socialism, Zionism, Marxism) found fertile ground in

---

77 From a speech by Vasyl' Kurdydyk at a meeting of the Ternopil' affiliate of the
  Kachkovs'kyi Society, cited in *Russkoe slovo*, VI, 24 and 25 (L'viv, 1895), p. 3 and p. 2.
78 From the speech of Chairman Didyts'kyi at the society's 1891 annual convention, cited in
  Russkoe slovo, II, 35 (L'viv, 1891), p. 2.

Galicia, Old Ruthenian spokespersons such as Didyts'kyi, whose own culture was still not fully respected, came to have an almost pathological fear of change. This was summed up poignantly in a speech on the meaning of the society by Osyp A. Markov (1849–1909), a long-time member of its central committee: "The Kachkovs'kyi Society wants that Rus' will always remain Rus', that our people will not lose one inch of its land, nor one letter from its alphabet, nor one prayer from its church."[79]

It is interesting that a few of the rival Ukrainophile national leaders in Galicia, among them the president of the Shevchenko Scientific Society, Mykhailo S. Hrushevs'kyi, respected the Old Ruthenian position and even called for greater cooperation with its representatives.[80] Hrushevs'kyi was an exception, however; most Ukrainophile leaders saw the Old Ruthenians and the Kachkovs'kyi Society as a Muscovite fifth column to be exorcised from their Galician midst.[81]

The final irony is that when, at the outset of the twentieth century, a few younger Galician politicians (Dmytro Markov, Volodymyr Dudykevych, Ivan Hrynevets'kyi) and newspaper editors (*Pridkarpatskaia Rus'*, *Golos naroda*) began to take what could be considered a classic Russophile position that favored the incorporation of Galicia into the Russian Empire and the adoption of standard literary Russian language for publications and education, the Kachkovs'kyi Society found it as difficult to deal with them as with the Ukrainian populists.[82] Therefore, it is not surprising that, with the outbreak of World War I and the rapid advance of tsarist Russian forces into Galicia in August 1914, the Kachkovs'kyi Society, like the Prosvita Society and other Ukrainian organizations, ceased functioning. In 1919, the Kachkovs'kyi Society was able to renew its activity; however, in the completely changed postwar political circumstances of Polish rule and with the ascendancy of the Ukrainian na-

---

79 O. Markov, "Chomu OMK mae dlia nas znachenie?," *Russkoe slovo*, IX, 44 (L'viv, 1898), p. 2.

80 See above, note 10.

81 A typical Ukrainophile view was expressed by Lon'gyn Tsehel's'kyi. He recognized that the "old Muscophiles [Old Ruthenians] de facto led a Ukrainian cultural life and expressed de facto the Ukrainian national position with regard to the Poles" (p. 402), but nonetheless argued that the whole movement was a pathological phenomenon in Galician-Ukrainian society. See his "Halyts'ke moskvofil'stvo v ostannii ioho fazi," *Literaturno-naukovyi vistnyk*, L (L'viv and Kiev, 1910), pp. 389–406.

82 See the negative views toward the Russophiles expressed by the chairman of the Kachkovs'kyi Society and prominent Old Ruthenian Bohdan Didyts'kyi, "Svoezhyt'evyy zapysky," pt. 2, *Vistnyk `Narodnoho Doma'*, XXVI, 3 (L'viv, 1908), pp. 50–54.

tional ideology, it was merely marking time until its final demise with the entry of Soviet troops into Galicia in September 1939.[83]

Conclusion

Despite such ominous signs on the eve of World War I, until that time the Kachkovs'kyi Society, during its four decades of existence under Austrian rule, succeeded in achieving its basic goal: to serve as a publisher of popular books intended to raise the educational, moral, and civic culture of the Rus'/Ukrainian population in Galicia. It was also partially successful in the more practical tasks of publication and instruction in agricultural matters for the rural population.

On the other hand, its ideology of looking backward and promoting the idea of Rus' cultural unity was eclipsed by that of the rival Prosvita Society and the Ukrainian national movement. The reason for the Kachkovs'kyi Society's failure can perhaps be found in its inability to develop and promote elements of higher culture rooted in the local Galician environment. For instance, while Prosvita and other Ukrainian cultural societies were promoting critical and scholarly publications, theatrical life, and the works of writers such as Ivan Franko, the Kachkovs'kyi Society sought its models of high culture in the works of Tolstoi, Pushkin, and other Russian writers who were culturally as well as linguistically distant from the local Galician-Rus'/Ukrainian environment.

The question of the degree to which higher forms of cultural endeavor can be divorced from the environment in which they are promoted is one that had faced the Galician intelligentsia throughout the whole period of the Ukrainian national revival between 1848 and 1914. In an effort to attain cultural prestige and self-confidence by associating with an undifferentiated historic East Slavic East, it seems that the Kachkovs'kyi Society (and the Old Ruthenian orientation it represented) went too far, thereby eventually alienating itself from the very population it had hoped to serve.

---

83 If the literature on the pre-World War I years of the Kachkovs'kyi Society is limited, that on the interwar period is virtually nonexistent.

Appendix 8.1
Statute of the Mykhail Kachkovs'ky Society*

СТАТУТЫ
ОБЩЕСТВА ИМЕНИ МИХАИЛА КАЧКОВСКОГО
въ КОЛОМЫѢ.

———

I. Назва и цѣль общества, его мѣстопребываніе и печать.

§. 1.

Общество имени „Михаила Качковского" вызначило собѣ задачу: розпространеніе наукъ, обычайности, трудолюбія, трезерезости и ощадности, гражданского сознанія и всякихъ честнотъ межи русскимъ народомъ въ Австріи.

Головнымъ мѣсто-пребываніемъ того общества и его выдѣла есть городъ Коломыя.

Общество тое употребляе печатки съ надписію: Общество „Михаила Качковского" въ Коломыѣ.

II. Средства общества.

§. 2.

Для достиженія задачи общества служатъ слѣдующіи средства:

а) издаванье популярныхъ и поучительныхъ, а дешевыхъ книжокъ религійно-обычайного, наукового, господарского и забавного содержанія;

б) основаніе читальней;

в) публичніи отчиты;

г) основаніе обществъ трезерезости;

д) основаніе громадскихъ позычковыхъ касъ и сыпбовъ збожа;

е) основаніе обществъ рукодѣльникбвъ.

§. 3.

Выдатки общества покрываются: вносами членбвъ, доброволь-

*Source: *Nauka*, IV (Kolomyia, 1875), pp.54–62.

нымн датками и жертвами, завѣщаніями н легатами якъ и приходами взыскуемыми изъ розпродажи книжокъ обществомъ издаваныхъ.

§. 4.

Весь мастокъ общества выказуе ннвентарь.

Маеткомъ орудуе ся такъ, щобы крбмъ покрытья текущихъ выдаткбвъ, основано фондъ коренный.

III. Составъ общества.

§. 5.

Общество состоитъ изъ членбвъ дѣйствительныхъ и почетныхъ.

§ (...).

Дѣйствительнымъ членомъ стаеся кождый австрійскій обыватель русской народности, который объявитъ свою волю, причинятись въ пользу общества грошевымъ даткомъ или другимъ якимъ способомъ на пр. трудомъ литературнымъ, и выдѣломъ общества буде принятый въ члены.

§. 7.

Почетными членами именуе общое собраніе общества лица, извѣстныи изъ чоловѣко- и народолюбія.

§. 8.

Особы допустившіи ся якого безчестного дѣла по карнымъ законамъ караемого, особенноже походящого изъ користолюбія, якъ и бтдаючіися неморальности или налогови піянства, не могутъ бути членами общества, а еслибы ними будучи попали въ подобный порокъ або противодѣйствовали цѣлямъ общества, рѣщеньемъ выдѣла изъ общества выключаются.

На случай отказанья приняитія въ члены общества или выключенья изъ того, служитъ оскорбленому право бтклика до общого собранія общества, которое жалобу рѣшае окончательно.

§. 9.

Также перестае бути членомъ кождый, кто съ уплатою датковою за два лѣта збстае въ заляглости п збставши до уплаты выдѣломъ упбмненый, въ теченіи 14 дней всеи заляглости не сложитъ.

IV. Обязанности членôвъ.

§. 10.

Каждый членъ дѣйствителный общества принимае слѣдующіи обязанности :

1. кождого года платити 1 зр. до касы общества;
2. старатися о позысканье новыхъ членôвъ для общества;
3. словомъ и дѣломъ заохочовати кождого до школьнои и всякои доброи и полезнои науки, якъ и подавати помôчь убогôй школьнôй молодежи.
4. неупотребляти нечемныхъ и поганыхъ слôвъ и проклонôвъ, и мерзкій звычай тотъ, где случится, искореняти.
5. словомъ и примѣромъ своимъ другихъ ôтъ піянства ôтводити и причинятися до основан'я обществъ воздержности (тверезости);
6. бути для всѣхъ добрымъ примѣромъ трудолюбія, порядка, чистоты, господарности и ощадности;
7. возбуджати и крѣпити въ народѣ почитаніе права и послушаніе законамъ;
8. старатись всѣми силами объ основаніи громадскихъ читалнеи, позысковати для нихъ якъ найбôльше членôвъ, и по возможности держати въ нихъ или слухати ôтчитôвъ о всякихъ полезныхъ рѣчахъ.
9. заложити у себе, если есть властителемъ грунту, школу садовины и роздавати или дешево продавати другимъ ублагороднену садовину — также старатися о обсадженье садовиною или хоть дикою деревиною дорôгъ и пустыхъ мѣстць.
10. старатися о заведеніе лучшои расы худобы, лучшихъ улісôвъ и роспространяти науку о раціональнôмъ веденію господарства, якъ о пôднесенье промысла — а тымъ самымъ, пособствовати добробытови народа.

V. Права членôвъ.

§. 11.

Кождый членъ дѣйствителный общества мае право :

1. при общихъ собраніяхъ забирати голосъ, ставляти внесенія, захвалювати къ именованію почетныхъ членôвъ, голосовати при выборахъ предсѣдателя общого собранія якъ и поодинокихъ секцій того собранія, дальше при выборѣ предсѣдателя и чле-

нôвъ выдѣла, наконецъ при ухвалахъ общого Собранія и вгля-
дати въ всѣ акта общому собранію предложеніи.

2. бути избраннымъ въ члены Предсѣдательства и выдѣла.

3. являтися на засѣданія выдѣла съ голосомъ совѣтующимъ, если
не есть членомъ выдѣла — або подавати до выдѣла внесенія
на письмѣ.

4. изъ всѣхъ книжокъ, обществомъ изданыхъ получати даромъ
по одному ексемпляру.

§. 12.

Кождый членъ получае ôтъ выдѣла грамоту принятія въ члены,
котора его яко члена легитимуе и управляе его до вступу на общое собраніе, на засѣданія выдѣла, якъ и на ôтчиты въ читальняхъ.

§. 1?.

Членъ почетный мае право до вступу на общіи собранія и засѣданія выдѣла, но не мае права забирати тутъ голосъ. Ему служитъ право посѣщати читальни и держати тутъ ôтчиты.

§. 14.

Списъ всѣхъ членôвъ удержуе выдѣлъ въ точнôй зримости и
оголошуе всякіи въ томже послѣдовавшіи змѣны въ способъ въ §. 30.
означеный.

§. 15.

Всѣми дѣлами общества управляютъ: общое собраніе и выдѣлъ.

А. Общое собраніе.

§. 16.

Общое собраніе ôтбувае ся по правилу разъ въ годъ и то о
скôлько возможно, въ день 8 (20) августа, яко въ день смерти б. п.
Михаила Качковского, а по обстоятельствамъ кождого року въ ин-
номъ мѣстци.

Коли 50 членôвъ того зажадаютъ или обстоятельства того тре-
бовати будутъ, долженъ выдѣлъ скликати надпорядочное общое собраніе.

§. 17.

Скликанье общого собранія должно дѣятись посредствомъ русскихъ красвыхъ часописей или особными листами и то четыри (4)

недѣли напередъ, въ наглыхъ же случаяхъ можна той речинецъ скоротити до 14 дней.

§. 18.

Общое собраніе проглашае предсѣдатель выдѣла що есть отворене, скоро явилось на тое 50 членовъ дѣйствительныхъ.

Онъ розпочинае дѣйствіе общого собранія короткою промовою и взывае, щобы собравшіися члены избрали предсѣдателя общого собранія, заступника предсѣдателя и двохъ секретарёвъ.

§. 19.

Выдѣлъ здае справу зъ веденія дѣлъ общества и предкладае счеты и внесенія.

Къ розсмотренію дѣлъ избирае собраніе потребне число комисій.

§. 20.

Общое собраніе ухваляе змѣну статутовъ общества, рѣшае внесенія, отклики и жалобы, именуе почетныхъ членовъ, избирае предсѣдателя выдѣла, тогоже членовъ и ихъ заступниковъ, заряжуе шконтра кассъ, склада книгъ и инныхъ засобовъ, удѣляе или отказуе абсолюторія выдѣлови, опредѣляе почетъ службы при выдѣлѣ якъ и платню или нагороду для поодинокихъ управненыхъ лиць и вообще розпоряжуе, якъ имѣніемъ общества оруловатися мае.

§. 21.

Общое собраніе ухвалюе важно абсолютнымъ большеньствомъ голосовъ присутствующихъ членовъ дѣйствительныхъ.

Предсѣдатель голосуе только при именованіи членовъ почетныхъ и при выборѣ выдѣла, въ прочемъ рѣшае при рôвности голосôвъ.

§ 22.

Якимъ способомъ голосоватися мае, т. е. чи поименно, картками, галками, черезъ аклямацію, пôднесеніе рукъ, повстаньс или черезъ сидженье, заряжае предсѣдатель.

Б. Выдѣлъ.

§. 23.

Выдѣлъ общества состоитъ изъ предсѣдателя, осьми (8) членôвъ и ихъ четырехъ (4) заступниковъ, всѣхъ общимъ собраніемъ избранныхъ.

Выдѣлъ же самъ избираетъ изъ посередъ себе мѣстопредсѣдателя и одного секретаря.

§. 24.

Мѣстопредсѣдатель заступае предсѣдателя отсутствуючого а заступникъ члена покликуеся, если который членъ есть перешкоджен҃ъ участвовати въ дѣлахъ выдѣла.

§. 25.

Выдѣлъ избираеся на одепъ годъ, онъ долженъ однакожь урядовати поти, поки новоизбранный выдѣлъ не отбере веденія дѣлъ общества.

Члены выдѣла могутъ быти поновно избранныи.

§. 26.

Кромѣ всѣхъ администраційныхъ дѣлъ общества належатъ до выдѣла: прпнятіе и выключеніе членовъ (§§. 6, 8.), оцѣнка рукописей до печатанья призначеныхъ, заключаніе уговора съ сочинителями взглядомъ выпагородъ, занятіеся печатаньемъ и розсылкою книгъ общества, веденіе касы общества, дальше оголошенія въ §§. 14, 17, 30, 34, 35, 36, паведеныи, потомъ надсмотръ читальней, также позамѣстцевыхъ, якъ и урядженье публичныхъ отчитовъ въ тыхже, также надсмотръ надъ обществами тверезости, громадскими позычковыми касами и ссыпами збожа якъ и надъ обществами рукодѣльникόвъ, наконецъ удѣлянье инструкцій всѣмъ отрослямъ общества.

§. 27.

Выдѣлъ ухвалюе важно, скоро кромѣ предсѣдателя (мѣстопредсѣдателя) собралося шесть (6) членόвъ или по крайной мѣрѣ три члены п три заступники членόвъ.

Секретарь всегда вчисляеся въ тое число.

Ухвалы выдѣла западаютъ абсолютною бόльшостію голосόвъ.

Предсѣдатель голосуе завсѣгды.

Голосованье отбуваеся явно или тайно (§. 22.) пόдля выбору и варяженія предсѣдателя.

§. 28.

Секретарь списуе всѣ ухвалы въ книгу выдѣла.

Кождый протоколъ якъ и всѣ письма и грамоты όтъ выдѣла выходящіи, пόдписуютъ предсѣдатели (мѣстопредсѣдатель) и секретарь.

Грамоты правнїй должнї кромѣ того содержати ссылку на ухвалу выдѣла и бути снабженыи вытисненіемъ печати общества.

§. 29.

Общество представляе на внѣ и заступае тоже передъ властями и судами предсѣдатель выдѣла — а въ его отсутсвію или перешкодѣ мѣстопредсѣдатель.

§. 30.

Состояніе касы съ всѣми сюда относящимися грамотами и квитами предкладае Выдѣлъ сжегодно общому собранію къ пересмотрови и одобренію и оголошус сумаричный выказъ касы въ русскихъ часописяхъ якъ и въ первой книжочцѣ изданой Обществомъ по отбытію кождократного общого собранія.

VII Читальнѣ.

§. 31.

Въ кождой мѣстцевости, въ котрой вписалося по крайной мѣрѣ 12 членовъ до общества, служитъ имъ право основати у себе читальню.

Въ той цѣли могутъ они возвати выдѣлъ общества къ содѣйствованю, которому также служитъ надзоръ основаной читальнѣ.

§. 32.

Кожда такая читальня получае даромъ по одному ексемпляру всѣхъ сочиненій обществомъ изданныхъ и на складѣ находящихся.

§. 33.

Члены общества маютъ свободный вступъ до читальнъ.

Зарядъ читальнѣ ухвалитъ, чи лица до Общества неналежащіи могутъ посѣщати читальню и подъ якими условіями.

§. 34.

Выдѣлъ общества якъ и зарядъ читальнѣ могутъ уряжати публичныи отчиты въ читальняхъ — и такъ одинъ якъ другіи о состояніи тѣхже подавати извѣстія до публичнои вѣдомости.

VIII. Общества тверезости.

§. 35.

Такъ выдѣлови общества якъ и поодинокимъ членамъ служитъ

право поспѣшествовати осипованію обществъ тверезости или воздержности.

Выдѣлъ провадитъ верховный надзоръ надъ ними и похвалы достойни событія подае до общой вѣдомости.

IX. Громадскіи пожичковыи касы и ссыпы збôжа.

§. 36.

За содѣйствіемъ выдѣла общества или членôвъ осипованыи пожичковыи касы или ссыпы збôжа въ поодинокихъ громадахъ удержуе выдѣлъ въ зримости и старася о періодичнôмъ обвѣщанію тыхже состоянія.

X. Общества рукодѣльникôвъ.

§. 37.

Выдѣлъ якъ и чоодинокіи члены общества должни улегчати сочленамъ-рукодѣльникамъ основаніе обществъ, маючихъ на цѣли спроваджуванье въ мѣсцевости, залишеныи въ промышленности, майстрôвъ и знатокôвъ — старатися о точное выученье ремеслъ черезъ поодинокихъ рукодѣльникôвъ якъ и о закупно потребныхъ матеріалôвъ гуртомъ.

XI. Розвязанье общества.

§. 38.

Тôлько общому собранію, къ той цѣли выразно скликаному, служитъ право ухвалити розвязанье общества.

Такую ухвалу якъ и опредѣленье, на якую общеполезную цѣль масся обернути все чистое имѣніе общества, становитъ общое собраніе важно, если по крайной мѣрѣ бôльшая половина дѣйствительныхъ членôвъ собранія и то три чвертины (³/₄) голосôвъ присутствуючихъ членôвъ дотычную ухвалу повзяла.

Еслибы же до такои ухвалы не прійшло, принадае все чистое имѣніе въ пользу русско-народного Института „Народный Дôмъ“ въ Львовѣ.

XII. Споры.

§. 39.

Всякого рода споры, изъ отношеній общества происходящіи

рѣшае окончательно и безъ всякого бтклика мировый судъ, въ составъ которого избирае кождая сторона по одному судіи, а тіи оба судіи избираютъ сверхника свого.

XIII. Переходныи опредѣленія.

§. 40.

Поки выдѣлъ общества не зостане по мысли §. 20. избранъ, комитетъ учредительный веде дѣла Выдѣлови препорученыи.

По затвержеиіи статутôвъ скличе комитетъ учредительный безпроволочно первое общое собраніе.

———

Appendix 8.2
Kachkovs'kyi Society Affiliates 1913*
(Names followed by parentheses refer to districts; all others are district centers.)

1. Brody
2. Buchach
3. Chortkiv
4. Drobromil'
5. Drohobych
6. Halych (Stanyslaviv)
7. Hrimno (Rudky)
8. Kalush
9. Kaminka Strumylova
10. Kolomyia
11. Krynica (Nowy S¹ cz)
12. Lisko
13. L'viv
14. Peremyshliany
15. Przemyśl
16. Rava Rus'ka
17. Rohatyn
18. Sambir
19. Sanok
20. Skalat
21. Sokal'

22. Stanyslaviv
23. Staryi Sambir (Sambir)
24. Stryi
25. Ternopil'
26. Turka
27. Ustryky Dolishni (Lisko)
28. Vysits'ko (Jaros»aw)
29. Zboriv
30. Zhovkva
31. Zolochiv

Other affiliates no longer existing in 1913
1. Berezhany
2. Hlyniany (Peremyshliany)
3. Iavoriv
4. Rudky
5. Sniatyn
6. Zhydachiv

*Source: *Russkaia nyva* (L'viv, 1913), p. 71.

Appendix 8.3
Kachkovs'kyi Society Chairmen and Secretaries

Chairmen		*Secretaries*	
1874–1877	Reverend Ivan Naumovych	1874–1878	Ivan E. Levyts'kyi
1877–1880	Vyktor M. Ploshchans'kyi	1876–1880	Fedir Olipnyk
1880–1884	Reverend Feofil Pavlykov	1878	Dmytro Vints'kovs'kyi
1884–1903	Bohdan Didyts'kyi	1879	F. Pleshkovych
1903–1914	Fylyp Svystun	1880–1882	Osyp A. Markov

(Secretaries continued)

1882–1884	Orest A. Avdykovs'kyi	1910–1912	Semen Bendasiuk
1884–1886	Osyp A. Monchalovs'kyi	1912–1914	Myron S. Zaiats'
1886–1910	Ivan N. Pelekh		

Appendix 8.4
Kachkovs'kyi Society Annual Conventions

1. Kolomyia	August 20, 1874	21. L'viv	September 18, 1894
2. Halych	August 24, 1875	22. Stanyslaviv	September 8, 1896
3. L'viv (extraordinary)	January 20, 1876	23. Drohobych	September 7, 1897
4. Stryi	August 22, 1876	24. Sambir	September 8, 1898
5. L'viv	September 20, 1877	25. L'viv	September 6, 1899
6. Przemyśl	August 20, 1878	26. Sanok	September 18, 1900
7. Stanyslaviv	September 11, 1879	27. Brody	September 12, 1901
8. Kolomyia	September 9, 1880	28. Sambir	September 16, 1902
9. Zolochiv	September 29, 1881	29. Przemyśl	September 29, 1903
10. L'viv	August 31, 1882	30. L'viv	September 8, 1904
11. Drohobych	September 18, 1883	31. Kolomyia	September 7, 1905
12. Ternopil'	September 29, 1884	32. L'viv	September 18, 1906
13. Sanok	September 8, 1885	33. Ternopil'	September 12, 1907
14. Brody	September 9, 1886	34. Jarosław	September 19, 1908
15. Kolomyia	September 8, 1887	35. L'viv	September 29, 1909
16. Drohobych	September 6, 1888	36. L'viv	September 29, 1910
17. Kalush	September 17, 1889	37. L'viv	September 29, 1911
18. Ternopil'	September 9, 1890	38. L'viv	September 24, 1912
19. L'viv	September 8, 1891	[39.L'viv	September 29, 1913]*
20. Stryi	September 8, 1892	*Convention cancelled because of cholera
[21.Stanyslaviv	September 12, 1893]*	epidemic.

Appendix 8.5
Kachkovs'kyi Society Membership

Members	Source and Date
1,439	*Russkaia rada*, V, 7 (Kolomyia, 1875), p. 50
2,600	*Slovo*, August 14, 1875, p. 1.
3,000	*Russkaia rada*, V, 18 (Kolomyia, 1875), p. 141.

Members	*Source and Date*
3,700	*Russkaia rada*, V, 24 (Kolomyia, 1875), p. 190.
3,562	*Russkaia rada*, VI, 1 (Kolomyia, 1876), p. 11.
6,000	*Russkaia rada*, VII, 11 (Kolomyia, 1877), p. 94.
over 5,000	*Slovo*, June 3, 1880, p. 1.
4,100	*Slovo*, September 24, 1881, p. 1.
3,500	*Slovo*, October 6, 1884, p. 1.
3,637	*Slovo*, November 23, 1885, p. 2.
5,000	*Russkaia rada*, XVIII, 15 (Kolomyia, 1888), p. 120.
4,136	*Russkaia rada*, XX, 17 (Kolomyia, 1890), p. 110; *Russkoe slovo*, I, 37 (L'viv, 1890), p. 6.
4,457	*Russkoe slovo*, II, 34 (L'viv, 1891), p. 4.
5,476	*Russkoe slovo*, III, 33 (L'viv, 1892), p. 5.
5,357	*Russkoe slovo*, V, 35 (L'viv, 1894), p. 7.
5,173	*Russkoe slovo*, VII, 35 (L'viv, 1896), p. 7.
5,875	*Halychanyn* , September 8, 1897, p. 1.
7,157	*Russkoe slovo*, XI, 37 (L'viv, 1900), p. 1; *Halychanyn*, September 19, 1900, p. 2.
7,444	*Halychanyn*, September 13, 1901, p. 2.
8,130	*Russkoe slovo*, XIII, 36 (L'viv, 1902), p. 2.
8,343	*Halychanyn*, September 30, 1903, p. 2.
7,972	*Halychanyn*, September 10, 1904, p. 2.
8,000	*Russkaia rada*, XXXIV, 16 (Kolomyia, 1905), p. 103.
9,229/7,888	*Russkoe slovo*, XVII, 37 (L'viv, 1906), p. 5; *Halychanyn*, September 19, 1906, p. 2.
9,872	*Dilo*, September 24, 1908, p. 1.
10,011	*Halychanyn*, October 1, 1909, p. 2.
10,700	*Halychanyn*, October 2, 1910, p. 2.
10,395	*Halychanyn*, September 21, 1912, p. 2.

chapter nine

Nationalism and National Bibliography: Ivan E. Levyts'kyi and Nineteenth-Century Galicia*

There are two basic essentials for the development of a nation's cultural life—a national library and a national bibliography.

Knud Larsen[1]

Bibliography ... is a true mirror upon which the whole intellectual creativity of a people is reflected.

Ivan E. Levyts'kyi[2]

The phenomenon of national bibliography has never really been discussed as an element in national movements. This is perhaps because at one level a bibliography simply records what has already been achieved. In that sense, national bibliographies are usually compiled during the second phase of a national movement, when the growth of national organizations makes the publication of such projects possible. We should also examine, however, what bibliographies contribute to the third phase, that is, a time when the growth of scholarship begins to provide a serious ideological basis for national movements.[3] In this sense, bibliographers do play a positive role in the growth of nationalism.

* First published in *Harvard Library Bulletin*, XXVIII, 1 (Cambridge, Mass., 1980), pp. 81–109; and reprinted in Harvard Ukrainian Research Institute Offprint Series, No. 28 (Cambridge, Mass., 1980).

1 Knud Larsen, "National Bibliographical Services," in *Essays on Bibliography*, ed. Vito J. Brenni (Metuchen, N.J., 1975), p. 204.

2 Ivan E. Levytskii, *Halytsko-ruskaia bybliohrafiia XIX-ho stolitiia*, Vol. I (L'viv, 1888), vi–vii.

3 On the various phases of national movements, see above, chapter 2.

The focus here is on only one national movement—that of nineteenth-century Galicia—and more specifically the role that the bibliographer and national biographer Ivan E. Levyts'kyi played in contributing to the cultural well-being of that region. The Ukrainians of Galicia entered the second, or organizational, phase of their national movement during the last decades of the nineteenth century, a time when Ivan Levyts'kyi was most active.

Ivan Emelianovych Levyts'kyi (1850–1913) was born in Berłohy, a small village in Kalush County at the foot of the Carpathian Mountains in eastern Galicia.[4] His father, Emelian, was a Greek Catholic clergyman, who, as well as fulfilling his duties as a village priest, also wrote historical works and other articles for the Galician-Ukrainian press in the 1850s and 1860s.[5] It is reasonable to suppose that Ivan Levyts'kyi acquired an appreciation for the power of the pen and its importance in the national movement from his father, whose literary endeavors were carried out during clerical assignments in isolated rural villages.[6]

4 Biographical data on Levyts'kyi, whether in published or unpublished form, are scanty. It seems the earliest biography of him appeared in a Czech encyclopedia: *Ottův slovník naučný*, Vol. XXVIII: *doplňky* (Prague, 1909), p. 888. This was followed by an extensive necrology by Ivan Krevets'kyi, "Ivan Em. Levyts'kyi: posmertna zhadka," *Zapysky Naukovoho tovarystva im. Shevchenka*, XXII, 1 [Vol. CXIII] (L'viv, 1913), pp. 155–159. It is interesting to note that neither of these sources is cited by Mykhailo P. Humeniuk, whose three relatively recent articles provide the most information on Levyts'kyi's life and work: "Levitskii—vydaiushchiisia ukrainskii bibliograf XIX stoletiia," *Sovetskaia bibliografiia*, No. 41 (Moscow, 1955), pp. 45–52; "Bibliohrafichna diial'nist' I O. Levyts'koho," *Arkhivy Ukraïny*, XXII, 6 (Kiev, 1968), pp. 30–36; and "Ivan Omelianovych Levyts'kyi," *Sotsialistychna kul'tura*, XXIII, 5 (Kiev, 1969).

   Brief biographical entries on Levyts'kyi have also appeared in *Ukraïns'ka zahal'na entsyklopediia*, Vol. II (L'viv, Stanyslaviv, and Kolomyia, 1932?), p. 448; *Entsysklopediia ukraïnoznavstva: slovnykova chastyna*, Vol. IV (Paris++New York, 1962), p. 1267; *Ukraïns'ka radians'ka entsyklopediia*, Vol. VIII (Kiev, 1962), p. 42; *Radians'ka entsyklopediia istoriï Ukraïny*, Vol. II (Kiev, 1970), p. 553; and V.R. Vavrik, *Kratkii ocherk galitskorusskoi pis'mennosti* (Louvain, 1973), p. 54. This last work incorrectly states that Fedor F. Aristov wrote a study on Levyts'kyi in 1930.

5 The writings of Emelian Levyts'kyi are listed in both volumes of the *Halytsko-russkaia bybliohrafiia*. The surname Levyts'kyi was one of the most widely known in nineteenth-century Galician life. Among the many influential leaders were the bishop Mykhailo Levyts'kyi (1774–1858), the grammarian Iosyf Levyts'kyi (1801–1861), the writer Volodymyr Lukych-Levyts'kyi (1856–1938), and the politician Kost' Levyts'kyi (1859–1941). There is no indication, however, that Ivan E. Levyts'kyi was related to any of these figures, or to the even more famous Dnieper-Ukrainian writer Ivan S. Levyts'kyi (1838–1918), who often wrote under the pseudonym "Ivan Nechui."

6 Levyts'kyi's daughter, Ivanna, wrote that later in life her father would often say of himself "In the service of the people, I am a worker with a pen." Cited from Ivanna's unpublished memoirs in Humeniuk, "Bibliohrafichna diial'nist'," p. 31.

At the age of twelve, the young Ivan left his native village for the nearest town, Stanyslaviv (now Ivano-Frankivs'k), where he was to attend secondary school (*gymnasium*). Before completing his eighth and last year, Levyts'kyi was drafted into the Austro-Hungarian Army. Despite this intrusion upon his student days, he continued to study in his free time and obtained permission to take his qualifying exams (which he passed) in Budapest, where his army unit had been stationed. As soon as he was discharged in 1871, Levyts'kyi entered the philosophical faculty at the University of Vienna, where he studied history and Slavistics under the renowned scholar František Miklosich (1813–1891).[7] In 1878, Levyts'kyi served again briefly in the army, then went back home to Galicia. He settled in the provincial capital and cultural center for Ukrainians, L'viv (German: Lemberg), where he was to remain for the rest of his life.

Notwithstanding his intellectual interests and training, Levyts'kyi did not enter the teaching profession. In fact, for thirty-four years, from 1879 until his death, he worked as a clerk in various insurance companies—Slavia, Azienda, and from 1892 in Dniester. His life was relatively uneventful. As an underpaid insurance clerk, he made barely enough money to support himself and his family. In his spare time, he devoted himself to writing. A rare insight into Levyts'kyi's lifestyle was provided many years later by his daughter, Ivanna: "[My father] worked hard from early morning until three in the afternoon at the Dniester [insurance company]. Then, after a half-hour's rest, he went to the library and worked there until seven or eight in the evening; finally, extremely exhausted, he would come home to eat. That was not the end, however, because he would write at home until midnight or one o'clock. Early in the morning he went again to the office and to his everyday regime."[8]

Levyts'kyi wrote in a variety of genres. Under his own name and a series of pseudonyms[9] he composed short stories, made several translations (especially from Polish), worked as a correspondent for Prague and L'viv newspapers, and published several historical, socioeconomic, bibliographical, and biographical studies.[10] He also served as editor and/or publisher of several journals and

---

7 Although Levyts'kyi finished the program, it is not certain whether he was awarded a doctorate. When his writings later were reviewed, all reviewers referred to him simply as "Mr. Levyts'kyi"; however, in one review, Ivan Franko called him "Dr. Levyts'kyi" (cf. below, note 55).

8 From Ivanna Levyts'kyi's unpublished memoirs, cited in Humeniuk, "Bibliohrafichna diial'nist'," p. 31.

9 "A"; "I"; "I.E."; "ii"; "X+Y+Z"; "Yvan yz Berloh"; "Yvan yz-nad Lukvŷ"; "Vladyslav Tsihel'skii."

10 The *Halytsko-ruskaia bybliohrafiia* and its supplements, which cover the period through 1893, indicate 108 entries by Levyts'kyi (including the individual fascicules of his

annual almanacs, such as *Narodna shkola* (1875), *Druh naroda* (1876), *Kalendar' karmannyi* (1882), *Kalendar' vydavnytstva narodnoho* (1884), and *Myr* (1885–87). The direction of his publishing activity was determined in part by his intellectual and national persuasion and in part by the need to supplement his income. Levyts'kyi seemed convinced that the educational system was a determining factor in national life, and among his earliest scholarly publications were studies of Ukrainian education in Galicia during the first decades of Austrian rule (1772–1848), a theme he was to return to again in later life.[11]

While it is commonly acknowledged that the Ukrainian national movement in Galicia enjoyed much success in the four decades before the outbreak of World War I, these achievements did not come easily and were frequently obtained at the cost of much external and internal friction, whether with the neighboring Poles, who had control over the Galician provincial administration, or among members of the Ukrainian intelligentsia itself, some of whom identified themselves as Old Ruthenians, as Ukrainians, or as Russians. Levyts'kyi tried to remain aloof from these controversies.

Having said that does not imply that Levyts'kyi was a recluse or merely an ivory-tower scholar completely removed from what was going on around him. Already in the 1870s he had joined cultural organizations such as the Academic Circle (Akademicheskii Kruzhok) and Kachkovs'kyi Society, and he wrote about contemporary problems in Galician periodicals such as *Slovo* and *Nauka*. At that time, these organizations and publications were relatively nonpartisan and had not yet adopted a particular stance concerning the problem of an appropriate national identity.[12] During these years, Levyts'kyi developed a talent for compromise and joined a group of political leaders who were hoping to reach an accommodation with the Poles. It was actually Levyts'kyi who hosted a coterie of Galicians that greeted the distinguished Ukrainian writer

bibliography). This may be quite representative of his total output, since the last two decades of his life were devoted largely to supplementing his *Halytsko-ruskaia bybliohrafiia* and publishing his national biography.

11 "Beiträge zur Entwicklung des galizischen Schulwesens unter der oesterr. Regierung vom Jahre 1772–1848," *Allgemeine oesterreichische Lehrerzeitung*, No. 17–18 (Prague, 1879); *Ruch Rusinów w Galicji w pierwszej połowie wieku panowania Austrji 1772–1820* (L'viv, 1879); "Pohliad na rozvii nyzshoho i vysshoho shkil'nytstva v Halychyni v rr. 1772–1800, i rozvii rus'koho narodnoho shkil'nytstva v rr. 1801–1820," in *Materialy do kul'turnoï istoriï Halyts'koï Rusy XVIII i XIX viku*, ed. Ivan Franko, in *Zbirnyk istorychno-fil'osofichnoï sektsiï NTSh*, Vol. V (L'viv, 1902), pp. 103–144.

12 These organizations and publications are often described incorrectly as Russophile. For a correct description of their traditionalist Galician-Old Ruthenian stance, see Mykola Andrusiak, *Narysy z istoriï halyts'koho moskvofil'stva* (L'viv, 1935), esp. pp. 15-45.

from Russia, Panteleimon Kulish (1819–1897), who had come several times to L'viv in the early 1880s, trying to work out a Polish-Ukrainian *modus vivendi*.[13] Although these efforts at compromise were eventually a failure, from Levyts'kyi's pen flowed a spate of short stories and historical tales which were careful to stress those instances of cooperation that had existed in the past between Ukrainian and Polish societies.[14] Moreover, most of his work appeared at this time under the imprint of a provincial government publishing house, which provided Levyts'kyi with the supplemental income he badly needed.[15]

With respect to the internal friction among the Galician-Ukrainian intelligentsia, Levyts'kyi tried to maintain a neutral position. Throughout most of his career he was able to maintain good relations with many Galician institutions and publications, whether they were of a traditionalist Rusynophile (Kachkovs'kyi Society), Russophile (Galician-Rus' Matytsia), or Ukrainophile (Shevchenko Scientific Society) orientation.[16] Levyts'kyi was first and foremost a Galician patriot, and because of his overriding sense of *lokalpatriotismus*, his national horizons did not go beyond the Ukrainian-inhabited territory within the boundaries of the Austro-Hungarian Empire. For this reason, during the last decades of his life he felt uneasy with both Galician Russophiles and Ukrainophiles, whose sympathies and national self-perceptions embraced lands beyond as well as within Austria-Hungary. Nevertheless, Levyts'kyi's activities and his national ideology, if that is what it can be called, were not terribly different from those of many other Galician leaders in the late nineteenth cen-

13 Vasyl' Shchurat, "Do istoryï ostannoho pobutu P. Kulisha u L'vovi," *Zoria*, XVIII (L'viv, 1897), p. 237. At Kulish's suggestion, plans were made to have Levyts'kyi edit two journals devoted to Polish-Ukrainian cooperation. One was to be called *Khutir*, the other (for which a masthead was found later among Levyts'kyi's papers) *Ukraina*. Cf. Ivan Franko, *Moloda Ukraïna*, pt. 1 (L'viv, 1910), p. 15; Krevets'kyi, "I.E. Levyts'kyi," p. 156.

14 Among typical tales in this genre were his *Dmytro Dietko, ruskïi voievoda pieriemÿskii* (L'viv, 1882); *Pôd Zborovom: opovîdanie z 1649 roku* (L'viv, 1884); and *Ne tak to buvalo!* (L'viv, 1885). Following his mentor, Kulish, Levyts'kyi was critical of Bohdan Khmel'nyts'kyi, the seventeenth-century Cossack leader who led a successful revolution against Polish rule. On the other hand, he did not hesitate to describe the exploitation of Ukraine by Polish aristocrats, as in his socioeconomic analysis: *Obozrînie obshchestven-no-èkonomychnoho stroia na Iuzhnoi Rusy v kniazheskii period y v vremia pol'skoho vladÿchestva* (L'viv, 1881).

15 Of the fifty brochures published by the Narodne vydavnytstvo during the 1880s, the majority were written by Ivan Levyts'kyi. Cf. Ivan Franko, *Narys istoriï ukraïns'koï literatury* (L'viv, 1910), pp. 349–350.

16 It is interesting to note that Levyts'kyi wrote in different "Galician national" languages. Until about 1890 he wrote in a traditional form of Slaveno-Rusyn (a kind of uncodified

tury. What makes us remember him, however, is his work as a bibliographer and, secondarily, as a national biographer.

Levyts'kyi began to consider compiling a retrospective national bibliography for Ukrainians in Austria-Hungary during the late 1870s, a time when the need for such a work was, so to speak, already in the air. The influential Ukrainian writer from the Russian Empire Mykhailo Drahomanov had travelled through Galicia in 1873 and tried to impress upon his acquaintances there the need to redress the "lack of knowledge about their own land"[17] and to prepare a bibliography. In 1877, the L'viv student journal *Druh* (1875–77), which included among its contributors Drahomanov's disciples Mykhailo Pavlyk (1853–1915) and Ivan Franko (1856–1916), began to solicit material for a bibliography, while a *Druh* editor, Ivan S. Mandychevs'kyi (1854–1925), actually began work on what was to be a Ukrainian-Rus' bibliography.[18]

Actually, there were already a few bibliographies about Galicia. In the early 1860s, Vladimir Mezhov (1830–1894) had published in St. Petersburg a bibliography of Galician-Ukrainian literature, while Professor Iakiv Holovats'kyi (1814–1888), who headed the Department of Ruthenian Language and Literature at L'viv University, had attempted the first retrospective national bibliography covering the years 1772 to 1848.[19] Then in the 1880s, several bibliographies on specific subjects appeared: for Church-Slavonic books published in L'viv (1574 to 1800); for the journal *Pravda* (1867 to 1883); for publications of the Galician-Rus' Matytsia (1848 to 1885); and for specific individuals (Anton

Galician recension of Church Slavonic); then for a decade or so he tried to write in literary Russian; finally, by the twentieth century he used Ukrainian. Cf. below, note 24, the variant titles on the different volumes of his bibliography. For Levyts'kyi's varied and sometimes contradictory views on language, see his *Halytsko-rus'ka bibliohrafiia za roky 1772–1800*, in *Zapysky Naukovoho tovarystva im. Shevchenka*, XII, 2 [Vol. LII] (L'viv, 1903), pp. 5–6.

17 Mykhailo Drahomanov, "Avstro-rus'ki spomyny (1867–1877)," in his *Literaturno-publitsystychni pratsi*, Vol. II (Kiev, 1970), p. 199.

18 On the Galician bibliographical environment in the 1870s, see Humeniuk, "Bibliohrafichna diial'nist'," pp. 32–33, and two works by Ihor I. Korneichyk: *Ukrainskie revoliutsionnye demokraty i bibliografiia* (Moscow, 1969), pp. 37–38, and *Istoriia ukraïns'koï bibliohrafiï: dozhovtnevyi period* (Kiev, 1971), pp. 175–178.

19 V. Mezhov, "Bibliograficheskii ukazatel' galitsko-russkoi literatury," *Osnova*, No. 6 (St. Petersburg, 1862), pp. 104–139; Iakov F. Holovatskii, "Bybliohrafiia halytsko-ruskaia s 1772–1848 hoda," *Halychanyn*, I, 3–4 (L'viv, 1863), pp. 309–327. Holovats'kyi also recorded older Galician publications printed in Church Slavonic by preparing a special supplement to a bibliography published in 1871 by V.M. Undol'skii, *Dopolnenie k ocherku slaviano-russkoi Bibliografii V.M. Undol'skago ... v osobennosti zhe perechen' galitsko-russkikh izdanii tserkovnoi pechati*, in *Zapiski Imperatorskoi Akademii Nauk*, XXIV, prilozhenie No. 3 (St. Petersburg, 1874), as well as a current bibliography covering

Petrushevych) or specific years (1885 to 1886).[20] In Prague, the leading center of solidarity for Austria's Slavs, a current Slavic bibliography including a special section for Galician-Ukrainian publications was even begun.[21] Finally, the distinguished Polish bibliographer Karol Estreicher (1827–1908) had already published several volumes of his monumental Polish bibliography, which also included some Galician-Ukrainian works.[22] None of these projects or bibliographic publications, however, came even close to achieving the goal of preparing a comprehensive retrospective national bibliography for Galicia. This task was left to Ivan E. Levyts'kyi.[23]

Clinging to the fashionable mode of dividing historical development by century, Levyts'kyi initially defined his time period as the nineteenth century. This

the years 1864 and 1865: "Bybliohrafycheskii spysok russkykh knyh," *Naukovŷi sbornyk*, I (L'viv, 1865), pp. 60–64, and II (1866), pp. 69–76.

20 A.S. Petrushevych, "Khronolohycheskaia rospys' tserkovnŷkh y mirskykh russko-slovenskykh knyh napechatannykh kyryllovskymy bukvamy v horodî L'vovî, nachynaia s 1574 do 1800 hoda," *Vremennyk Stavropyhiiskoho Ynstytuta ... na hod prostŷi 1885* (L'viv, 1884), pp. 113–133; Ivan Franko, "Bibliohrafichnyi pokazhchyk statei pechatanykh v Pravdi v vsikh 13 rochnykakh [1867–1883]," *Pravda*, XIII (L'viv, 1884), pp. 273–315; B.A. Dîdytskii, "Rospys' yzdanii Halytsko-russkoi Matytsŷ [1848–1885]," *Lyteraturnŷi sbornyk Halytsko-russkoiu Matytseiu* (L'viv, 1885), pp. 47–60, and Dîdytskii, "Sochyneniia Antoniia S. Petrushevycha," *Lyteraturnŷi sbornyk Halytsko-russkoiu Matytseiu*, pp. 220–234; "Yzdaniia halytsko-russkii za 1886 h.,"*Lyteraturnŷi sbornyk Halytsko-russkoiu Matytseiu* (1886), pp. 234–242; Ieronym Kalytovskii, "Bybliohrafichnŷi pokazchyk za rôk 1885," *Zoria*, VII, 7, 9, 11–14, 18–19 (L'viv, 1886).

21 *Slovanský katalog bibliografický za roky 1877–1881*, ed. A. Michálek and J. Klouček (Prague, 1878–82). The "bybliohrafiia maloruska" was prepared by Aleksandr Stefanovych for 1877, 1878, and 1879, and by A.N. Shcherban for 1880 and 1881.

22 The first series of Estreicher's multiseries bibliography, dealing with the nineteenth century, was already completed before the appearance of Levyts'kyi's bibliography: *Bibliografia polska XIX stólecia*, 7 vols. (Cracow, 1872–82). Estreicher's coverage of Galician-Ukrainian publications was haphazard and unreliable. For instance, in the introduction to his bibliography, Estreicher claimed that 250 "Ruthenian" works appeared in Galicia between 1837 and 1863 (Volume I, p. iv); for that same period Levyts'kyi uncovered 1,483 individual titles (*Halytsko-ruskaia bybliohrafiia*).

23 When placed in a general Ukrainian context, Levyts'kyi is often compared to his contemporary, Mykhailo Komarov (1849–1913), who published a retrospective bibliography of modern Ukrainian literary works that appeared between 1798 and 1883 in the Dnieper (Russian) Ukraine: *Pokazhchyk novoi ukrains'koi literatury* (Kiev, 1883). But this work pales in comparison with Levyts'kyi's, since Komarov intended to list only belletristic works. Even in that regard the Komarov bibliography was sorely incomplete as evidenced by the many contemporary critical reviews and finally by a revised version of the work by Dmytro Doroshenko, "Pokazhchyk literatury ukraïns'koho movoiu v Rosii za 1798–1897 roky," in *Naukovyi iubyleinyi zbirnyk Ukraïns'koho universytetu v Pratsi prysv... . T.G. Masarykovi* (Prague, 1925), pp. 142–238.

clear why, but Levyts'kyi decided to make 1886 the cut-off date for volume two. Thus, the first volume appeared in 1888 under the title *Halytsko-ruskaia bybliohrafiia XIX-ho stolîtiia s uvzhliadneniem ruskykh yzdanii poiavyvshykhsia v Uhorshchynî y Bukovynî (1801–1886): khronolohycheskii spysok publykatsii, 1801–1860* (Galician-Rusyn Bibliography for the nineteenth Century, also Comprising Rusyn Publications That Appeared in Hungary and Bukovina, 1801–1886: Chronological List of Publications, 1801–1860). The second volume appeared in 1895 and covered the years 1861 to 1886.[24] Both volumes were published by the author, although he received some financial help from the Galician Diet and local cultural societies, including the Stavropegial Institute's print shop where the book was produced.[25]

The *Halytsko-ruskaia bybliohrafiia* was monumental in both size and scope. Set in a large format (eight and a half inches by twelve and a half), its two volumes looked (and weighed) very much like the bibles and other religious books used in churches. Together the volumes comprised 930 pages (xxiv, 162, and [viii], 736) with a total of 4,774 bibliographic entries. Each volume also included a complete title and author index. Levyts'kyi followed the *de visu* principle, and it was in only a few exceptional cases that he did not actually see the work he was describing. Accessibility was a great problem in it-

the work by Dmytro Doroshenko, "Pokazhchyk literatury ukraïns'koho movoiu v Rosii za 1798–1897 roky," in *Naukovyi iubyleinyi zbirnyk Ukraïns'koho universytetu v Pratsi prysv... . T.G. Masarykovi* (Prague, 1925), pp. 142–238.

On these and earlier bibliographical developments in Dnieper Ukraine, see Korneichyk, *Istoriia*, pp. 47–183, *passim*, and Bohdan Krawciw, "Bibliography," in *Ukraine: A Concise Encyclopedia*, Vol. II, ed. V. Kubijovyč (Toronto, 1971), pp. 431–434.

24 The wording of the title in the second volume changed slightly to reflect a period in Levyts'kyi's life when he tried to write in literary Russian. Thus, the first word in the second volume reads "Galitsko-russkaia" compared with "Halytsko-ruskaia" in the first volume, while the subtitle is given in Russian: "dopolnennaia russkimi izdaniiami vyshedshimi v Vengrii i Bukovinie." Levyts'kyi's use of Russian also reflected a hope of receiving a large number of subscribers from the Russian Empire. But this did not occur after the appearance of the first volume (1888); moreover, in 1894 his work was listed in the official tsarist governmental catalog of books banned from importation into the Russian Empire. Korneichyk, *Istoriia*, pp. 179–180.

25 The Stavropegial Institute guaranteed the first volume's appearance by arranging for prepublication subscriptions to the individual fascicules that appeared periodically. Besides this, the National Home (Narodnyi Dom) and Galician-Rus' Matytsia donated 100 guldens and the Galician Diet 200 guldens. Levyts'kyi, *Halytsko-ruskaia bybliohrafiia*, Vol. I, p. vi, note 1.

It seems that the publication of Volume II was delayed until 1895, after the initial promise of the Ukrainophile Prosvita Society to guarantee subscribers was cancelled, because that organization's chairman, the literary historian Omelian Ohonovs'kyi, was opposed to Levyts'kyi's ostensible "Russophile" inclinations. In the end, assistance from self, because Galicia did not have a national or other library where all Ukrainian publications were held. Thus, it took Levyts'kyi a full decade to survey a wide variety of public, university, religious, organizational, and private libraries in Galicia in order to obtain the necessary materials.[26]

In practice, the content of any national bibliography varies.[27] Levyts'kyi sought to include (1) all publications printed in Austria–Hungary in Rusyn [Ukrainian] both in the Cyrillic and civil scripts as well as in the Latin alphabet, notwithstanding the nationality of the author; and (2) all collections appearing in print, both in Austria–Hungary and abroad, in Polish, German, Latin, and other languages, whose authors were born Galician Rusyns [Ukrainians].[28]

The organizing principle was chronological, with all the works for a given year being listed alphabetically according to the name of the author or title. Levyts'kyi did not offer a simple list of books, however; he also reproduced titles in their original languages and alphabets, gave information on format, price, and size of edition, reproduced tables of contents for collected works, and, most invaluable, provided analytics for each volume of journals and other periodical literature. For many historically significant books, he also supplied information on their publication background.

The reception given the *Halytsko-ruskaia bybliohrafiia* was universal praise. Whether in the Galician-Ukrainian and Polish press or in the many periodicals which reviewed the work in the Russian Empire, Levyts'kyi was lauded for his objectivity and impeccable scholarship.[29]

the Stavropegial Institute print shop made possible the second volume's appearance. Korneichyk, *Istoriia*, p. 179.

26 In the introductions to each volume Levyts'kyi singles out the libraries of the National Home, the Prosvita Society, and the personal collection of the writer Ivan Franko, all in L'viv.

27 A national bibliography may contain publications (1) issued within a given territory (i.e., nation-state or ethnolinguistic territory); (2) issued in the language(s) of a given territory; (3) issued by natives of a given territory regardless of where they may reside or the language used; (4) about a given territory; (5) copyrighted in a given territory; (6) for a given territory. Cf. Leory H. Linder, "National Bibliography," in *Essays on Bibliography*, p. 218.

28 Levytskii, *Halysko-ruskaia bybliohrafiia*, Vol. I, p. viii.

29 A respected historical journal in the Russian Empire proclaimed that Levyts'kyi's bibliography was a "classic, monumental work, which gives the author the right to be considered in the ranks of the most outstanding bibliographers of our time." N. Ryzhkov in *Istoricheskii viestnik*, LXIII (St. Petersburg, 1896), pp. 301–302. For a discussion of the many other favorable reviews in contemporary Polish, Ukrainian, and Russian publications, see Humeniuk, "Levitskii," pp. 50–51; and Korneichyk, *Istoriia ukraïns'koï bibliohrafiï*, p. 179.

It seems that the only criticism came from Omelian Ohonovs'kyi, "Ôdpovîd' na tendentsiinu napast' p. Yvana Em. Levytskoho v halytsko-ruskôi Bybliohrafiy," *Zoria*, IX,

Levyts'kyi's bibliography included publications only through 1886, omitting the last fifteen years of the nineteenth century. Thus, even before the second volume of the retrospective bibliography appeared, he embarked on a project of current bibliography. For each of the three years, 1887 through 1889, he published an annual bibliography, first in the journal of the Galician-Rus' Matytsia, then in individual volumes.[30] It is not clear why, but after 1890 Levyts'kyi's current bibliographical coverage stopped. Indeed, he must have been preoccupied with getting out the second volume of the retrospective bibliography, which was finally completed in 1895, as well as with the national biographical project which he began in 1887. Therefore, Levyts'kyi's next bibliographical work did not appear until 1903. This was his retrospective national bibliography for the years 1772–1800, published in the scholarly journal of the Shevchenko Scientific Society.[31] In this work, he uncovered ninety-nine publications, three to four times more than any previous bibliography had shown to have appeared during the last decades of the eighteenth century.[32]

By the early part of the twentieth century, Levyts'kyi's relations with the older Galician cultural organizations seem to have soured;[33] he began to publish almost exclusively in Ukrainian, especially with the dynamic Shevchenko Scientific Society. In May 1909, that Ukrainophile organization decided to establish its Bibliographical Commission, which was constituted the following November. The commission included the leading Ukrainian scholars of the day, among them Mykhailo Hrushevs'kyi, Volodymyr Hnatiuk, and Mykhailo Vozniak. Yet for its chairman the commission decided to go beyond the mem-

---

10 (L'viv, 1888), p. 179, who complained about the description of the journal *Lada*, and to which Levyts'kyi published a reply: "Otvît d-ru Om. Ohonovskomu," *Chervonaia Rus'*, I, 60–62, 67 (L'viv, 1888).

30 "Halytsko-russkaia bybliohrafiia za 1887 h.," *Lyteraturnyĭ sbornyk Halytsko-russkoi Matytsȳ* (L'viv, 1887), pp. 278–348; "za 1888 h.,"*Lyteraturnyĭ sbornyk Halytsko-russkoiu Matytseiu* (1889), 127 p.; "za 1889 i 1890 h.,"*Lyteraturnyĭ sbornyk Halytsko-russkoiu Matytseiu* (1890), 130 p. These same works were published as three separate volumes (L'viv, 1888, 1889, 1890).

31 "Halyts'ko-rus'ka bibliohrafiia za roky 1772–1800," *Zapysky Naukovoho tovarystva im. Shevchenka*, XII, 2 [Vol. LII] (L'viv, 1903), 44 p.

32 For that same period, Holovats'kyi's work, "Bybliohrafiia halytsko-ruskaia," listed eighteen publications and his *Dopolnenie*, twenty publications, while Petrushevych's "Khronolohycheskaia rospys'" listed thirty publications.

33 Beginning with the 1890s, a small group of younger Galicians—Iuliian Iavors'kyi, Symeon Labens'kyi, Ilarion Sventsits'kyi—began to have greater influence in the older cultural organizations and publications. As Russophiles, they were committed to the use of standard Russian and to association with Great Russian culture. As a result, they rejected what they believed to be the "confused, provincial patriotism" of Galician Old Ruthenian

bership rolls of the Shevchenko Scientific Society, and out of respect for his bibliographic achievements it chose Ivan E. Levyts'kyi.[34] In subsequent meetings, the commission outlined its intention to continue where the second volume of the *Halytsko-ruskaia bybliohrafiia* left off. Levyts'kyi was to be responsible for the years 1887 to 1900, Mykhailo Vozniak for 1901 to 1905, and Volodymyr Doroshenko for 1906 to 1910.[35] These goals were only partly achieved. In 1909, a new series, *Materialy dlia ukraïns'koï bibliohrafiï* (Materials for a Ukrainian Bibliography), was begun, in which Levyts'kyi's bibliography appeared under a new title—*Ukraïns'ka bibliohrafiia Avstro–Uhorshchyny za roky 1887–1900* (Ukrainian Bibliography in Austria–Hungary for the Years 1887–1900). But between 1909 and 1911 only three volumes were published, the first containing a reprint of the previously published years 1887 to 1889, the other two covering 1890 through 1893. These volumes contained 2,529 new bibliographic entries.[36] Levyts'kyi's material for the last years of the century was never destined to appear in print because in 1911 his health began to fail.[37] Bedridden with asthma for most of the next two years, Levyts'kyi died on January 30, 1913 at the age of sixty-three.[38]

Although Levyts'kyi's bibliography does not cover the last few years of the nineteenth century, it still remains to this day a primary source for the historian of Galicia.[39] Levyts'kyi knew that he was not engaged in an antiquarian hobby to be pursued each evening after coming home from the office. He was fully

traditionalists such as Levyts'kyi. Cf. Iavors'kyi's critical review of the initial fascicules of Levyts'kyi's biographical dictionary in *Nauchno-literaturnyi sbornik*, I, 1 (L'viv, 1901), pp. 88–94.

34 *Khronika Naukovoho tovarystva im. Shevchenka*, III, 39 (L'viv, 1909), p. 18, and. ibid, IV, 40, p. 20.

35 Ibid., II, 42 (1910), p. 20.

36 *Materiialy do ukraïns'koï bibliohrafiï: Ukraïns'ka bibliohrafiia Avstro-Uhorshchyny za roky 1887–1900*, 3 vols. [1887-1893] (L'viv, 1909–11).

37 The volume for 1894 was edited by Ivan Krevets'kyi, vice-chairman of the Shevchenko Scientific Society's Bibliographical Commission, but it, together with the remaining bibliographic materials of Levyts'kyi, remains in the manuscript division of the Stefanyk State Scientific Library in L'viv.

38 Levyts'kyi did publish two other bibliographic works before he died: "Reiestr naukovykh i literaturnykh prats' prof. Mykhaila Hrushevs'koho," in *Naukovyi zbirnyk prysviachenyi profesorovi Mykhailovi Hrushevs'komu* (L'viv, 1906), pp. 1–64; and *Bibliographie des Fedorowiczs* (L'viv, 1910).

39 No bibliography can ever be complete, and Levyts'kyi's is no exception. Despite his praise, Ivan Franko, writing under the pseudonym "Miron," was forced to conclude in his review of volume I of the *Halytsko-ruskaia bybliohrafiia* that "in the end, despite 10 years of work, it seems that the bibliography of Mr. Levyts'kyi is still not complete even for

aware of the significance of his work for the national movement and of its relevance for contemporary and future scholarship. In the introduction to the first volume, he wrote: "The task of scholarship should be to study by means of critical analysis the historical process of the national awakening as well as the intellectual movement of Galician Rus.' ... Recognizing the importance of this task, I worked for a full decade in gathering the appropriate material. ... "[40] Other writers quickly realized that Levyts'kyi's bibliography was a model "for other Slavic literatures, for which it would also be possible to extract interesting data on the national renaissance."[41]

In the context of a French encyclopedic survey dealing with history as a scholarly discipline, one author recently wrote: "All historians, or more properly all scholars, should acquire a bibliographic education."[42] I would rephrase this: No historian or scholar is worth his salt if he is not first a competent bibliographer. In this regard, Levyts'kyi's *Halytsko-ruskaia bybliohrafiia* is particularly valuable. His principle of chronological organization not only had the practical function of allowing him to continue easily at whatever point in time he left off, it has also made it possible to see at a glance the intellectual and cultural status of Galicia at one period during the nineteenth century. His own introduction actually includes eleven statistical tables that analyze the places, languages, subjects, and sizes of publications. Besides these numerical data, Levtys'kyi's precise reproduction of the titles, with their varying alphabets, for each bibliographic entry provides invaluable information for those interested in language, whether from a purely linguistic point of view or from the standpoint of the sociology of language and the closely related language question, so crucial to understanding the national movement in nineteenth-century Galicia. The analytics of journals, almanacs, and newspapers on a year-by-year basis provide in some cases the only source of information on rare or ephemeral serial publications. They also make it possible to understand the changing intellectual environment of Galician-Ukrainian society and to see how certain individuals worked together during one period on publications representing a certain national or social ideology, while they may have been

Galician Rus'." *Kievskaia starina*, XXI (Kiev, 1888), p. 32. Franko was particularly critical of Levyts'kyi's incomplete coverage for Bukovina and Subcarpathian Rus', especially the lack of Hungarian-language publications dealing with the latter region. Franko himself published two studies in 1898 and 1912 supplementing Levyts'kyi's coverage for Galicia. Cf. Korneichyk, *Ukrainskie revoliutsionnye demokraty*, pp. 41–44.

40 *Halytsko-ruskaia bybliohrafiia*, Vol. I, p. vi.
41 *Viestnik Evropy*, XXIV, 10 (St. Petersburg, 1888), p. 839.
42 Pierre Marot, "Les outils de la recherche historique," in *L'histoire et ses méthodes*, ed. Charles Samarin, Encyclopédie de la Pléiade, Vol. XI (Paris, 1973), p. 1431.

part of an entirely different ideological setting at another time.

The most impressive feature of Levyts'kyi's bibliography is its reliability. Ivan Franko and Kyrylo Studyns'kyi already note this in their scholarly work. Citing Levyts'kyi was almost as necessary in establishing one's scholarly credibility as, in a completely different context, citing Marx or Lenin. Because of the rarity of the material involved, it is no longer possible to check each of Levyts'kyi's 7,402 entries for the period 1772 to 1892; what is extraordinary, however, is to discover time and again, when one may have occasion to check an original publication against Levyts'kyi, that he is invariably correct.

While Levyts'kyi's efforts in preserving the national heritage of Galicia are best known in the field of bibliography, this is not the only area in which he worked. He also became the region's first national biographer. Writing more than half a century later about the biographical approach to history, the distinguished Elizabethan scholar Sir John E. Neale stated: "we cannot fully understand the nature and functioning of any human group without knowing about the individuals who compose it. This knowledge must come from a series of biographies."[43] Of course, the writing of biographies had been going on for centuries, and the art had reached a particular vogue throughout Europe in the later nineteenth century. But for the modern historian, the classic biographical literature frequently falls short of what is needed. To quote Neale again: "We must first know what questions we hope to answer from the biographies, and if at all possible the necessary information must be got. This is a very different proposition from writing ordinary biographies."[44]

Levyts'kyi knew in advance what he wanted from biography: he hoped to describe in the fullest terms that group of people who had created the national movement in eastern Galicia. In that sense, he set out to do what in recent years has come to be known as prosopography, i.e., "the investigation of the common background characteristics of a group of actors in history by means of a collective study of their lives."[45]

With these principles in mind, Levyts'kyi planned a six-volume work which was to contain 2,000 biographies.[46] Considering future analytical needs, he attempted to ensure that the data were comparable, and with this in mind dis-

---

43 J.E. Neale, "The Biographical Approach to History," *History*, N.S., XXXVI, [128] (London, 1951), p. 196.

44 Ibid.

45 Lawrence Stone, "Prosopography," *Daedalus*, C, 1 (Boston, 1971), p. 46.

46 The fullest description of Levyts'kyi's national biographical project, from which much of the following discussion derives, is Ia. R. Dashkevych, "Materialy I.O. Levyts'koho iak dzherela dlia biohrafichnoho slovnyka," *Istorychni dzherela ta ikh vykorystannia*, Vol. II (Kiev, 1966), pp. 35–53.

tributed a standardized fourteen-part questionnaire in 1887. Besides typical questions on name, pseudonyms, dates, and place of birth, he also called for information on professional status, activity, and published works. Most important for an understanding of the ideological formation of a group of persons was the question of educational background—specifically, with which lecturers or professors the person studied. While we do not know how many questionnaires Levyts'kyi sent out in 1887, we do know that the initial results were meager—a scant thirty replies. Undaunted, he proceeded with his research. From his bibliographic work, he had become fully conversant with Galician periodical literature and knew all the biographies and necrologies already in print.[47] For historic individuals from the earlier part of the century, he made use of unpublished documents, diaries, and other resources in local archives.

In 1895, Levyts'kyi published the first two sample biographies in the Ukrainian-language journal *Zhytie i slovo*.[48] The following year, Osyp A. Monchalovs'kyi (1858–1906), editor of the Russian-language Galician journal *Besieda*, publicized Levyts'kyi's biographical project.[49] This publicity, as well as Levyts'kyi's growing reputation as author of the *Halytsko-ruskaia bybliohrafiia* (the second volume appeared in 1895), made his new questionnaire, sent out in 1896 and 1897, more successful. He now received more than 100 autobiographical responses. This was still much less than he had hoped for, and even those that he did receive were, for various reasons, incomplete. For instance, the biochemist and future academician Ivan Ia. Horbachevs'kyi (1854–1942) agreed to send a list of his publications, but out of modesty, false or otherwise, wrote: "I am writing nothing about details. First, it is unpleasant for me to write about myself [*pro domo sua*]; second, I really remember well very little; finally, I must say there isn't really much that could be of general interest."[50] The writer and journalist Volodymyr F. Lutsyk (1858–1909) was even more candid. In response to the question, "other significant moments in your life," he wrote: "I served in the army, but never saw the front; they threw me out of the [editorial board of the journal] *Myr* at the instigation of Aristov; I drank from time to time; I had a few love affairs—that's it."[51]

47   In particular, the journals *Zoria* (L'viv, 1880–97), which often had comprehensive biographies of contemporary Galicians, and *Nauka* (Kolomyia, L'viv, and Vienna, 1871–1914), which from 1884 to 1893 published an ongoing series entitled, "Slovar' slavnýkh liudei" (A Dictionary of Famous Persons).

48   I. Levyts'kyi, "Modest Hrynevets'kyi," *Zhytie i slovo*, III, 2 (L'viv, 1895), pp. 313–315, and "Hryhorii Tarkovych," *Zhytie i slovo*, III, 3, pp. 465–466.

49   O.A. Monchalovskii, "Prikarpatskaia Rus' v XIX st.," *Besieda*, X, 2–3 (L'viv, 1896), pp. 27–28.

50   Cited in Dashkevych, "Materialy," pp. 44–45.

51   Cited in ibid., p. 45. The reference is to Fedor F. Aristov, the Russian specialist on

In spite of his unpredictable still-living subject matter, Levyts'kyi published the first fascicule of his national biographical dictionary in 1898 under the title: *Prykarpatska Rus' v XIX viki v biohrafiiakh y portretakh iey diitelei uvzhliadnen'em zamichatel'nykh liudei, kotrykh 1772 g. zastav pry zhyzhny* (Carpathian Rus' in the Nineteenth Century through Biographies and Portraits of Distinguished People since 1772). The original plan was to have a new fascicule of 56 pages appear every two months. Unfortunately, Levyts'kyi took ill in 1899, so that by 1901 only four fascicules, a total of 224 pages, had appeared.[52]

Levyts'kyi's *Prykarpatska Rus'* was truly national. It was conceived to include not only "the more well-known and popular figures or those famous because of their official position," but also "all outstanding activists in Austrian Rus' who in some area of our cultural life put forth their might in the sacrifice of national progress."[53] This meant writers, artists, composers, priests, lawyers, scientists, teachers, civil servants, businessmen, laborers, peasants, and even those who did not have a direct impact on Galician life but who had attained success abroad. Like his bibliography, the first fascicules of Levyts'kyi's *Prykarpatska Rus'* were greeted favorably in local and foreign circles. He was praised for his accuracy in gathering hard-to-obtain data and for his complete objectivity in dealing with all leaders, regardless of their national orientation.[54] It seems the only serious criticism to arise was directed not at Levyts'kyi the scholar but at Levyts'kyi the man—with his human limitations. Ivan Franko remarked all too prophetically that the "plan of the author goes beyond the strength of one man" and would at best require at least thirty years to complete.[55] Franko concluded by pointing out how other national biographies, like Germany's *Allgemeine deutsche Biographie*, were undertaken by whole com-

Galicia, who in 1907 established a Carpatho-Russian Museum in Moscow.

52 *Prykarpatska Rus' v XIX viki...*, Vol. I, 4 pts. (L'viv, 1898–1901). This work was published by the author with help from the Stavropegial Institute print shop where it was produced. It is unknown how many copies of each fascicule were printed, but the work has become a bibliographic rarity. There are no copies in any of the major research libraries in either western Europe or the Americas, and even the rich collections of Galician materials found in several libraries in Prague do not have a copy.

53 From the author's preface to the first fascicule, cited in Dashkevych, "Materialy," p. 39.

54 Levyts'kyi's objective description of Ukrainophile leaders seems to have prompted the Russophiles to reject him. Cf. above, note 33. The reaction of some reviewers to *Prykarpatska Rus'* is discussed in Dashkevych, "Materialy," pp. 40–41; Dashkevych does not, however, mention a review by František Řehoř in *Slovanský přehled*, I (Prague, 1899), p. 209.

55 I. Franko, in *Zapysky Naukovoho tovarystva im. Shevchenka*, XI, 2 [Vol. XLVI] (L'viv, 1902), pp. 26–29.

missions, and he wondered if Levyts'kyi would not consider such an approach, implicitly suggesting cooperation with the Shevchenko Scientific Society.

The independent-minded Levyts'kyi did not follow Franko's well-placed advice. As a result, *Prykarpatska Rus'* never got beyond the letter B, the fourth and last fascicule actually stopping half-way through the biography of Volodymyr Barvins'kyi (1850–1883).[56] More than 3,596 small packets of autobiographical data still remain, but they are virtually untouched in the manuscript division of the Stefanyk State Scientific Library in L'viv.[57] It is particularly unfortunate to note that, after all these years, no one has yet undertaken to rework Levyts'kyi's biographical materials or to publish a new biographical dictionary.[58]

The work of Ivan Levyts'kyi in national bibliography, and secondarily in national biography, speaks for itself. Those few Soviet scholars who have been fortunate to have access to his published materials know how essential they are for any serious work on nineteenth- and early-twentieth-century Galicia. But how does Levyts'kyi hold up in a broader context? What else was going on at the time in the fields of national bibliography and national biography not only in eastern Europe but in western Europe as well?

56 For a list of those biographies that did appear in the first four fascicules and for more than 100 others for which there is substantial material in Levyts'kyi's archive, see Dashkevych, "Materialy," pp. 40, 48–52. A few other biographies were published by Levyts'kyi elsewhere. See his treatment of the early-nineteenth-century leaders Mykhailo Levyts'kyi, Ivan Mohyl'nyts'kyi, and Iosyf Iaryna in Levyts'kyi, "Pohliad na rozvii nyzshoho i vysshoho shkil'nyts'tva," pp. 131–137.

57 The fact that this material has hardly been used by contemporary Soviet scholars is underscored in the articles by Dashkevych, "Materialy," p. 52, and Humeniuk, "Levitskii," p. 52. Also among Levyts'kyi's materials is an unpublished dictionary of pseudonyms and cryptonyms for more than 800 western-Ukrainian writers.

58 The Ukrainian national biographic tradition has witnessed several attempts, but a biographical dictionary still does not exist. Among the earlier published efforts were P.I. Keppen on Kharkov writers (1828); H.N. Gennadi and G.A. Miloradovych on "outstanding personages of Little Russia" (1856–59); P.I. Bodianskii on famous people from Poltava (1865)—all of which appeared as part of other works; and the proposed multivolume work "historical personages of South-West Russia," by V.B. Antonovych and V.A. Bets, of which only one volume (with nine biographies) appeared (1883). S.I. Ponomarev planned a biographical dictionary for the Dnieper Ukraine (i.e., within the Russian Empire), but nothing more than his plan ever appeared (1898). More ambitious was the project for a general Ukrainian biographical dictionary begun in 1893 under the direction of Mykhailo Hrushevs'kyi. Six years later the volumes for A to M comprising 200 to 300 persons per letter were ready for simultaneous publication in Kiev (in Russian) and L'viv (in Ukrainian). However, as a result of editorial disagreements, nothing ever saw the light of day.

After the appearance of Levyts'kyi's uncompleted work (1898–1901), a few subject-oriented biographical guides were published: D. Bahylii et al. on Kharkov University

The work of Ivan Levyts'kyi in national bibliography, and secondarily in national biography, speaks for itself. Those few Soviet scholars who have been fortunate to have access to his published materials know how essential they are for any serious work on nineteenth- and early-twentieth-century Galicia. But how does Levyts'kyi hold up in a broader context? What else was going on at the time in the fields of national bibliography and national biography not only in eastern Europe but in western Europe as well?

It is essential to remember that Galicia was a mere province of Austria–Hungary. And within that province Ukrainians were a political and social, if not numerical, minority. As such, they did not enjoy the direct and indirect advantages that usually accrue from having political autonomy or independence. They did not, like some other regions in contemporary Europe, have state-supported organizations that might undertake to sponsor at public expense a national bibliography, current or retrospective.

Local Galician-Ukrainian national leaders traditionally felt these disadvantages. As early as 1842, the writer Iakiv Holovats'kyi declared in a German-language publication, "Among all the Slavic peoples, the Rusyn or Little Russian branch [in Galicia] has sunk the lowest."[59] Galician self-perception had not improved much by the latter part of the century. The prolific Ivan Franko, who was always fond of criticizing his own Galician society, wrote in 1878, "The whole thirty-year span of our 'national renaissance' [since 1848] has not produced one important writer or scholar, not one intelligent politician, nor one activist in education or public enlightenment—in a word, it has produced nothing which would reflect the existence of a healthy intelligentsia."[60] Even Levyts'kyi prefaced the second volume of the *Halytsko-ruskaia bybliohrafiia* with these words: "Without question, there is not any other cultured society in the world that is so little

literatury, 2 vols. (1966–73, others still in preparation). On the above developments, see Korneichyk, *Istoriia*, pp. 184–187, 260–262; and I.M. Kaufman, *Russkie biograficheskie i biobibliograficheskie slovari* (Moscow, 1955), pp. 545–551.

More recently, the journal *Arkhivy Ukraïny* (Kiev) began to publish a series entitled "Materialy do ukraïns'koho biohrafichnoho slovnyka," which was to include writers and scholars from two oblasts in the Ukrainian S.S.R.—Poltava and Ivano-Frankivs'k (comprising much of former Galicia). The series on Poltava, including several hundred biographies written by P. Rotach, was published in parts in almost every issue of *Arkhivy Ukraïny* between 1965 and 1971. The series on Ivano-Frankivs'k, compiled by V. Poliek, was begun in 1969, but after only four installments (seventy-three biographies for the letters A to V—the third Ukrainian letter) it was discontinued.

59 Havryło Rusyn [Iakiv Holovats'kyi], "Zustände der Russinen in Galizien," *Jahrbücher für slawische Literatur, Kunst und Wissenschaft*, IV, 9–10 (Leipzig, 1846), p. 361.

60 Yvan Franko, "Krytychni pys'ma o halyts'kij intelihentsiji," *Molot*, I (L'viv, 1878)—reprinted in Ivan Franko, *Tvory*, Vol. XVI (Kiev, 1955), p. 24.

interested in the fate of its literary productivity as is our Rus'-Carpathian society. This is not an overstatement but the present-day truth."[61]

But was this not indeed an overstatement? Was Galicia culturally so badly off? Or were these comments simply echoes of the frustrations of well-meaning if myopic national leaders whose tendencies toward self-pity and self-denigration were characteristics all too common among representatives of national minorities? To answer these questions, it is necessary to look at the larger European picture.

The first attempts to create a bibliography that would systematically list all publications that had appeared in a single national area have been traced back to sixteenth-century England.[62] Often, however, these early so-called national bibliographies really consisted of biographies of writers (usually only belletrists) from a given territory, to which a list of their published works would be attached.

It was not until the late eighteenth century that the first real national bibliographies, in the manner that we know them today, were produced. The evolution of printing technology, better systems for distribution, and improved standards of living and education were the important preconditions for this new bibliographic stage. By the early nineteenth century, the impact of the French Revolution, combined with the classical/romantic interest in the past and nationalism's demands for greater pride in the cultural heritage of one's own people, all contributed to a greater awareness of the need for national retrospective bibliographies: that is, the compilation of works, usually multivolume, which listed all the publications that appeared on a given territory either since the first printed book or during some designated time period.[63] The nineteenth century also saw the birth of current national bibliographies (first in France,

---

61 *Galitsko-russkaia bibliografiia XIX stolietiia*, Vol. II (L'viv, 1895), p. [v].

62 Louise Noëlle Malclès, *Bibliography* (New York, 1961), pp. 22–29; Theodore Besterman, *Les débuts de la bibliographie méthodique* (3rd rev. ed.; Paris, 1950), p. 43 *et passim*.

63 Malclès, *Bibliography*, pp. 101–108. Aside from the general work of Malclès, there is a decided lack of literature dealing with the phenomenon of modern retrospective national bibliography. Writers like Joris Vorstius, L.H. Linder, Wilhelm Totok, and Roger C. Greer, who have dealt with the subject (cf. references in *Handbuch der Bibliographischen Nachschlagewerke* [4th rev. ed.; Frankfurt am Main, 1972], p. 19), generally treat the subject from the perspective of the theoretical and practical problems involved in compiling current national bibliographies. One exception is the work of Rudolf Blum, "Vor- und Frühgeschichte der nationalen Allgemeinbibliographies," *Archiv für Geschichte des Buchwesens*, II (Frankfurt-am-Main, 1960), pp. 233–303, which discusses western-European developments during the late sixteenth and seventeenth centuries. Let us hope that someone will continue Blum's work and discuss retrospective national bibliographies as a cultural phenomenon in the modern period.

If we look at a list of the first modern retrospective national bibliographies of European countries or ethnonational territories/groups (Appendix 9.1a),[64] we are not surprised to discover that some of the earliest examples of the genre were produced in western Europe, especially in countries with relatively high economic and cultural standards such as Germany, France, and Great Britain. The appearance of Ireland and Russia so early might come as somewhat of a surprise. What is particularly surprising, however, is to find that out of the total of forty-six countries and ethnonational territories/groups, arranged in chronological order according to when they produced their first national retrospective bibliographies, Ukrainian Galicia comes fourteenth, with the 1863 bibliography of Holovats'kyi. In the same list, Levyts'kyi's *Halyts'ko-ruskaia bybliohrafiia* comes twenty-seventh. If we were to take this list and treat comparable units, that is, ethnonational territories/groups that did not have their own state in the late nineteenth century, then Holovats'kyi's bibliography would come seventh and Levyts'kyi's thirteenth (Appendix 9.1b).

If we look at the record for the first national biographical dictionaries, Ukrainian Galicia, as represented by Levyts'kyi's 1898 *Prykarpatska Rus'*, comes thirtieth out of a total of forty-one (Appendix 9.2a),[65] and as number fifteenth if we consider only those territories/groups that did not have independence (Appendix 9.2b). Finally, if we focus on eastern Europe (that is the area east of Germany), it is interesting to note that Ukrainian Galicia had its first national bibliography before all other neighboring cultures except Russia, Bohemia, and Croatia, and the beginnings of its first national biographical dictionary before all other neighbors except Bohemia–Moravia, Livonia, the Transylvanian Germans, Austria, Poland, Russia, and Hungary.

It is certainly true that ratings of this kind have limited value. One could quibble with the relative position of some areas on the chronological schema, or with the criteria for considering some works and not others. Nonetheless, it is useful to look at a given culture in a larger context, provided that context has

---

64 The following information is based on L.-N. Malclès, *Les sources du travail bibliographique*, Vol. I (Geneva and Lille, 1950), pp. 120–212, 279–336; Georg Schneider, *Handbuch der Bibliographie* (Leipzig, 1930), pp. 168–349; and Olga Pinto, *Le bibliographie nazionali* (2nd rev. ed., Florence, 1951). It is interesting to note that the *Halytsko-ruskaia bybliohrafiia* of Levyts'kyi is mentioned in each of these works.

65 The following information is based primarily on Robert B. Slocum, *Biographical Dictionaries and Related Works*, 2 vols. (Detroit, 1967–72), which has been supplemented by Malclès, *Les sources*, pp. 231–237, 279–336, and by Schneider, *Handbuch*, pp. 481–531. None of these, however, mentions the biographical dictionary of Levyts'kyi, *Prykarpatska Rus'*. Even more surprising is that it is also not listed in the standard biobibliography of the Russian Empire by Kaufman (see note 58), which does mention several other uncompleted Ukrainian works.

quibble with the relative position of some areas on the chronological schema, or with the criteria for considering some works and not others. Nonetheless, it is useful to look at a given culture in a larger context, provided that context has built-in comparable components. I believe that Europe as a whole in the nineteenth century had many of these components, and when we look at Ukrainian Galicia in this larger European context—if only from the standpoint of national retrospective bibliography and national biography (in themselves not insignificant indicators of the cultural level of a people)—then the province certainly does not look as bad as some of its own illustrious sons, including Ivan Levyts'kyi, had thought.

Yet within any cultural context, the role of individual initiative, drive, and accomplishment cannot be denied. In this sense, Ivan E. Levyts'kyi contributed much to the high level of culture and scholarship that eastern Galicia attained during the decades previous to World War I, a level, it might be added, that has not really been repeated anywhere else in Ukrainian scholarship since then.

Moreover, Levyts'kyi was not even a professional scholar. In spite of, or perhaps because of this, he was able to make a great contribution. As an ordinary clerk in an insurance company, he was liberated from having to dazzle students through academic lectures or from having to participate in the normal and frequently burdensome administrative tasks faced by faculties of high schools, universities, and research institutes. Finally, he was free from having to maintain a "proper professional stance" in a highly status-conscious society. The simple Mr. Levyts'kyi could file insurance forms until three o'clock in the afternoon, then do what was recently said at Harvard University about the great Jewish scholar Soloman Baron—retire to his study, close the door, and write.

Ivan Levyts'kyi was a loner. He tried to maintain a middle-ground position in the increasingly polarized intellectual climate of his day. He was neither a Russophile, a Ukrainophile, nor a Polonophile. Nor was he a theorizer, formulating ideas about how to compile a national bibliography or a national biographical dictionary. He had little time to speculate; he was too busy carrying out concrete tasks. Perhaps being beyond an academic setting and carrying out scholarly pursuits only "after hours" provided him with the necessary discipline. Whatever the reason, Ivan Emelianovych Levyts'kyi has left us with a national bibliography and with the beginnings of a national biographical dictionary for one part of Ukrainian territory that have not since been matched. For these achievements, we, more than half a century later, remain deeply in his debt. *Vichnaia iomu pamiat'.*

Appendix 9.1a
Retrospective National Bibliographies[*]
(Arranged according to the first to have appeared for a given country or ethnonational territory)[**]

Country/Territory/ Group	Work	Coverage	Date of Publication
1. Ireland	John Jones, *A General Catalogue of Books in all Languages, Arts, and Sciences, That Have Been Printed in Ireland and Published in Dublin*	1700–1790	1791
2. Germany	Wilhelm Heinsius, *Allgemeines Bücherlexikon*, 19 vols.	1700–1892	1793–1894
3. Russian (Old Slavonic)	Vasilii S. Sopikov, *Opyt rossiiskoi bibliografii*, 5 vols.	15th century – 1813	1813–21
4. Great Britain	Robert Watt, *Bibliotheca Britannica*, 4 vols.	–1824	1824
5. France	Joseph–Marie Quérard, *La France littéraire ou Dictionnaire bibliographique*, 10 vols.	1700–1827	1827–39
6. Scotland	John Reid, *Bibliotheca Scoto–Celtica*	–1832	1832
7. Netherlands	Johannes De Jong, *Alphabetische naamlijst van boeken*, 4 vols.	1790–1831	1832
8. Bohemia	Antonín Hansgirg, *Katalog Katalog českých knih*	1774–1839	1840

[*] Based on L.–N. Malclès, *Les sources du travail bibliographique*, Vol. I (Geneva and Lille, 1950), pp. 120–212, 279–336; Georg Schneider, *Handbuch der Bibliographie* (Leipzig, 1930), pp. 168–349; Olga Pinto, *Le bibliographie nazionali* (2nd rev. ed.; Florence, 1951).
[**] This list does not include current bibliographies, book dealers' lists, or bibliographies limited to a specific subject (literature, history, etc.). It also does not include works that were basically conceived as biographical dictionaries with bibliographical data appended. The dates of publication refer to first editions, not revised or supplemented editions.

Appendix 9.1a (continued)

Country/Territory/ Group	Work	Coverage	Date of Publication
9. Basque territory	Francisque Michel, *Bibliographie basque*		1847
10. Finland	Fredrik w. Pipping, *Förteckning öfver i tryck utgifna Skrifter på Finska*	1542–1856	1856–57
11. Portugal	Innocencio F. de Silva, *Diccionario bibliografico portuguez*	–1923	1858–1923
12. Croatia	Ivan Kukuljević Sakcinski, *Bibliografia hrvatska*, 2 vols.	1483–1860	1860–63
13. Spain	Dionisio Hidalgo, *Diccionario general de bibliografia española*, 7 vols.	–1881	1862–81
14. GALICIA (Austrian Ukraine)	Iakiv Holovats'kyi, *Bybliohrafiia halytsko–ruskaia*	1772–1848	1863
15. Estonia	M. Jürgens, *Ramatute nimme–kirri.*	1553–1863	1864
16. Greece	Émile Legrand, *Bibliographie hellénique*, 11 vols.	1476–1900	1865–1928
17. Romania	Dimitrie Iarcu, *Annale bibliografice române*	1550–1865	1865
18. Serbia	Stojan Novaković, *Srpska bibliogrqfija za noviju književnost.*	1741–1867	1869
19. Wales	William Rolands, *Cambrian Bibliography*	1546–1800	1869
20. Poland	Karol Estreicher, *Bibliografja polska*, 37 vols.	1474-1900	1872–1939

Appendix 9.1a (continued)

Country/Territory/ Group	Work	Coverage	Date of Publication
21. Denmark	Christian V. Bruun, *Bibliotheca Danica*, 4 vols.	1482–1830	1877–1902
22. Hungary	Karoly Szabó, *Régi magyar könyvtár*, 4 vols.	1531–1711	1879–98
23. Belgium	*Bibliotheca Belgica*, 54 vols.	1473–1600	1880–1922
24. Sweden	Hjalmar Linnström, *Svenskt Boklexikon*, 2 vols.	1830–1865	1883–84
25. Armenia	Garegin Zarbhanelean, *Bibliographie arménienne? Haikakan matenagituthiun*	1565–1883	1883
26. Iceland	Daniel Willard Fiske, *Books Printed in Iceland*, 4 vols.	1578–1844	1886–1907
27. GALICIA (Austrian Ukraine)	Ivan E. Levyts'kyi, *Halytsko–ruskaia bybliohrafiia XIX–ho stolîtiia*, 2 vols.	1801–1886	1887–95
28. Lithuania	Silvestr Baltramaitis, *Spisok litovskikh i drevne–prusskikh knig*	1553–1890	1891
29. Flanders	Frans De Potter, *Vlaamsche Bibliographie*	1830–1890	1893–1902
30. Russia (civil script)	Semen A. Vengerov, *Russkie knigi*, 3 vols.	1708–1897	1897–98
31. Norway	Hjalmar Pettersen, *Bibliotheca Norvegica*, 4 vols.	1643–1814	1899–1924
32. Italy	Attilio Pagliaini, *Catalogo generale della libreria italiana*, 16 vols.	1847–1930	1901–35
33. French Switzerland	Alexandre Julien, *Catalogue des éditions de la Suisse romande*, 4 vols.	1900–1945	1902–1945

Appendix 9.1a (continued)

Country/Territory/ Group	Work	Coverage	Date of Publication
34. Luxembourg	Martin Blum, *Bibliographie luxembourgeoise*, 2 vols.	–1900	1902–32
35. Slovenia	Franc Simonič, *Slovenska bibliografija*, 3 vols.	1550–1900	1903–05
36. Bulgaria	Alexandŭr Teodorov Balan, *Bŭlgarski knigopis za sto godini*	1806–1905	1901
37. Switzerland	Bibliographie Nationale Suisse, *Liste alphabetique des imprimés*, 2 vols.	–1900	1910
38. Albania	Émile Legrand, *Bibliographie albanaise*	–1900	1912
39. Austria	Eduard Langer, *Bibliographie der österreichischen Drucke des XV. und XVI. Jahrhunderts*	1400–1600	1913
40. Catalonia	Mariano Agulo y Fuster, *Catalogo de obras en lengua catalana*	1474–1860	1924
41. Latvia	Jahnis Missins, *Latweeschu rakstneezibas rahditajs*, 2 vols.	1585–1925	1924–37
42. Belarus	*Letapis belaruskaha druku*, 3 vols.	1835–1924	1927–29
43. Jews	Bernhard Friedberg, *Bet 'eged sefarim: Lexique bibliographique de tous les ouvrages de la littérature hébraique et judéo–allemande*	1475–1900	1928–31

Appendix 9.1a (continued)

Country/Territory/Group	Work	Coverage	Date of Publication
44. Slovakia	L'udovít Rízner, *Bibliografia písomníctva slovenského*, 6 vols.	–1900	1929–33
45. Romansch	*Bibliografia retoromontscha*	1552–1930	1938
46. Georgia	*K'art'uli Cigni: Bibliograp'ia*	1629–1920	1941

Appendix 9.1b
Retrospective National Bibliographies
(Arranged according to the first to have appeared for ethnonational territories/groups that were not independent in the late nineteenth century.)

Ethnonational Territory/Group	Date of Publication
1. Ireland	1791
2. Scotland	1832
3. Bohemia	1840
4. Basque territory	1847
5. Finland	1856–57
6. Croatia	1860–63
7. GALICIA (Holovats'kyi)	1863
8. Estonia	1864
9. Wales	1869
10. Poland	1872–1939
11. Armenia	1883
12. Iceland	1886–1907

Appendix 9.1b (continued)

Ethnonational Territory/Group	Date of Publication
13. GALICIA (Levyts'kyi)	1887–95
14. Lithuania	1891
15. Flanders	1893–1902
16. Norway	1899–1924
17. French Switzerland	1902–45
18. Slovenia	1903–05
19. Albania	1912
20. Catalonia	1924
21. Latvia	1924–37
22. Belarus	1927–29
23. Jews	1928–31
24. Slovakia	1929–33
25. Romansch	1938
26. Georgia	1941

Appendix 9.2a
National Biographical Dictionaries[*]
(Arranged according to the first to have appeared for a given country or
ethnonational territory)[**]

Country/Territory/ Group	Work	Date of Publication
1. Germany	Melchior Adam, *Dignorum laude virorum, quos musa vetat mori, immortalitas . . . maximam partem Germanorum*, 5 vols.	1615–53
2. Denmark	Tycho de Hofman, *Portraits historiques des hommes illustres de Dannemark*	1746
3. Switzerland	Johann Jakob Leu, *Allgemeines helvetisches, eydgenössisches, oder schweitzerisches Lexicon*, 20 vols.	1747–65
4. Great Britain	*Biografia Britannica*, 5 vols.	1747–66
5. Malta	Ignazio S. Mifsud, *Biblioteca maltese*	1764
6. Bohemia– Moravia	Ignaz von Born, *Effigies virorum eruditorum atque artificium Bohemiae et Moraviae*, 4 vols.	1773–75
7. Livonia	Friedrich K. Gadebusch, *Livländische Bibliothek*, 3 vols.	1777
8. Sweden	Georg Gezelius, *Försök til et biographiskt lexicon öfver namnkundige och lärde svenske män*, 4 vols.	1778–87
9. France	François Henri Turpin, *La France illustre, ou Le Plutarque français*, 4 vols.	1780–84
10. Italy	Andrea Rubbi, *Elogi italiani*, 12 vols.	1782–83

[*]   Based primarily on Robert B. Slocum, *Biographical Dictionaries and Related Works*, 2 vols. (Detroit, 1967–72).
[**]   The choice of works to be included in this list was difficult. An attempt was made to indicate only those works that were conceived as national biographical dictionaries and not those limited to a short period of time, profession, social class, organization membership, or to collections of portraits with brief biographical data. No encyclopedias or contemporary Who's Who publications were considered. The dates of publication refer to first editions, not revised or supplemented editions.

Appendix 9.2a (continued)

Country/Territory/ Group	Work	Date of Publication
11. Transylvania (Germans)	Johann Seivert, *Nachrichten von siebenbürgischen Gelehrten und ihre Schriften*	1785
12. Belgium	*Dictionnaire historique; ou, histoire abrégée de tous les hommes, nés dans les XVII provinces belgiques*, 2 vols.	1786
13. Austria	Johann Pezzl, *Oesterreichische Biographien*, 4 vols.	1791
14. Netherlands	Jacques Alexandre de Chalmot, *Biographisch woordenboek der Nederlanden*, 8 vols.	1798–1800
15. Jews	Philipp Yung, *Alphabetische Liste aller gelehrten Juden und Jüdinnen.*	1817
16. Ireland	Richard Ryan, *Biographia Hibernica*, 2 vols.	1819–21
17. Wales	John H. Perry, *The Cambrian Plutarch*	1824
18. Poland	Ignacy Chodynicki, *Dykcjonarz uczonych Polaków*, 3 vols.	1833
19. Russia	Dmitrii N. Bantysh–Kamenskii, *Slovar' dostopamiatnykh liudei Russkoi zemli*, 5 vols.	1836
20. Sardinia	Pasquale Tola, *Dizionario biografico degli uomini illustri di Sardegna*, 3 vols.	1837–38
21. Scotland	William Anderson, *The Popular Scottish Biography*	1842
22. Brittany	Prosper Jean Levot, *Biographie bretonne*, 2 vols.	1852
23. Spain	Manuel Ovilo y Otero, *Memorias para formar un catálogo alfabético de los españoles, americanos y extranjeros célebres que más se han señalado en España*, 2 vols.	1854–67

Appendix 9.2a (continued)

Country/Territory/ Group	Work	Date of Publication
24. Luxembourg	Auguste Neyen, *Biographie luxembourgeoise*, 3 vols.	1860
25. Portugal	Manuel Pinheiro Chagas, *Portuguezes illustres*	1869
26. Galicia (Spain)	Teodosio Vesteiro Torres, *Galéria de gallegos illustres*, 6 vols.	1874–75
27. Alsace–Lorraine	Alphonse Cerfberr de Medelsheim, *Biographie alsacienne–lorraine*	1879
28. Finland	*Elämäkertoja Suomen entisiltä ja nykyajoilta toimittanut Suomen Historiallinen Seura*	1879–89
29. Hungary	József Szinnyei, *Magyar írók élete és munkái*, 14 vols.	1891–1914
30. GALICIA (Austrian Ukraine)	Ivan E. Levyts'kyi, *Prykarpatska Rus' v XIX vîkî v biohrafiiakh y portretakh*	1898–1902
31. Croatia	Milan Grlović, *Album zaslužnih Hrvata XIX stoljeća*, 2 vols.	1898–1900
32. Serbia	Andra Gavrilović, *Znameniti srbi XIX veka*, 3 vols.	1901–04
33. Catalonia	*Catalanes ilustres*	1905
34. Armenia	Arsen G. Ghazikean, *Hajkakan nor matenagitouthium eu hanragitaran haj keankhi*	1909
35. Norway	*Illustrert biografisk Leksikon over kjendte norske Maend og Kvinder.*	1916–20
36. Slovenia	*Slovenski biografski leksikon*, 2 vols.	1925–52
37. Estonia	*Eesti biograafiline leksikon*	1926–29
38. Iceland	Páll Eggert Ólason, *Íslenzkar aeviskrár frá landnámstínum til ársloka 1940*, 5 vols.	1948–53

Appendix 9.2a (continued)

Country/Territory/ Group	Work	Date of Publication
39. Greece (modern)	*Maga Hellēnikon biographikon lexikon*	1958
40. Basque territory	*Fausto Arocena Arrequi, Diccionario biográfico vasco*	1963–
41. Slovakia	*Slovenský biografický slovník, 6 vols.*	1986–94

Appendix 9.2b
National Biographical Dictionaries
(Arranged according to the first to have appeared for ethnonational territories/groups that were not independent in the late nineteenth century.)

Ethnonational Territory/Group	Date of Publication
1. Malta	1764
2. Bohemia-Moravia	1773–75
3. Livonia	1777
4. Transylvania (Germans)	1785
5. Jews	1817
6. Ireland	1819–21
7. Wales	1824
8. Poland	1833
9. Sardinia	1837–38
10. Scotland	1842

Appendix 9.2b (continued)

Ethnonational Territory/Group	Date of Publication
11. Brittany	1852
12. Galicia (Spain)	1874–75
13. Alsace–Lorraine	1879
14. Finland	1879–89
15. GALICIA (Austrian Ukraine)	1898–1902
16. Croatia	1898–1900
17. Catalonia	1905
18. Armenia	1909
19. Norway	1916–20
20. Slovenia	1925–52
21. Estonia	1926–29
22. Iceland	1948–53
23. Basque territory	1963–
24. Slovakia	1986–94

chapter ten

Vienna as a Resource for Ukrainian Studies: With Special Reference to Galicia*

There exists a rather widespread myth among scholars of eastern Europe that Vienna, the once powerful capital of the Austro-Hungarian Empire and the repository for a wide variety of archival and printed materials dealing with the peoples of the Habsburg state, was largely depleted of its rich holdings after World War I. Allegedly, most material pertaining to countries that had just arisen in whole or in part from the ruins of the Habsburg Empire—Poland, Czechoslovakia, Hungary—was "returned" to those new states in the 1920s. Hence, in Austrian and east-European scholarly circles, one frequently hears the uninformed statement, "Such material is not in Vienna any longer. It is in Cracow, or Prague, or Budapest." Fortunately for the student interested in modern Ukrainian history, especially in nineteenth-century Galicia, the above description is indeed largely a myth.

This is not to say that no materials were sent from Vienna to Poland or to Czechoslovakia as a result of international agreements reached during the 1920s. While certain archival materials were removed, much still remains in the capital of the old Habsburg Empire, and this study will outline briefly what printed materials can be found there for the study of Ukrainian Galicia.[1]

1. **Österreichische Nationalbibliothek** (Austrian National Library, I. Josefsplatz 1). Under its present name since 1922, this institution is the successor to

---

* First published in *Eucharisterion: Essays Presented to Omeljan Pritsak*, special issue of *Harvard Ukrainian Studies*, III–IV, Pt. 2 (Cambridge, Mass., 1979–80), pp. 609–626.

1 A topic worthy of discussion is archival holdings in Vienna related to Galician-Ukrainian subjects. Although beyond the scope of this study, it is still useful to note that each of the six divisions of the Österreichisches Staatsarchiv has material on Galicia. Of greatest importance are the Haus-, Hof-, und Staatsarchiv (for foreign affairs and internal political developments), the Allgemeines Verwaltungsarchiv (for education and religious affairs),

the Hofbibliothek (Imperial Library) founded by the Habsburgs in the six-teenth century. By the nineteenth century, the Hofbibliothek served the func-tion of a national deposit library, because in 1808 an imperial decree was passed requiring that at least one copy of every publication that appeared in the terri-tory of Austria–Hungary be sent to this library.[2]

The so-called old catalog, which was actually recopied onto modern cards and made available to the public for the first time in the 1960s, contains 1.3 million author-title cards for books printed between 1501 and 1929. An esti-mated 12 percent (156,000 volumes) of this collection, together with another 44,000 volumes published since 1930, may be classified as Slavica.[3] Of these, the amount of printed materials (books, pamphlets, journals, newspapers, year-books, *schematisma*, etc.) originating from Ukrainian Galicia is both quantita-tively as well as qualitatively impressive. And since Habsburg Austria was for several decades the only place where Ukrainian cultural activity was permitted relatively unhampered development, this material has significance for Ukrain-ian studies well beyond the confines of Galicia.

Perhaps the most impressive part of the Nationalbibliothek's Ukrainian col-lection consists of newspapers and journals.[4] For instance, the Nationalbiblio-

and the Finanz- und Hofkammerarchiv (for economic developments).

General descriptions of Vienna's archives can be found in Arthur J. May and Marrim L. Brown, "Austria," in *The New Guide to the Diplomatic Archives of Western Europe*, ed. Daniel H. Thomas and Lynn M. Case (Philadelphia, 1975), pp. 3–19; and in the section "Austrian State Archives," in the *Austrian History Yearbook*, VI-VII (Houston, 1970–71), pp. 3–77. A comprehensive description of the oldest and most important archives is Ludwig Bettner, ed., *Gesamtinventar des wiener Haus-, Hof-, und Staatsarchivs*, 5 vols. (Vienna, 1936–1940).

2 For general descriptions of this institution, see Ernst Trenkler, "The History of the Austrian National-Bibliothek," *Library Quarterly*, XVII (1947), pp. 224–231, and Josef Stummvoll and Rudolf Fiddler, "National Library of Austria," *Encyclopedia of Library and Information Science*, Vol. II (New York and London, 1969), pp. 119–127.

3 Stanislaus Hafner, "Slavica der österreichischen Nationalbibliothek," *Österreichische Osthefte*, V, 2 (Vienna, 1963), pp. 161–165. Only the collection of books since 1930 contains a subject catalog (the "Schlagwort" or "key word" catalog), which contains the headings "Galizien," "Lemberg," and "Ukrajina." Since the Österreichische Nationalbibliothek adopted after 1930 the cataloging procedures used in Germany, the books and serials in both the "old" and "new" post-1930 catalogs are arranged according to the initial noun in a title. Thus, *Halyčo-ruskjij vîstnyk* would be found under *Vîstnyk*, *halyčo-ruskjij*, or *Červonaja Rus'* under *Rus', červonaja.*

4 It was Professor Ihor Ševčenko, associate director of the Harvard Ukrainian Research Institute (HURI), who originally proposed that the serial holdings of the Österreichische Nationalbibliothek be surveyed. Edward Kasinec, HURI research bibliographer, prepared a list of titles, which were then checked in Vienna by Maria Razumovsky. I wish to express deep appreciation to the staff of the Österreichische Nationalbibliothek, and most

thek holds as much as 65 percent of the 209 titles listed in V. Ihnatijenko's comprehensive bibliography of newspapers published in Galicia between 1848 and 1916.[5] For Bukovina, the other Austrian Habsburg province with a Ukrainian population, the figure is 48 percent of the 44 titles published during the same period. (For a complete list of titles, see appendixes 10.1 and 10.2).

Among the titles available are the first serial publications for Austria–Hungary's Ukrainians that appeared during the post-1848 decade (*Dnewnyk ruskij, Zorja halycka, Vîstnyk*), as well as complete runs of the earliest populist-Ukrainophile literary journals from the 1860s (*Večernycî, Meta, Rusalka*).[6] For the period of national and political controversy that occurred during the last decades of the nineteenth and early twentieth centuries, the Nationalbibliothek holds the most influential newspapers of the three competing factions: the Old Ruthenians (*Slovo, Halyčanyn*), the Ukrainophiles (*Dilo, Batkôvščyna, Svoboda*), and the Russophiles (*Prikarpatskaja Rus', Golos naroda*). The collection also includes complete or nearly complete runs of the publications of Galician national organizations: the *Vremennyk* of the Stauropegial Institute, the *Naukovŷj* (later *Lyteraturnŷj*) *sbornyk* of the Galician-Rus' Matytsia, the *Vîstnyk* of the National Home (Narodnyj Dom), and the *Naukovi zapysky* of the Ševčenko Scientific Society. Finally, there are several publications available that are basic to an understanding of pre-1914 developments in Galician-Ukrainian literature (*Pravda, Zorja, Druh, Žytje i slovo, Besěda, Literaturno-naukovyj vistnyk*), education and student life (*Učytel', Moloda Ukrajina, Naša škola*), church affairs (*Sion ruskij, L'vôvsko archieparchijal'ny vîdomosty, Osnova*), law (*Časopys pravnyča, Pravnyča, Pravnyčyj vistnyk*), economic life (*Hospodar'y promyšlennyk*), and socialism (*Narod, Hromads'kyj holos, Vpered*).

The years of World War I heralded not only the decline of the Habsburg Empire but also a marked decrease in the Nationalbibliothek's Ukrainian serial holdings. Certain publications, such as the influential daily newspaper *Dilo*, which continued to appear after the war, were no longer collected systematically after 1914. Still to be found, however, are the *Vistnyk* of the Vienna-based Union for the Liberation of the Ukraine, which appeared during the war years, and several issues of the Russian-language *L'vovskij věstnik*, published in the

especially to Ms. Razumovsky, whose knowledge of the collection made my research more fruitful than it might otherwise have been.

5   This is meant to include both Ukrainian newspapers published in Galicia (in particular L'viv) as well as those published elsewhere (especially Vienna) by or for Galician Ukrainians. V. Ihnatijenko, *Bibliohrafija ukrajins'koji presy, 1816–1916* (Kharkiv, 1930).

6   Titles of newspapers and journals reflect the forms that appeared on the mastheads of the first issues of a given publication. The international transliteration system is employed with the supplements for the alphabet used in Galician-Ukrainian publications devised by the journal *Recenzija* (Cambridge, Mass.).

course of the tsarist army's occupation of eastern Galicia during the autumn and winter of 1914–1915.

Although the Nationalbibliothek's systematic acquisition of Galician-Ukrainian serials ended after 1918, the collection does contain a few publications from the postwar era, such as the first émigré Communist and socialist organs (*Pracja, Naša pravda*) and a few interwar periodicals from Polish Galicia (*Stara Ukrajina, Novi šljachi, Šljach naciji, Peremoha*). The Österreichische Nationalbibliothek's interests did not transcend the boundaries of the Austrian half of the Habsburg Empire, however. Thus, there are no serials published by or for Rusyn/Ukrainians in Hungary (the preserve of the Széchényi National Library in Budapest),[7] nor any by immigrants from Galicia to the United States.

The Nationalbibliothek's collection of Galician-Ukrainian books, pamphlets, grammars, and political tracts is as impressive as its holdings of serials. The national movement in Ukrainian Galicia had its modest beginnings during the first half of the nineteenth century, and the Nationalbibliothek has a good selection of rare volumes from this period, including Josyf Levyc'kij's *Grammatik der ruthenischen oder kleinrussichen Sprache in Galizien* (1834), Josyp Lozyns'kyj's *Ruskoje wesile* (1835) and *Gramatyka języka ruskiego* (1846), Denys Zubryckij's *Rys do historyi narodu ruskiego w Galicyi* (1837) and *Kronika miasta Lwowa* (1844), Ivan Vahylevyč's *Gramatyka języka małoruskiego w Galicyi* (1845), and Ivan Holovac'kij's two-volume anthology of literature, *Vinok rusynam* (1846–47). It is interesting to note, however, that the most famous book from this period, Markijan Šaškevyč's *Rusalka dnistrovaja* (1837), is not to be found in a first edition. This is perhaps because it was printed in Budapest, a publishing source of secondary concern to Vienna.

The revolutionary year 1848 was a crucial turning point in the political and cultural history of Galician Ukrainians and other Austrian Slavs, and many valuable brochures and tracts from this period are in the Nationalbibliothek: Kaspar Cieglewicz, *Die Roth-reussischen Angelegenheiten* (1848) and *Rzecz czerwono-ruska 1848 r.* (1848); Antoni Dąbczanski, *Wyjasnienie sprawy ruskiej* (1848) and *Denkschrift der ruthenischen Nation* (1848). After a decade of centralization and general negative reaction to the liberal direction that followed 1848–1849, the so-called constitutional period of Austrian history began in 1861. It lasted until the outbreak of World War I and witnessed enormous scholarly and literary productivity among Galicia's Ukrainians. The holdings of the Nationalbibliothek reflect these achievements in the works of leading scholars and publicists such as Bohdan Didyc'kyj, Ivan Franko, Mychajlo

---

7 Unfortunately, this institution does not have complete runs of the oldest Rusyn newspapers from the Hungarian Kingdom.

Lozyns'kyj, Josyp Mončalovs'kyj, Omeljan Ohonovs'kyj, Anton Petruševyč, and Izydor Šaranevyč, all of whose writings are well represented.

Important for both historical and especially literary works are the various series known as the Biblioteka. The Nationalbibliothek has an impressive complete (or nearly complete) collection of forty-one of these series, including the Byblioteka najznamenytšych povîstej (33 vols., 1881–93), Biblioteka vydavnyčnoji spilky NTŠ (11 vols., 1899–), Rus'ka istoryčna biblioteka (24 vols., 1886–1904), Teatral'na biblioteka (26 vols., 1899–1904), and the Ukrajins'ko-ruska biblioteka NTŠ (8 vols., 1902–11). Also important in this regard are the annual almanacs (*kalendary*), which were destined primarily for the peasant masses and which reflect the historical, social, and cultural ideologies that prevailed during the period. The Nationalbibliothek has twenty-six series of *kalendary* from Galicia and four more from Bukovina, among which the most popular were the *kalendary* issued by the Kačkovs'kyj Society and the Prosvita Society.

Finally, among printed source materials are the yearbooks of the Greek Catholic church (known as *schematisma*) and the yearbooks of the various *gymnasia* (known as *zvity*). These volumes are extremely important because they provide histories and reports of the annual activity of the individual institution, as well as lists of all the staff (priests, teachers, students), often with data on birth, social background, profession, and so on. Thus, the *schematisma* and *zvity* are invaluable tools for analyzing the social composition of nineteenth-century Galician society. The Nationalbibliothek has complete sets of *schematisma* for Galicia's three Greek Catholic eparchies: Przemyśl (1828–1918), L'viv (1832–1989), and Stanyslaviv (1886–1914), and *zvity* for Ukrainian *gymnasia* in Kolomyja (1900/01–1913/14), Ternopil' (1905/06–1913/14), Stanyslaviv (1912/13–1913/14), Przemyśl (1910/11–1917/18), Turka (1913/14), Javoriv (1912/13–1913/14), Rohatyn (1912/13), Zbaraž (1912/13); and for female *gymnasia* in Przemyśl (1906/07–1917/18), L'viv (1906/07–1913/14), and Stanyslaviv (1912/13).

2. **Parliamentsbibliothek** (Parliamentary Library, I. Reichratsstrasse, 3).[8] The Parliamentsbibliothek was founded in 1869, and fourteen years later it was moved to new quarters in the impressive neo-Greek Parliament building, where it is still located today. It was designed to serve members of the Austrian Imperial Parliament (Reichsrat), whose number had grown by 1907 to 516 in

---

8 I am very grateful to Dr. Rudolf Stöhr, director of the Parliamentsbibliothek, who not only permitted me to work when the library was closed to outside readers (i.e., when the Austrian parliament is in session), but who also allowed me unlimited direct access to the stacks, where I made discoveries that would not have been likely from use of the card catalog.

the House of Deputies (Haus der Abgeordneten) and 118 in the House of Lords (Herrenhaus). Between 1861 and 1918, when Ukrainians from Galicia served in the House of Deputies, their number varied from a low of three in 1867 to twenty-seven in 1907.

The Parliamentary Library contains the complete stenographic record of the proceedings and publications of the House of Deputies (374 volumes) and House of Lords (74 volumes) for the years 1861 through 1918.[9] Most important are the published indexes for the stenographic record of both houses.[10] Using these tools, it is easy to find the complete texts of the speeches, inquiries, and law proposals of all Ukrainian deputies, among them the influential Aleksander Barvins'kyj, Stepan Kačala, Kost' Levyc'kyj, Jevhen Petruševyč, and Julijan Romančuk. The Parliamentsbibliothek also includes the rare guides by Sigmund Hahn and Fritz Freund, which provide complete biographical data on each member of parliament,[11] and a set of the annual Handbook of the Austro-Hungarian Monarchy, which describes in great detail the administrative structure of Galicia and Bukovina.[12]

Even more valuable for understanding local developments are the Parliamentsbibliothek's holdings of the complete stenographic record for the diets in each of the empire's seventeen crownland provinces. This, of course, includes the proceedings of both the Galician (178 volumes) and Bukovinian (71 volumes) diets between the years 1861 and 1914.[13] Here it is possible to find the

9 *Stenographische Protokolle áber die Sitzungen des Hauses der Abgeordneten des österreichischen Reichrathes*, 374 vols. (Vienna, 1862–1918); *Stenographische Protokolle über die Sitzungen des Herrenhauses des österreichischen Reichrathes*, 74 vols. (Vienna, 1862–1918).

10 *Index zu den stenographischen Protokollen des Abgeordnetenhauses des österreichischen Reichsrathes*, 28 vols. (Vienna, 1862–1920); *Index zu den stenographischen Protokollen des Herrenhauses des österreichischen Reichsrathes*, 22 vols. (Vienna, 1869–1920).

11 Sigmund Hahn, *Reichsraths-Almanach für die Session* [in 1867–1892], 5 vols. (Vienna, 1867–91); Fritz Freund, *Das österreichische Abgeordnetenhaus: ein biographishch-statistisches Handbuch* [1907–1913 and 1911–1917] (Vienna, 1907–11).

12 *Schematismus des kaiserlichen auch kaiserlich-königlichen Hofes und Staates*—later *Hof- und Staats-Schematismus* (or *Handbuch*) *des österreichischen Kaiserthumes* (Vienna, 1778–1868); *Hof- und Staats-Handbuch der oesterreichisch-ungarischen Monarchie*, Vols. I–XLIV (Vienna, 1874–1918). Beginning in 1856, these annual volumes allotted about 100 pages to Galícia and 50 to Bukovina. The triple-column pages provide lists of all officials in the provincial diets and administration, educational institutions, justice department, financial administration, trade department, land department, military, and churches. Each volume also has a complete name index.

13 *Stenograficzne Sprawozdania Sejmu Krajowego Królestwa Galicyi i Lodomeryi wraz z Wielkiem Księstwem Krakowskiem: Posiedzenie* [1861–1914], 54 vols.; *Alegatey* [1865–1914], 90 vols.; *Protokoły, 1876–1914*, 34 vols. [L'viv], 1861–1914. *Stenographische*

complete speeches and law proposals of all Ukrainian members. Very useful in this regard are the indexes to the proceedings of the Galician Diet prepared for the years 1861 through 1895.[14]

Because the Parliamentsbibliothek has since its establishment functioned uninterruptedly as the library of the Austrian national parliament, it has continued to collect the stenographic records of parliamentary institutions in major countries throughout the world. Hence, it contains the complete stenographic record of the senate and diet in both interwar Poland (52 volumes) with the speeches of all Ukrainian senators and deputies,[15] and interwar Czechoslovakia (187 volumes), with the speeches by Rusyn/Ukrainian representatives from Subcarpathian Rus' and the Prešov Region.[16]

3. **Institut für osteuropäische Geschichte und Südostforschungen** (IOGS). The IOGS (I. Liebiggasse, 5) has had its present name since 1956 when it succeeded the Seminar für osteuropäische Geschichte, which traces its beginnings at the University of Vienna back to 1907. The present institute serves as a regional-studies research center for eastern and southeastern Europe, with its own library numbering close to 50,000 volumes.[17]

The Ukrainian materials include a few works on pre-1918 Galicia not found in the Österreichische Nationalbibliothek and an interesting collection of

Protokolle des Bukowinaer Landtags, 71 vols. (Chernivtsi, 1863–1913).

    Speeches in the Galician Diet by Ukrainian deputies are mostly in Ukrainian (although printed in a Polish-based Latin alphabet).Speeches in the Bukovinian Diet are, with minor exceptions, in German.

14 Władysław Koziebrodzki, *Repertorjum czynności galicyjskiego sejmu krajowego*, 2 vols., 1861–1889 (L'viv, 1885–89); Stanisław Miziewicz, *Repertoryum czynności Gallicyjskiego Sejmu krajowego*, 1889–1895 (L'viv, 1896). Unfortunately, there are no separately published indexes for the Bukovinian Diet nor for the Galician Diet between 1896 and 1914, although each volume of the stenographic record (see above, note 12), does contain comprehensive speaker and subject indexes.

15 *Sprawozdanie stenograficzne Sejmu Ustawodawczego* [1919–21] and *Sprawozdanie stenograficzne Senatu Rzeczypospolitej* [1922–37], 44 vols.; *Sprawozdanie stenograficzne Senatu Rzeczypospolitej* [1922–37], 8 vols. These volumes have no indexes.

16 *Těsnopisecké zprávy o schůzich Národního shromáždění, poslanecké sněmovny* [and] *Senátu*, 88 vols. (Prague, 1919–37); *Tisky k těsnopiseckým zprávam o schůzi poslanecké sněmovny* [and] *Senátu*, 99 vols. (Prague, 1920–38). The Parliamentsbibliothek also has the rare comprehensive indexes to these volumes: *Index k těsnopiseckým zprávám o schůzich Poslanecké sněmovny* [and] *Senátu Národního shromáždění republiky československé*, 12 vols. (Prague, 1920–50).

17 General descriptions of the IOGS are found in "Das Institut für Osteuropäische Geschichte und Südostforschung der Universität Wien," *Österreichische Osthefte*, I, 2 (Vienna, 1959), pp. 118–123; and Thorvi Eckhardt, "Zehn Jahre Slavica-Zentralkatalog," *Österreichische Osthefte*, IV, 2 (1962), pp. 160–163. The IOGS card catalog does not have a subject catalog for Galicia, but it does have a good author-title catalog.

Ukrainian serials largely from the twentieth century. Most of the latter are from culturally active World War I prisoner-of-war camps (*Rozvaha*, 1915–18; *Vil'ne slovo*, 1917–18; *Rozs'vit*, 1916–18; *Hromads'ka dumka*, 1917–18; *Pros'vitnyj lystok*, 1916–17; *Vil'ne slovo*, 1916–18) or from interwar Austria (*Volja*, 1919–21; *Chliborobs'ka Ukrajina*, 1920–25; *Ukrajins'kyj skytalec'*, 1920–23; *Nova hromada*, 1923–24), Czechoslovakia (*Ukrajins'kyj student*, 1922–24; *Praci Ukrajins'koho istoryčno-filologičnoho tovarystva*, 1926–42), and Germany (*Die Ukraine*, 1919–21; *Ukrainische Kulturberichte*, 1933–38). The IOGS also has some important older Ukrainian serials, including complete collections of the L'viv Ševčenko Scientific Society's *Zapysky* (1892–1939), the Kiev Ukrainian Scientific Society's *Zapysky* (1892–1939), the Kiev Ukrainian Scientific Society's *Zapysky* (1908–25), and the rare *Halyčanyn* (L'viv, 1862) and *Galicko-russkij věstnik* (St. Petersburg, 1894).

4. **Institut für Slavistik** (Institute for Slavistics, I, Liebiggasse, 5). The Institut für Slavistik is part of the University of Vienna and specializes in the languages and literatures of Slavic peoples. It has its own library with holdings under the subject headings "Ukrainian language" and "Ukrainian literature" that indicate a rich collection, including several nineteenth-century grammars and first editions of literary works.

5. Other institutions. The **Universitätsbibliothek in Wien** (University of Vienna Library, I. Dr. Karl Lueger Ring, 1), which was badly damaged during the last years of World War II, holds some Ukrainian materials, but none that cannot be found in any of the above-mentioned libraries.

The **Sankt Barbara Kirche** (Saint Barbara Church, I. Postgasse 10, adjacent to the Main Post Office) and the **Seminary (Barbareum)** have had a long tradition of cultural leadership among the Habsburg Empire's Greek Catholics, most especially Galician Ukrainians, since their establishment in the late eighteenth century.[18] There are, however, no materials in the church building itself, and the rectory, located a few blocks away, contains only a small library of no special significance.

The **Mechitaristen Kloster** (Mechitarist Monastery, VII. Mechitaristengasse) has since the nineteenth century housed a Cyrillic printing press operated by Armenian Roman Catholic monks who printed works in fifty different languages, including several Ukrainian periodicals destined for Galicians.[19] There

18 For a recent comprehensive history, see Willibald M. Plöchl, *St. Barbara zu Wien*, 2 vols. (Vienna, 1975).
19 These include *Vistnyk dlja Rusynov avstrjijskoj deržavŷ* (1850–66), *Otječestvjennŷj sbornyk* (1853–66), *Domova škola* (1854–56), *Horod nebesnŷj* (Altenmarkt-Windischgratz, 1888); *Dilo* (Viennese edition, 1914–15); *Vistnyk Sojuza vyzvolennja Ukrajiny* (1914–15), and *Hospodars'kyj lystok* (1914).

are perhaps records of financial dealings with Ukrainian publishers and maybe even some copies of older publications, but the chaotic condition of the monastery's archives makes access to such material difficult if not impossible.

The importance of Vienna as a resource for Ukrainian studies, in particular as they pertain to nineteenth- and early-twentieth-century Galicia, cannot be overstated. Despite this, the city's Ukrainian holdings have been decidedly underused. Only a handful of dissertations on Ukrainian topics have been written in Austria after World War II,[20] and western-Ukrainian specialists seem unaware of the amount of material—most of which is readily accessible—that the city has to offer. In this era of burgeoning Ukrainian scholarship in the United States and Canada, serious attention should be focused on Vienna. More scholars should make direct use of its libraries and archives, while centers of Ukrainian scholarship, such as the Ukrainian Research Institute at Harvard, should make every effort to microfilm for preservation and easy access the rare nineteenth-century Galician and Bukovinian newspapers and journals that might otherwise not survive for much longer. All Ukrainians, not only those of Galician descent, should seek to prevent such an irreparable cultural loss from occurring.[21]

20 Among those to make use of Vienna's resources on Galicia are Roman Drazniowsky's University of Innsbruck doctoral dissertation (1957) on Galicia under Austrian and Polish rule,!and the University of Vienna doctoral dissertations by Michael Jaremko on Ukrainians in the Viennese Parliament (1944) and by Nicholas Dutka on the language question in Galicia before 1848 (1951). Professor Günther Wytrzens, head of the Department of Slavic Studies at the University of Vienna, reported that the interest in Ukrainian topics is very limited, and, as indicated by the annual survey in the *Austrian History Yearbook*, no doctoral dissertations have been written in Austria on Galicia or any other Ukrainian topic at least since 1965.

21 In 1982, Peter Jacyk of Mississauga, Ontario, made available a grant of $47,000 to the Chair of Ukrainian Studies at the University of Toronto. Under the direction of Professor Paul Robert Magocsi, these funds were used to microfilm all Ukrainian-related serials at the Austrian National Library that date from the period 1848–1918. Several other titles from those years that were not in Vienna were added from the Czech National Museum and the Slavonic Library in Prague; the Széchényi National Library in Budapest; and the Pontifical Institute for Oriental Studies in Rome. See Paul Robert Magocsi, comp., *The Peter Jacyk Collection of Ukrainian Serials: A Guide to Newspapers and Periodicals* (Toronto, 1983).

Appendix 10.1
Galician, Bukovinian, and Viennese Ukrainian Serials in the
Austrian National Library
(Asterisks indicate that holdings are complete.)

Title	Place of Publication	Years of Appearance	Holdings
1. *Dnewnyk ruskij	L'viv	1848	1848
2. Zorja halycka	L'viv	1848–57	1853–57
3. *Halyčo-ruskjij vîstnyk	L'viv	1849–50	1849–50
4. *Novyny	L'viv	1849	1849
5. *Obščjij zakonov deržavných pravytel'stva vîstnyk dlja cîsarstva Avstrjij	Vienna	1849–53	1849–53
6. *Pčola	L'viv	1849	1849
7. Vîstnyk . . . dlja Rusynov Avstrjijskoj djeržavŷ	L'viv	1850–66	1853–66
8. Vseobščjij dnjevnyk (later Vîstnyk) zjemskych zakonôv y pravytel'stva dlja koronnoj oblasty Halycjij y Volodymjerjij	L'viv	1849–65	1849–60
9. Otječestvjennŷj sbornyk	Vienna	1853–59, 1861, 1862, 1866	1853, 1857–62
10. *Semejnaja byblioteka	L'viv	1855–56	1855–56
11. *Sion, Cerkov, Škola	Vienna	1858–59	1858–59
12. *Slovo	L'viv	1861–87	1861–87

Title	Place of Publication	Years of Appearance	Holdings
13. Večernycî	L'viv	1862–63	1862–63
14. Dom y škola	L'viv	1863–64	1863–64
15. Meta	L'viv	1863–65	1863–65
16. Pys'mo do hromadŷ	L'viv	1863–65, 1867–68	1864
17. Strachopud	Vienna	1863–67	1863–67
18. Vremennyk Stavropyhijskoho Ynstytuta	L'viv	1864–1915, 1923–1939	1870–92, 1894–95, 1898–1902, 1905, 1909–14
19. Zolotaja hramota	Vienna	1864–67	1865, 1867
20. Naukovŷj (later Lyteraturnŷj) sbornyk Halycko-russkoj Matycŷ	L'viv	1865–73, 1885–90, 1896–97	1865–73, 1885–87, 1897
21. Nedîlja	L'viv	1865–66	1865–66
22. Škola	L'viv	1865	1865
23. Vîstnyk zakonov y rosporjaženjij krajevých dlja koroljevstva Halycjij	L'viv	1866–67, 1872–1916	1866–67 1872–1916
24. Rusalka	L'viv	1866	1866
25. Pys'mo do hromadŷ: dodatok do 'Slova'	L'viv	1867–68	1867–68

Title	Place of Publication	Years of Appearance	Holdings
26. Pravda	L'viv	1867–80, 1884, 1888–96	1867–69, 1872–77, 1879–96
27. *Rus'	L'viv	1867	1867
28. Hospodar'	L'viv	1869–72	1869
29. Lastovka	L'viv	1869–81	1869–80
30. Učytel'	L'viv	1869–74, 1880	1869, 1871–74
31. *Osnova	L'viv	1870–72	1870–72
32. Nauka	Kolomyja, L'viv, Vienna, Černivci, L'viv	1871–1914, 1924–39	1884–98, 1902–03, 1906–08
33. Russkaja Rada	Kolomyja	1871–1912	1872–73, 1875–82, 1900–06, 1912
34. Ruskij sion	L'viv	1871–85	1872–79, 1883–85
35. *Vîstnyk zakonôv deržavných dlja korolevstv y krajev v Deržavnoj Dumî zastupljených	Vienna	1872–1916	1872–1916
36. *Strachopud	L'viv	1872–73	1872–73
37. *Druh	L'viv	1874–77	1874–77

Title	Place of Publication	Years of Appearance	Holdings
38. Narodna škola	Kolomyja	1875	1875
39. Druh naroda	L'viv	1876	1876
40. Lopata	Černivci	1876	1876
41. Vesna	Kolomyja	1878–80	1878–80
42. Sel'skij hospodar'	Černivci	1878–79	1878
43. Bat'kôvščyna	L'viv	1879–96	1886–96
43. Bat'kôvščyna	L'viv	1879-96	1886-96
44. Hospodar' y promŷšlennyk	Stanyslaviv, L'viv	1879-87	1880-87
45. Rodymŷj lystok	Černivci	1879-82	1879-81
46. Viče	L'viv	1880-82	1880-82
47. Halyckij sion	L'viv	1880-82	1880-82
48. Dîlo	L'viv	1880-1939	1880-1914
49. Zorja	L'viv	1880-97	1880, 1882-97
50. Prolom	L'viv	1880-82	1880-82 (incompl.)
51. Novost'	L'viv	1881-83	1883
52. 'Prijatel' dîtej	L'viv	1881	1881

Title	Place of Publication	Years of Appearance	Holdings
53. S'vit	L'viv	1881–82	1881–82 (incompl.)
54. Vîstnyk Narodnoho Doma	L'viv	1882–1914, 1918–19, 1921, 1924	1882–1908, 1910–14
55. Nove zerkalo	L'viv	1883–85	1884
56. Bukovyna	Černivci	1885–1910, 1913–18	1895–1910
57. *Myr	L'viv	1885–87	1885–87
58. Prykarpatskaja Rus'	L'viv	1885	1885 (incompl.)
59. *Rus'	L'viv	1885–87	1885–87
60. Strachopud	L'viv	1886–95	1894–95
61. Besěda	L'viv	1887–97	1894–97
62. Dušpastŷr'	L'viv	1887–94	1887–88
63. *Russka pravda	Vienna	1888–92	1888–92
64. *Červonaja Rus'	L'viv	1888–91	1888–91
65. L'vôvsko-archieparchijal'nŷ vîdomosty	L'viv	1889–1944	1910–13
66. Poslannyk	Berežany, L'viv, Ternopil', Przemyśl	1889–1911	1894–1904

Title	Place of Publication	Years of Appearance	Holdings
67. Zerkalo	L'viv	1889–1909	1889–1891
68. *Učytel'	L'viv	1889–1914	1889–1914
69. Časopys' pravnyča	L'viv	1889–1900 (?)	1889, 1891–96, 1898–1900
70. *Dzvinok	L'viv	1890–1914	1890–1914
71. Narod	L'viv, Kolomyja	1890–95	1890–94
72. Russkoe slovo	L'viv	1890–1914	1890–1914 (incompl.)
73. Narodna časopys	L'viv	1891–1914, 1918	1891–1909
74. *Chliborob	L'viv, Kolomyja	1891–94	1891–94
75. Zapysky Naukovoho Tovarystva im. Ševčenka	L'viv	1892–1937	1892–1910, 1911–1924
76. Hromads'kyj holos	L'viv	1892–1914, 1917, 1922–39	1898–1900 1904–05
77. *Galičanin	L'viv	1893–1913	1893–1913
78. Pravoslavnaja Bukovina	Vienna, Černivci	1893–1905	1899–1905
79. *Prosvěščenie	Vienna	1893–1902	1893–1902

	Title	Place of Publication	Years of Appearance	Holdings
80.	*Čytal'nja	L'viv	1893–96	1893–96
81.	*Žytje i slovo	L'viv	1894–97	1894–97
82.	Bukovynskŷ vîdomosty	Černivci	1895–1909	1895
83.	*Hromada	Kolomyja	1896	1896
84.	Misionar	Žovkva	1897–1944	1897–1913
85.	*Vinočok dlja russkych dîtočok	Vienna	1897	1897
86.	Ruslan	L'viv	1897–1914	1897–1910, 1912–14
87.	Svoboda	L'viv	1897–1939	1897–1907, 1915
88.	Hospodar'	Przemyśl	1898–1913	1900–01
89.	*Zerkalo	L'viv	1898–1909	1898–1909
90.	Literaturno–naukovyj vistnyk	L'viv, Kiev	1898–1914, 1917–19, 1922–32	1896–1913, 1924, 1930
91.	Ruska rada	Černivci	1898–1908	1898–1901, 1906–08
92.	*Budučnist'	L'viv	1899	1899
93.	Bohoslovskij vîstnyk	L'viv	1900–03	1900–01
94.	Moloda Ukrajina	L'viv	1900–03, 1905, 1910	1900–03, 1910

Title	Place of Publication	Years of Appearance	Holdings
95. *Časopys' pravnyča i ekonomična	L'viv	1900–12	1900–12
96. Naučno–literaturnyj sbornik	L'viv	1901–02, 1904–06, 1908, 1930, 1934	1902, 1930
97. *Zorja	Kolomyja	1902–03	1902–03
98. Vistnyk Sojuza russkych chljiborobskych spilok na Bukovyni 'Seljans'ka Kasa'	Černivci	1903–07	1904–07
99. *Iskra	L'viv	1903	1903
100. Malyj misionarčyk	Žovkva	1903–14, 1939	1904
101. *Postup	Kolomyja	1903–05	1903–05
102. *Ruthenische Revue	Vienna	1903–05	1903–05
103. *Chlops'ka pravda	Kolomyja	1903, 1909	1903, 1909
104. *Vînoček	L'viv	1904–08	1904–08
105. Ekonomist	L'viv	1904–14	1904–13
106. Katolyc'kyj vschid	L'viv	1904–07	1904–06
107. *Misjačnyj kaljendar	Vienna	1904–05	1904–05
108. *Molodiž	Ternopil'	1904	1904
109. *Narodnaja Rada	Černivci	1904–08	1904–08

Title	Place of Publication	Years of Appearance	Holdings
110. *Promin'	Vaškivci nad Čeremošem	1904–07	1904–07
111. *Nova Sič	Stanyslaviv	1904	1904
112. *Chliborob	Černivci	1904–14	1904–14
113. Artystyčnyj vistnyk	L'viv	1905–07	1905
114. *Narodna biblioteka	Černivci	1905	1905
115. Zemlja i volja	Černivci, L'viv	1906–12, 1919–24	1906, 1911
116. *Osnova	L'viv	1906–13	1906–13
117. *S'vit	L'viv	1906–07	1906–07
118. Ukrainische Rundschau	Vienna	1906–17	1906–17 (incompl.)
119. *Dodatok ekonomičnyj- hospodars'kyj i pravnyčyj 'Narodnoho slova'	L'viv	1907	1907
120. *Dodatok istoryčno-literaturnyj 'Narodnoho slova'	L'viv	1907–08	1907–08
121. Narodna sprava	Černivci	1907–10	1908
122. Narodne slovo	L'viv	1907–11	1907–08, 1910, 1911
123. *Seljans'ka rada	Przemyśl	1907–09	1907–09

Title	Place of Publication	Years of Appearance	Holdings
124. *Listok	L'viv	1907–14	1907–14
125. Borba	Hliboka, Černivci	1908–14, 1918	1908–13
126. *Narodne bohatstvo	Černivci	1908–10	1908–10
127. Kamenjari	Mamajivci	1908–14, 1921–22	1913–14
128. Prapor	L'viv, Kolomyja	1908–12	1910–11
129. Čorna rada	Vienna	1908–11	1908–10
130. Budučnist'	L'viv	1909–10	1909
131. Golos naroda	L'viv	1909–15	1911–15
132. *Golos truda	L'viv	1909–10	1909–10
133. Narodnyj holos	Černivci	1909–15, 1921, 1923	1909–10, 1912
134. Naša škola	L'viv	1909–14, 1916–18	1911–13
135. Peremys'kyj vistnyk	Przemyśl	1909–14	1909–11
136. *Pravoslavnaja Rus'	Černivci	1909–10	1909–10,
137. Prikarpatskaja Rus'	L'viv, Kiev	1909–15, 1918–20	1909–13, 1915
138. *Rus'	L'viv	1909	1909
139. Samopomič	L'viv	1909–14	1910

Title	Place of Publication	Years of Appearance	Holdings
140. Hospodars'ka časopys'	L'viv	1910–18, 1920	1913–14
141. Djakôvskŷ vîdomosty	Lukavec'	1910–14	1910–12
142. *Pravnyčyj vistnyk	L'viv	1910–13	1910–13
143. *Russkaja pravda	Černivci	1910–13	1910–13
144. *Emihrant	L'viv	1911–14	1911–14
145. *Vpered	L'viv	1911–13	1911–13
146. *Nova Bukovyna	Černivci	1912–14	1912–14
147. Nove slovo	L'viv	1912–15	1915
148. Pidhirs'kyj dzvin	Sanok, Nowy Sącz	1912–15	1912
149. *Stanjislavivs'ki visty	Stanyslaviv	1912–13	1912–13
150. *Strachopud	L'viv	1912	1912
151. *Zdorovlje	L'viv	1912–14	1912–14
152. Dobra novyna	L'viv	1913–14	1913–14 (incompl.)
153. *Russkaja niva	L'viv	1913	1913
154. *Ukrajina	Černivci	1912–14	1912–14
155. Šljachy	L'viv	1914–17	1915–17

Title	Place of Publication	Years of Appearance	Holdings
156. Vistnyk Sojuza Vyzvolennja Ukrajiny	Vienna	1914–18	1914–18 (incompl.)
157. Kolomyjs'ke slovo	Kolomyja	1914	1914 (incompl.)
158. *Pracja	L'viv, Vienna	1914, 1918	1914, 1918
159. *Svît	Nowy Sącz	1914	1914
160. *Torhovi visty	L'viv	1914	1914
161. *Ukrainische Nachrichten	Vienna	1914–17	1914–17
162. *Ukrajins'ke slovo	L'viv	1915	1915
163. L'vovskij věstnik	L'viv	1915	1915 (incompl.)
164. Ukrainisches Korrespondenzblatt	Vienna	1914–18	1916–18
165. Chliborobs'ka Ukrajina	Vienna	1920–25	1922–25
166. *Na perelomi	Vienna	1920	1920
167. *Naša pravda	Vienna	1921–23	1921–23
168. *Soborna Ukrajina	Vienna	1921–22	1921–22
169. *Naša pravda	L'viv	1923–24	1923–24
170. *Stara Ukrajina	L'viv	1924–25	1924–25

Title	Place of Publication	Years of Appearance	Holdings
171. Nova zorja	L'viv	1926–39	1931, 1934
172. Litopys Červonoji Kalyny	L'viv	1929–39	1931
173. Novi šljachi	L'viv	1929–32	1932
174. Dzvinočok	L'viv	1931–39	1931
175. Samostijna dumka	Černivci	1931–37	1933
176. Students'kyj šljach	L'viv	1931–34	1931–33
177. Naš front	L'viv	1933–?	1933
178. Komar	L'viv	1933–39	1935, 1938
179. Zorna	L'viv	1933–34	1933–34 (incompl.)
180. Peremoha	L'viv	1933–39	1933
181. Visnyk	L'viv	1933–39	1933–36
182. *Katolyc'ka akcija	L'viv	1934–39	1934–39
183. Nazustrič	L'viv	1934–39	1936
184. Torhovlja i promysl'	L'viv	1934–38	1937–38
185. *Šljach naciji	L'viv	1935–36	1935–36
186. Šljach molodi	L'viv	1936–39	1939
187. Na slidi	L'viv	1936–39	1937–38

Title	Place of Publication	Years of Appearance	Holdings
188. Ukrajins'kyj invalid	L'viv	1937–39	1938
189. Students'kyj prapor	L'viv	1943–44	1944

Appendix 10.2
Index of Galician, Bukovinian, and Viennese Ukrainian Serials in the Austrian National Library
(Numbers in parentheses refer to Appendix 10.1.)

Artystyčnyj vistnyk (113)
Bat'kôvščyna (43)
Besěda (61)
Bohoslovskij vîstnyk (93)
Borba (125)
Budučnist' (92)
Budučnist' (130)
Bukovynskŷ vîdomosty (82)
Bukovyna (56)
Časopys' pravnyča (69)
Časopys' pravnyča i ekonomična (95)
Červonaja Rus' (64)
Chliborob (74)
Chliborob (112)
Chliborobs'ka Ukrajina (165)
Chlops'ka pravda (103)
Čorna rada (129)
Čytal'nja (80)
Dîlo (48)
Djakôvskŷ vîdomosty (141)
Dnewnyk ruskij (1)
Dobra novyna (152)
Dodatok ekonomičnyj-hospodars'kyj i
    pravnyčyj 'Narodnoho slova' (119)
Dodatok istoryčno-literaturnyj
    'Narodnoho slova' (120)

Dom y škola (14)
Druh (39)
Druh naroda (37)
Dušpastŷr' (62)
Dzvinočok (174)
Dzvinok (70)
Emihrant (144)
Ekonomist (105)
Galičanin (77)
Golos naroda (131)
Golos truda (132)
Halyckij sion (47)
Halyčo-ruskjij vîstnyk (3)
Hospodar' (28)
Hospodar' (88)
Hospodar' y promŷšlennyk (44)
Hospodars'ka časopys' (140)
Hromada (83)
Hromads'kyi holos (76)
Iskra (99)
Kamenjari (127)
Katolyc'ka akcija (182)
Katolyc'kyj vschid (106)
Kolomyjs'ke slovo (157)
Komar (178)
Lastôvka (29)